Think, Code, Create

Advanced Python Programming Series

Northward House Publishing

A series of twelve advanced programming books for secondary students.

Each book is a standalone resource. Read alone or as part of the full series.

Designed for Years 9–12

Australian Curriculum Version 9 — Digital Technologies

Prerequisite: Think, Code, Create — A Python Programming Journey for Students

ISBN 978-1-7640698-0-9

Think, Code, Create — Advanced Python Programming Series

BOOK 2

File Handling & Exception Management

Read, write, and manage data files; handle errors gracefully in real-world programs

M. North

BEd. (Sec), BSc, MInfoTech

Northward House Publishing

Brisbane, Queensland, Australia

2025

Prerequisite:

Think, Code, Create — A Python Programming Journey for Students

About the Author

M. North holds a Bachelor of Education (Secondary), a Bachelor of Science, and a Master of Information Technology. He has worked as a secondary school teacher of Digital Technologies, Mathematics, and Science across Queensland, Australia, before turning to educational publishing full time.

His teaching practice has centred on making abstract computational thinking concrete and accessible for students at every level — from those encountering programming for the first time to advanced students pursuing algorithmic thinking and software engineering. The Think, Code, Create series grew directly from classroom experience: the need for structured, curriculum-aligned materials that treat secondary students as capable thinkers, not passive recipients of watered-down content.

The foundation text, Think, Code, Create — A Python Programming Journey for Students (ISBN 978-1-7640698-0-9), established the pedagogical approach: clear explanations, worked examples with annotated code, guided exercises with hints, and challenge tasks for extension. The twelve-book advanced series extends that approach through specialised programming domains — from object-oriented design and data structures through to concurrency, networking, and automation — with the same rigour and the same respect for the reader.

M. North is based in Brisbane, Queensland, Australia, and publishes through Northward House Publishing.

Northward House Publishing

Brisbane, Queensland, Australia

www.northwardhouse.com.au

Feedback, corrections, and curriculum enquiries are welcome. Contact the publisher via the website above.

Publication Information

First published 2026
Published by Northward House Publishing, Brisbane, Queensland, Australia

This book is part of the Think, Code, Create — Advanced Python Programming Series.
This volume ISBN: 978-1-7640698-5-4

Acknowledgements

The author and publisher gratefully acknowledge the contribution of all teachers and students who provided feedback during the development of this series. The Python programming language is created and maintained by the Python Software Foundation (python.org).

Disclaimer

The information in this book is provided in good faith and is accurate to the best of the author's knowledge at the time of publication. Programming languages, libraries, and tools change over time. The publisher and author accept no liability for errors, omissions, or outcomes arising from the use of code or information in this publication.

All example programs are written for educational purposes. Any resemblance to real persons, organisations, or events in example scenarios is coincidental.

The Complete Series

The twelve books in the Think, Code, Create Advanced Series are designed for students who have completed the foundation text. Each book is a standalone resource — you may read them in any order based on your interests or curriculum pathway. The recommended pathways below are a guide, not a requirement.

01 Object-Oriented Programming in Python
Design and build programs using classes, objects, and the four pillars of OOP
Prerequisite: Foundation text Chapters 14–15 **Audience:** Years 9–12

02 File Handling & Exception Management
Read, write, and manage data files; handle errors gracefully in real-world programs
Prerequisite: Foundation text Chapters 3–4, 11–12 **Audience:** Years 9–12

03 Modules, Packages & the Python Ecosystem
Organise, share, and reuse code with modules, packages, and the broader Python library
Prerequisite: Foundation text Chapters 14–15 **Audience:** Years 9–12

04 Data Structures & Algorithms
Understand, implement, and analyse core data structures and fundamental algorithms
Prerequisite: Foundation text Chapters 11–13 **Audience:** Years 10–12

05 Functional Programming & Advanced Iterables
Master Python's functional tools — generators, comprehensions, closures, and more
Prerequisite: Foundation text Chapters 14–15 **Audience:** Years 10–12

06 Regular Expressions & Advanced Text Processing
Search, validate, and transform text data using Python's powerful re module
Prerequisite: Foundation text Chapter 10 **Audience:** Years 10–12

07 Database Programming with Python
Store and retrieve data persistently using SQLite, SQL queries, and Python ORMs
Prerequisite: Books 01–02 recommended **Audience:** Years 10–12

08 Web Scraping & Working with APIs
Collect real-world data from websites and web services using Python
Prerequisite: Books 02–03 recommended **Audience:** Years 10–12

09 Data Analysis with Python
Explore, clean, and visualise real-world datasets using NumPy, Pandas, and Matplotlib
Prerequisite: Book 03; spreadsheet literacy **Audience:** Years 11–12

10 GUI Programming with Tkinter

Design and build graphical desktop applications using Python's built-in GUI toolkit
Prerequisite: Book 01 (OOP) **Audience:** Years 10–12

11 **Testing, Debugging & Code Quality**
Write reliable, maintainable code using testing frameworks, debugging tools, and style standards
Prerequisite: Books 01 and 03 **Audience:** Years 11–12

12 **Concurrency, Networking & Automation**
Write programs that do multiple things at once, communicate over networks, and automate tasks
Prerequisite: Books 01, 02, and 03 **Audience:** Years 11–12

How to Use This Book

Each book in the Advanced Series is structured in the same way. Understanding the format will help you get the most from each chapter.

Chapter Structure

Every chapter opens with a blockquote that describes what the chapter covers and connects it to what you already know. This is followed by seven numbered sections, each with worked examples, a note callout for important warnings or tips, and closing paragraphs that lead to the next concept.
At the end of each chapter you will find:

- **Chapter Summary** — Eight bullet points summarising the key concepts from the chapter.
- **Guided Exercises** — Five hands-on tasks with hints to help you get started. Complete these before moving on.
- **Challenge Tasks** — Three open-ended tasks with no hints. These require independent problem-solving and are suitable for extension or assessment.

Code Examples

All code is shown in shaded blocks. Every non-obvious line has an inline comment. Each section contains three examples: an Introduction example that introduces the concept in isolation, a Variation example that extends or explores an edge case, and a Real-world application example set in a recognisable context — school, finance, or commerce.
Output blocks immediately follow their code and show exactly what the program prints when run. You should be able to reproduce every output exactly by running the code in a Python 3.10 or later interpreter.

Prior Knowledge

This series assumes you have completed Think, Code, Create — A Python Programming Journey for Students. Foundational concepts (variables, data types, loops, functions, lists, dictionaries) are not re-explained. Where a prior chapter or book is relevant, you will see a brief cross-reference in the text.
Within this book, chapters build on each other. Earlier chapters are referenced with a note rather than a full explanation. If you encounter an unfamiliar concept, check the chapter cross-reference and review that material before continuing.

Table of Contents

CHAPTER 1 Why Files and Exceptions Matter

Book 02: File Handling & Exception Management

Every program that does something genuinely useful either reads data from somewhere or writes data somewhere — and in most cases, both. That somewhere is almost always a file. This chapter establishes why files are fundamental to real programming, what can go wrong when working with them, and why Python's approach to error handling is built around expecting problems rather than pretending they will not occur. By the end of this chapter you will understand the difference between volatile and persistent storage, the landscape of common errors, two competing philosophies for handling them, and how to set up your working environment with the tools that all remaining chapters rely on.

1.1 Programs Without Persistence

Every program stores data in memory as it runs — variables, lists, objects, and every value your code creates. The moment execution ends, all of that disappears. This is not a bug; it is simply how computer memory works. RAM is volatile: it holds whatever the running program needs and releases it the instant that program exits. Switch off the power, close the terminal, or let the script finish — the data is gone.

Persistence means storing data so it outlives the program that created it. When you open a spreadsheet, the figures were not regenerated from scratch — they were read from a file on disk. When a school database records a student's results, those results survive the program restarting, the computer rebooting, and the network dropping, because they were written to persistent storage. Without persistence, every program starts blank every time, which makes it useless for nearly any real-world purpose.

Files are the simplest and most universal form of persistence. Before databases, APIs, and cloud storage existed, nearly every program that needed to remember anything used files. Even today, most programs interact with files in some form: configuration files that store settings, log files that record what happened, CSV exports from databases, JSON responses cached to disk, and plain text reports for users. Understanding how to read and write files is a fundamental skill, not an optional extra.

Example 1 — Introduction

A score tracker that loses all data every time the script exits — the persistence problem demonstrated.

```
# score_volatile.py  —  data disappears each run

scores = []   # starts empty every single run

print("Enter scores (blank line to finish):")
while True:
    entry = input("  Score: ")
    if entry == "":
        break
    scores.append(int(entry))

if scores:
    average = sum(scores) / len(scores)
    print(f"Average: {average:.1f}  (from {len(scores)} scores)")
else:
    print("No scores entered.")

# Run again — the list is empty again. Nothing was saved.
```

Output:
```
Enter scores (blank line to finish):
  Score: 85
  Score: 92
  Score: 78
  Score:
Average: 85.0  (from 3 scores)

# —— Second run ——
Enter scores (blank line to finish):
  Score:
No scores entered.
```

Example 2 — Variation

The same tracker rewritten to save scores to a file and reload them on the next run.

```
# score_persistent.py  —  scores survive between runs
import os

SCORES_FILE = "scores.txt"

# Load any existing scores from disk
if os.path.exists(SCORES_FILE):
    with open(SCORES_FILE, "r") as f:
        scores = [int(line.strip()) for line in f if line.strip()]
else:
    scores = []

print(f"Loaded {len(scores)} existing score(s).")

print("Enter new scores (blank line to finish):")
while True:
    entry = input("  Score: ")
    if entry == "":
        break
    scores.append(int(entry))

# Save all scores back to disk
with open(SCORES_FILE, "w") as f:
    for score in scores:
        f.write(f"{score}\n")

if scores:
    average = sum(scores) / len(scores)
    print(f"Average: {average:.1f}  (from {len(scores)} scores total)")
```

Output:
```
# —— First run ——
Loaded 0 existing score(s).
Enter new scores (blank line to finish):
  Score: 85
  Score: 92
  Score:
Average: 88.5  (from 2 scores total)

# —— Second run ——
Loaded 2 existing score(s).
Enter new scores (blank line to finish):
  Score: 74
  Score:
Average: 83.7  (from 3 scores total)
```

Example 3 — Real-world application

A student grade logger for St Lucia State High School that appends results to a persistent record file.

```
# grade_logger.py  —  persistent grade log for a class
import os
from datetime import date

LOG_FILE  = "grade_log.txt"
SEPARATOR = "-" * 52

def load_grades(filepath):
    """Return a list of [date, name, subject, grade] rows."""
    if not os.path.exists(filepath):
        return []
    records = []
    with open(filepath, "r") as f:
        for line in f:
            parts = line.strip().split(",")
            if len(parts) == 4:
                records.append(parts)
    return records

def save_grade(filepath, name, subject, grade):
    """Append one grade entry to the log file."""
    today = date.today().isoformat()   # e.g. 2025-08-14
    with open(filepath, "a") as f:     # "a" = append mode
        f.write(f"{today},{name},{subject},{grade}\n")

def display_summary(records):
    print(SEPARATOR)
    print(f"  Grade log — {len(records)} record(s)")
    print(SEPARATOR)
    for date_str, name, subject, grade in records:
        print(f"  {date_str}  {name:<20} {subject:<15} {grade}")
    print(SEPARATOR)

records = load_grades(LOG_FILE)
display_summary(records)

name    = input("Student name:   ")
subject = input("Subject:        ")
grade   = input("Grade (A–E):    ")

save_grade(LOG_FILE, name, subject, grade)
print(f"Saved. Log now contains {len(records) + 1} record(s).")
```

Output:

```
----------------------------------------------------
  Grade log — 2 record(s)
----------------------------------------------------
  2025-08-12  Anika Patel          Mathematics     B
  2025-08-13  Liam Torres          English         A
----------------------------------------------------
Student name:   Priya Nair
Subject:        Science
Grade (A-E):    A
Saved. Log now contains 3 record(s).
```

These three examples illustrate the core problem and its solution. The rest of this book teaches you how to read, write, and manage files reliably — and how to handle every error that can arise along the way.

1.2 The Anatomy of a File

Text Files and Binary Files

Every file stored on a computer is ultimately a sequence of bytes. What distinguishes one file type from another is how those bytes are interpreted. Text files store data as human-readable characters encoded in a character set — most commonly UTF-8. When you open a .txt, .csv, .py, or .json file in a text editor, you see recognisable letters, numbers, and punctuation because the encoding maps each byte (or sequence of bytes) to a character.

Binary files store data in formats that are not directly human-readable — images, audio, compiled programs, compressed archives, and Word documents are all binary. Trying to open a binary file in text mode produces garbled output. Python distinguishes the two when opening files: the default mode reads text, while adding "b" to the mode string (e.g. "rb" or "wb") reads and writes raw bytes. This book focuses on text-mode files throughout; binary handling is introduced where needed.

File Paths

Every file is identified by its path — the address that tells the operating system where to find it. An absolute path specifies the complete location from the root of the file system (e.g. /home/anika/data/scores.txt on Linux and macOS). A relative path specifies location relative to the current working directory — the folder from which the program is running (e.g. data/scores.txt means "inside the data subfolder of wherever I am running from").

Relative paths are generally preferable in programs because they make code portable — it does not matter which drive or user folder the project lives in, provided the relative structure is maintained. However, relative paths silently break if the working directory is not what you expect. The os.getcwd() function tells you the current working directory at runtime, which is invaluable when debugging path errors.

Line Endings

Text files encode the end of each line using special characters. Unix and macOS use a single linefeed (\n). Windows traditionally uses a carriage return followed by a linefeed (\r\n). When Python opens a file in text mode (the default), it automatically translates all line endings to \n on reading, and writes \n on all platforms. This universal newlines mode means you can generally ignore line-ending differences when reading text files in Python — but knowing they exist is essential when exchanging files between operating systems.

> **Note:** Always open text files in text mode (the default) and binary files in binary mode ("rb"/"wb"). Opening a binary file in text mode causes errors or data corruption, particularly on Windows where \r\n translation is applied to all bytes.

Example 1 — Introduction

Inspecting file path components using os.path functions.

```
import os

filepath = "/home/anika/school/data/grades.csv"

print("Full path: ", filepath)
print("Directory:", os.path.dirname(filepath))    # everything before the last
separator
print("Filename: ", os.path.basename(filepath))   # just the file name
print("Stem:     ", os.path.splitext(os.path.basename(filepath))[0])
print("Extension:", os.path.splitext(filepath)[1])

# Build a path safely — works on Windows and Unix alike
safe = os.path.join("school", "data", "grades.csv")
print("Built:    ", safe)
```

Output:

```
Full path:  /home/anika/school/data/grades.csv
Directory: /home/anika/school/data
Filename:  grades.csv
```

```
Stem:      grades
Extension: .csv
Built:     school/data/grades.csv
```

Example 2 — Variation

Demonstrating what happens with a correct relative path, a wrong relative path, and os.path.abspath().

```
import os

print("Working directory:", os.getcwd())

# A relative path that is wrong for the current working directory
wrong = "data/missing_file.txt"
if not os.path.exists(wrong):
    print(f"Not found at relative path: {wrong!r}")
    print("  Common cause: script run from a different directory.")

# Convert a relative path to its absolute equivalent
relative = "grades.csv"
absolute = os.path.abspath(relative)
print(f"\nRelative {relative!r} expands to:")
print(f"  {absolute}")
```

Output:

```
Working directory: /home/anika/school
Not found at relative path: 'data/missing_file.txt'
  Common cause: script run from a different directory.

Relative 'grades.csv' expands to:
  /home/anika/school/grades.csv
```

Example 3 — Real-world application

A file inspection utility that reports the type, size, and line-ending style of a text file.

```
# file_inspector.py  —  examine a file before processing it
import os

TEXT_EXTENSIONS = {".txt", ".csv", ".json", ".py", ".html", ".md", ".log"}

def inspect_file(filepath):
    if not os.path.exists(filepath):
        print(f"Error: {filepath!r} does not exist.")
        return

    size = os.path.getsize(filepath)
    ext  = os.path.splitext(filepath)[1].lower()
    kind = "text" if ext in TEXT_EXTENSIONS else "binary (likely)"

    print(f"File:      {os.path.basename(filepath)}")
    print(f"Size:      {size} bytes")
    print(f"Type:      {kind}")
    print(f"Extension: {ext}")

    if kind == "text" and size > 0:
        with open(filepath, "rb") as f:   # binary mode to see raw bytes
            sample = f.read(512)
        if b"\r\n" in sample:
            ending = "Windows (\\r\\n)"
        elif b"\r" in sample:
            ending = "Old Mac (\\r)"
        else:
            ending = "Unix (\\n)"
        print(f"Line ends: {ending}")
    print()
```

```
inspect_file("grades.csv")
inspect_file("photo.jpg")
inspect_file("nonexistent.txt")
```

Output:

```
File:       grades.csv
Size:       1042 bytes
Type:       text
Extension:  .csv
Line ends:  Unix (\n)

File:       photo.jpg
Size:       84320 bytes
Type:       binary (likely)
Extension:  .jpg

Error: 'nonexistent.txt' does not exist.
```

Understanding path mechanics and file types upfront prevents a large class of frustrating errors. When a file operation fails, the first questions to ask are always: is the path correct for the current working directory, and is the file being opened in the right mode?

1.3 What Can Go Wrong — Common File Errors

File operations interact with the operating system, the file system, and hardware — all of which can fail in ways that have nothing to do with your program's logic. A file might not exist because a user typed the wrong name. A program might lack permission to read a protected file. A path that points to a directory might be passed where a file is expected. These are not edge cases; they are routine situations in any program that handles real data.

Python maps OS-level errors to a clear hierarchy of exception types. The base class for all file and OS-related errors is OSError (also known as IOError in older code — they are the same class in Python 3). From OSError, Python derives more specific types: FileNotFoundError when a path does not exist, PermissionError when the process lacks the necessary access rights, IsADirectoryError when a directory path is passed where a file is expected, and others. Catching the specific subclass rather than the broad OSError produces more informative error messages and makes code easier to debug.

The principle of failing early and failing clearly is central to robust file handling. When a required file is missing, report it immediately with a meaningful message — do not let the program continue in a broken state and produce a confusing error five steps later. Every traceback Python shows you is a gift: it tells you exactly where the problem occurred, what type of error it was, and what value caused it. Learning to read tracebacks fluently is as important as learning to write code.

Example 1 — Introduction

A FileNotFoundError raised and its traceback examined line by line.

```
# Attempt to open a file that does not exist
f = open("missing_data.txt", "r")

# Python raises:
# FileNotFoundError: [Errno 2] No such file or directory: 'missing_data.txt'
#
# Reading the traceback:
#   Line 1  – "Traceback (most recent call last)": Python is about to show the
call stack.
#   Line 2  –  File "demo.py", line 2: where in the source the error occurred.
#   Line 3  –  The exact statement that failed.
```

```
#   Line 4  —  Exception type + OS error code + filename in quotes.
#
# [Errno 2] is the POSIX error code for "No such file or directory".
# The filename is shown in quotes so you can verify the exact path used.
```

Output:

```
Traceback (most recent call last):
  File "demo.py", line 2, in <module>
    f = open("missing_data.txt", "r")
FileNotFoundError: [Errno 2] No such file or directory: 'missing_data.txt'
```

Example 2 — Variation

Triggering and identifying IsADirectoryError and PermissionError.

```
import os

# IsADirectoryError  —  passing a directory path where a file is expected
try:
    open(".")   # "." is the current directory, not a file
except IsADirectoryError as e:
    print(f"IsADirectoryError: {e}")

# PermissionError  —  attempting to write to a protected system file
(Linux/macOS)
try:
    open("/etc/hosts", "w")
except PermissionError as e:
    print(f"PermissionError: {e}")

# Confirm both are subclasses of OSError
print(issubclass(FileNotFoundError, OSError))
print(issubclass(PermissionError,   OSError))
print(issubclass(IsADirectoryError, OSError))
```

Output:

```
IsADirectoryError: [Errno 21] Is a directory: '.'
PermissionError: [Errno 13] Permission denied: '/etc/hosts'
True
True
True
```

Example 3 — Real-world application

A diagnostic function that attempts to open each of three files and provides a specific, clear message for each type of failure.

```
# file_diagnostics.py  —  identify exactly why each file cannot be opened

def diagnose_file(filepath):
    """Attempt to open filepath and report the exact reason for any failure."""
    print(f"Checking: {filepath!r}")
    try:
        with open(filepath, "r") as f:
            content = f.read()
        print(f"  OK — {len(content)} characters read.")
    except FileNotFoundError:
        print("  ERROR: File does not exist. Check the filename and path.")
    except IsADirectoryError:
        print("  ERROR: That path is a directory, not a file.")
    except PermissionError:
        print("  ERROR: Insufficient permissions to read this file.")
    except OSError as e:
        print(f"  ERROR: OS error — {e}")
    print()

diagnose_file("student_records.csv")   # does not exist
```

```
diagnose_file(".")                    # a directory
diagnose_file("config.json")          # exists and is readable
```

Output:

```
Checking: 'student_records.csv'
  ERROR: File does not exist. Check the filename and path.

Checking: '.'
  ERROR: That path is a directory, not a file.

Checking: 'config.json'
  OK — 142 characters read.
```

Notice that the most specific exception types are caught first, with the broader OSError as a catch-all at the end. This ordering matters: Python evaluates except clauses from top to bottom and stops at the first match. Placing a broad type at the top would swallow all the specific cases below it. Section 7.3 covers this ordering in full.

1.4 What Can Go Wrong — Common Runtime Errors

File errors are only one category of failure. Once data has been successfully read from a file, your program must interpret it — and interpretation can go wrong in a completely different set of ways. A line expected to contain a number might contain text. A row expected to have five columns might have three. A dictionary key you assumed would exist might be absent. These failures are not caused by the file system; they are caused by data that does not match your program's expectations.

Python's exception hierarchy is organised as a tree. At the root is BaseException, the ultimate parent of every exception. Below it sits Exception, the parent of all "normal" errors that programs are expected to handle. The exceptions you will encounter constantly when processing file data are: ValueError (a value has the right type but wrong content, such as converting "abc" to an int), TypeError (an operation applied to the wrong type entirely), IndexError (accessing a list position that does not exist), KeyError (accessing a dictionary key that is not present), and ZeroDivisionError (dividing by zero, often the result of an empty dataset).

Understanding that exceptions are objects in a class hierarchy matters because it lets you catch them at different levels of specificity. Catching ValueError handles only value-related errors. Catching Exception handles almost everything that inherits from it. The hierarchy makes it possible to write code that is precise where precision matters and broad where it does not — a skill developed fully through Chapters 7 and 8.

> **Note:** Never write a bare "except:" with no exception type. This catches BaseException, including SystemExit and KeyboardInterrupt, and can make a program impossible to stop from the keyboard. Always name the exception type — at minimum, use "except Exception:".

Example 1 — Introduction

A ValueError raised when converting non-numeric text to an integer — the most common data-cleaning error.

```
# Simulating data read from a file  —  some values are not valid numbers
raw_values = ["85", "92", "N/A", "74", ""]

for raw in raw_values:
    try:
        score = int(raw)
        print(f"  Parsed: {score}")
    except ValueError:
        print(f"  Skipped {raw!r}  —  not a valid integer")
```

Output:

```
  Parsed: 85
  Parsed: 92
  Skipped 'N/A'  —  not a valid integer
  Parsed: 74
  Skipped ''  —  not a valid integer
```

Example 2 — Variation

IndexError and KeyError raised by a short CSV row and a missing dictionary key.

```
# IndexError  —  a CSV row shorter than expected
rows = [
    ["Priya", "Mathematics", "A"],
    ["Liam",  "English"],             # missing the grade column
    ["Anika", "Science",    "B"],
]

for row in rows:
    try:
        name, subject, grade = row[0], row[1], row[2]
        print(f"  {name}: {subject} — {grade}")
    except IndexError:
        print(f"  Skipped {row!r}  —  missing column")

print()

# KeyError  —  accessing a key absent from a loaded dict
record = {"name": "Priya", "subject": "Mathematics"}
try:
    grade = record["grade"]
except KeyError as e:
    print(f"  KeyError: key {e} not found in record")
```

Output:

```
  Priya: Mathematics — A
  Skipped ['Liam', 'English']  —  missing column
  Anika: Science — B

  KeyError: key 'grade' not found in record
```

Example 3 — Real-world application

A record-processing function that catches ValueError, IndexError, and KeyError separately, reporting a clear message for each.

```
# data_loader.py  —  process raw CSV-style records with full error reporting

def process_record(raw_row, line_number):
    """
    Parse [name, subject, score_str] into a dict.
    Returns the dict on success, or None on failure.
    """
    try:
        name    = raw_row[0].strip()              # IndexError if row is too
short
        subject = raw_row[1].strip()
        score   = int(raw_row[2].strip())         # ValueError if not numeric
        if not name:
            raise ValueError("name cannot be blank")
        return {"name": name, "subject": subject, "score": score}
    except IndexError:
        print(f"  Line {line_number}: fewer than 3 columns — skipped")
    except ValueError as e:
        print(f"  Line {line_number}: invalid data ({e}) — skipped")
    return None

raw_data = [
```

```
    ["Anika Patel", "Mathematics", "88"],
    ["Liam Torres", "English"],              # only 2 columns
    ["Priya Nair",  "Science",     "abc"],   # non-numeric score
    ["",            "History",     "75"],    # blank name
    ["Sam Wong",    "Physics",     "91"],
]

results = [r for r in (process_record(row, i) for i, row in enumerate(raw_data,
1)) if r]

print(f"\nSuccessfully loaded {len(results)} record(s):")
for r in results:
    print(f'  {r["name"]:<20} {r["subject"]:<15} {r["score"]}')
```

Output:

```
  Line 2: fewer than 3 columns – skipped
  Line 3: invalid data (invalid literal for int() with base 10: 'abc') –
skipped
  Line 4: invalid data (name cannot be blank) – skipped

Successfully loaded 2 record(s):
  Anika Patel          Mathematics     88
  Sam Wong             Physics         91
```

This pattern — attempt the operation, catch specific exceptions, report clearly, continue — appears throughout real-world data processing code. Rather than crashing on the first bad record, the program reports the problem and moves on. This is almost always the correct behaviour when processing batches of data from external sources.

1.5 The Two Approaches: LBYL and EAFP

When writing code that might fail, you must choose how to deal with that possibility before it occurs. There are two distinct philosophies, each with a memorable acronym from the Python community.

Look Before You Leap (LBYL)

LBYL means checking conditions before attempting an operation. Before opening a file, check that it exists. Before accessing a list index, check that the list is long enough. Before dividing, check the divisor is not zero. This approach is common in languages like C and Java, where exceptions are expensive or deliberately avoided. In Python, LBYL looks like a series of if statements guarding each potentially risky operation.

Easier to Ask Forgiveness than Permission (EAFP)

EAFP means attempting the operation directly and handling any exception that arises. Rather than checking whether a file exists before opening it, you simply open it and catch FileNotFoundError if it fails. This is Python's idiomatic style. The Python documentation explicitly recommends EAFP for most situations because it is cleaner, faster, and avoids a class of subtle bugs called race conditions.

The Race Condition Problem

A race condition occurs when two operations happen so close together that the result depends on timing. With LBYL, you check whether a file exists and then open it — but between those two operations, another process could delete the file. The check passed; the open fails anyway. With EAFP, there is no gap between checking and acting: you open the file and handle failure if it occurs. This makes EAFP inherently safer in concurrent or multi-user environments.

That said, LBYL is genuinely more appropriate in some situations. When validating user input before attempting any operation — such as checking a field contains a valid date before parsing it — pre-checking is cleaner and produces better error messages. The choice is not dogmatic; it is contextual.

Note: The Python glossary explicitly defines both LBYL and EAFP and describes EAFP as "the preferred Python style." When in doubt, default to EAFP with try/except for any operation that touches external resources: files, network, databases.

Example 1 — Introduction

The LBYL approach to opening and reading the first line of a file.

```
import os

def read_first_line_lbyl(filepath):
    """LBYL: check conditions before attempting the operation."""
    if not os.path.exists(filepath):
        print(f"  LBYL: {filepath!r} does not exist.")
        return None
    if not os.path.isfile(filepath):
        print(f"  LBYL: {filepath!r} is not a file.")
        return None
    with open(filepath, "r") as f:
        return f.readline().strip()

result = read_first_line_lbyl("data.txt")
if result is not None:
    print(f"  First line: {result!r}")

read_first_line_lbyl("missing.txt")
read_first_line_lbyl(".")
```

Output:

```
  First line: 'StudentID,Name,Score'
  LBYL: 'missing.txt' does not exist.
  LBYL: '.' is not a file.
```

Example 2 — Variation

The EAFP approach to the same task — cleaner code, no window between check and action.

```
def read_first_line_eafp(filepath):
    """EAFP: attempt the operation and handle failure if it occurs."""
    try:
        with open(filepath, "r") as f:
            return f.readline().strip()
    except FileNotFoundError:
        print(f"  EAFP: {filepath!r} does not exist.")
        return None
    except IsADirectoryError:
        print(f"  EAFP: {filepath!r} is a directory.")
        return None

for path in ["data.txt", "missing.txt", "."]:
    result = read_first_line_eafp(path)
    if result is not None:
        print(f"  {path!r}: first line = {result!r}")
```

Output:

```
  'data.txt': first line = 'StudentID,Name,Score'
  EAFP: 'missing.txt' does not exist.
  EAFP: '.' is a directory.
```

Example 3 — Real-world application

A configuration loader using EAFP for file access and LBYL for validating values already in memory.

```
# config_loader.py  —  EAFP for file I/O, LBYL for value validation
import os
```

```
DEFAULT_CONFIG = {
    "school":  "Brisbane State High",
    "year":    2025,
    "log_dir": "logs",
}

def load_config_eafp(filepath):
    """
    EAFP: open and parse; handle errors as they occur.
    Race-condition safe — no gap between checking and opening.
    """
    try:
        with open(filepath, "r") as f:
            config = {}
            for line in f:
                line = line.strip()
                if "=" in line and not line.startswith("#"):
                    key, _, value = line.partition("=")
                    config[key.strip()] = value.strip()
            return config
    except FileNotFoundError:
        print(f"Config {filepath!r} not found — using defaults.")
        return DEFAULT_CONFIG.copy()

def validate_config_lbyl(config):
    """
    LBYL: check required keys before using the config.
    Appropriate here — we are inspecting values already in memory.
    """
    required = ["school", "year", "log_dir"]
    missing  = [k for k in required if k not in config]
    if missing:
        raise ValueError(f"Config missing required key(s): {missing}")
    return True

cfg = load_config_eafp("school.conf")
print("Loaded:", cfg)
validate_config_lbyl(cfg)
print("Config validated.")
```

Output:

```
Config 'school.conf' not found — using defaults.
Loaded: {'school': 'Brisbane State High', 'year': 2025, 'log_dir': 'logs'}
Config validated.
```

The key insight is that EAFP and LBYL are complementary rather than mutually exclusive. Use EAFP when interacting with external resources (files, network, databases) where conditions can change between a check and an action. Use LBYL when validating values that are already in memory and will not change during the check.

1.6 Why This Chapter Matters for Real Programs

Every program that does something genuinely useful reads or writes data. A grade calculator reads a spreadsheet. A student information system writes records to a database. A configuration tool reads a settings file. A logging system appends to a log file. File handling is not a niche skill for systems programmers — it is the bridge between a program and the real world. Without it, a program can only process data typed in manually during a single session.

Exception handling is equally fundamental — not as a mechanism for suppressing errors, but for responding to them intelligently. The difference between a fragile program and a robust one is not that the robust program never encounters bad data. It is that the robust program recognises bad data, handles it appropriately, and continues to function. In a real school environment, student records can contain typos, missing fields, or inconsistent formats. A program that crashes on the first anomaly is useless. A program that reports the anomaly, skips the bad record, and processes the rest is genuinely valuable.

The following examples show the same grade calculator written two ways: one that crashes immediately on unexpected data, and one that handles every likely failure and continues processing. The difference in code length is modest; the difference in practical usefulness is enormous.

Example 1 — Introduction

A fragile grade calculator with no error handling — it crashes on the first problem it encounters.

```
# fragile_grades.py  —  no error handling; crashes on first bad record

raw_data = [
    "Anika Patel,88",
    "Liam Torres,N/A",   # bad score  —  will crash here
    "Priya Nair,91",
    "Sam Wong,",         # missing score
]

total = 0
count = 0

for line in raw_data:
    parts = line.split(",")
    name  = parts[0]
    score = int(parts[1])   # ValueError on "N/A"
    total += score
    count += 1
    print(f"  {name}: {score}")

print(f"Class average: {total / count:.1f}")
```

Output:

```
  Anika Patel: 88
Traceback (most recent call last):
  File "fragile_grades.py", line 16, in <module>
    score = int(parts[1])   # ValueError on "N/A"
ValueError: invalid literal for int() with base 10: 'N/A'
```

Example 2 — Variation

The robust version: handles every likely failure, reports skipped records, and continues processing.

```
# robust_grades.py  —  handles every failure and continues

raw_data = [
    "Anika Patel,88",
    "Liam Torres,N/A",
    "Priya Nair,91",
    "Sam Wong,",
    "Maya Chen,95",
]

total   = 0
count   = 0
skipped = []

for line in raw_data:
    try:
        parts = line.split(",")
        name  = parts[0].strip()
        score = int(parts[1].strip())   # ValueError if not numeric
        if not name:
            raise ValueError("blank name")
        total += score
```

```
        count += 1
        print(f"  {name}: {score}")
    except (ValueError, IndexError) as e:
        skipped.append((line.strip(), str(e)))

if skipped:
    print(f"\n  Skipped {len(skipped)} record(s):")
    for raw, reason in skipped:
        print(f"    {raw!r}  —  {reason}")

if count > 0:
    print(f"\nClass average ({count} students): {total / count:.1f}")
else:
    print("No valid records to process.")
```

Output:

```
  Anika Patel: 88
  Priya Nair: 91
  Maya Chen: 95

  Skipped 2 record(s):
    'Liam Torres,N/A'  —  invalid literal for int() with base 10: 'N/A'
    'Sam Wong,'  —  invalid literal for int() with base 10: ''

Class average (3 students): 91.3
```

Example 3 — Real-world application

A complete file-based grade report generator with graceful error handling at every stage of processing.

```
# grade_report.py  —  reads a CSV file and produces a summary report
import os

GRADES_FILE = "class_grades.csv"   # Format: Name,Subject,Score

def load_grades(filepath):
    """Load grades from CSV; return (records, errors) tuple."""
    records, errors = [], []
    try:
        with open(filepath, "r", encoding="utf-8") as f:
            lines = f.readlines()
    except FileNotFoundError:
        return records, [f"File not found: {filepath!r}"]
    except PermissionError:
        return records, [f"Permission denied: {filepath!r}"]

    for i, line in enumerate(lines[1:], start=2):   # skip header
        line = line.strip()
        if not line:
            continue
        parts = line.split(",")
        try:
            name, subject = parts[0].strip(), parts[1].strip()
            score = int(parts[2].strip())
            if not 0 <= score <= 100:
                raise ValueError(f"score {score} out of range 0-100")
            records.append({"name": name, "subject": subject, "score": score})
        except IndexError:
            errors.append(f"Line {i}: too few columns")
        except ValueError as e:
            errors.append(f"Line {i}: {e}")
    return records, errors

def print_report(records, errors):
    print("=" * 52)
    print("  GRADE REPORT")
    print("=" * 52)
```

```
    if records:
        for r in records:
            print(f'  {r["name"]:<20} {r["subject"]:<14} {r["score"]:>3}')
        avg = sum(r["score"] for r in records) / len(records)
        print("-" * 52)
        print(f"  Average: {avg:.1f}  |  Students: {len(records)}")
    else:
        print("  No valid records.")
    if errors:
        print(f"\n  Warnings ({len(errors)}):")
        for e in errors:
            print(f"    - {e}")
    print("=" * 52)

records, errors = load_grades(GRADES_FILE)
print_report(records, errors)
```

Output:

```
====================================================
  GRADE REPORT
====================================================
  Anika Patel          Mathematics     88
  Priya Nair           Science         91
  Sam Wong             Physics         95
  Maya Chen            English         79
----------------------------------------------------
  Average: 88.3  |  Students: 4

  Warnings (2):
    - Line 3: invalid literal for int() with base 10: 'N/A'
    - Line 5: too few columns
====================================================
```

The robust version is longer — but only because it does more. Every additional line is work that was previously being done by the crash and the confused user manually fixing their data. Exception handling is not extra code; it is the code that makes programs genuinely usable in the real world.

1.7 Setting Up: File Paths and the os Module — First Look

Before writing any serious file-handling code, it pays to establish a small toolkit of path-management utilities. Python provides two interfaces for this work: the older os.path module (part of the standard library since the earliest Python versions) and the newer pathlib module (introduced in Python 3.4), which represents paths as objects rather than plain strings. Both are widely used; pathlib is generally preferred in modern code for its cleaner syntax and richer feature set.

The most useful os.path functions for this book are: os.getcwd() (returns the current working directory as a string), os.path.join() (builds a path from components using the correct OS separator), os.path.exists() (True if the path exists), os.path.isfile() (True if it is a regular file), and os.path.abspath() (converts a relative path to absolute). These five cover the majority of path operations you will need.

pathlib.Path wraps all of these into a single object. You construct a Path from a string, then use the / operator to build child paths (Path("data") / "grades.csv"), .exists() and .is_file() for existence checks, .read_text() to read a file's contents in one call, and .write_text() to write a string to a file. Chapter 9 covers pathlib in depth; here we introduce enough to use it throughout this book.

> **Note:** os.path.join() is critical for cross-platform code. Never concatenate path strings with "+" or hard-code "/" or "\\" as separators. Always use os.path.join() or the pathlib / operator — they insert the correct separator for the current operating system automatically.

Example 1 — Introduction

Key os and os.path functions for inspecting and constructing file paths.

```
import os

# Current working directory
cwd = os.getcwd()
print(f"Working directory: {cwd}")

# Build paths safely  —  no hard-coded separators
data_dir = os.path.join(cwd, "data")
csv_path = os.path.join(data_dir, "students.csv")
print(f"Data dir:  {data_dir}")
print(f"CSV path:  {csv_path}")

# Existence checks
print(f"data/ exists:        {os.path.exists(data_dir)}")
print(f"students.csv exists: {os.path.exists(csv_path)}")

# Convert relative to absolute
print(f"Absolute of 'results/term3.txt':")
print(f"  {os.path.abspath('results/term3.txt')}")
```

Output:

```
Working directory: /home/anika/school
Data dir:  /home/anika/school/data
CSV path:  /home/anika/school/data/students.csv
data/ exists:        True
students.csv exists: False
Absolute of 'results/term3.txt':
  /home/anika/school/results/term3.txt
```

Example 2 — Variation

The same operations using pathlib.Path — the modern, object-oriented approach.

```
from pathlib import Path

# Path object from the current directory
cwd = Path.cwd()
print(f"Working directory: {cwd}")

# Build child paths with the / operator
data_dir = cwd / "data"
csv_path = data_dir / "students.csv"
print(f"Data dir:  {data_dir}")
print(f"CSV path:  {csv_path}")

# Path component properties
print(f"Name:   {csv_path.name}")     # students.csv
print(f"Stem:   {csv_path.stem}")     # students
print(f"Suffix: {csv_path.suffix}")   # .csv
print(f"Parent: {csv_path.parent}")

# Existence checks
print(f"data/ exists:  {data_dir.exists()}")
print(f"data/ is dir:  {data_dir.is_dir()}")
```

Output:

```
Working directory: /home/anika/school
Data dir:  /home/anika/school/data
CSV path:  /home/anika/school/data/students.csv
Name:   students.csv
Stem:   students
Suffix: .csv
Parent: /home/anika/school/data
data/ exists:  True
data/ is dir:  True
```

Example 3 — Real-world application

A setup helper using pathlib that creates a config directory and default file on first run, then reads the file back safely.

```
# setup_helper.py  —  create, write, and read back a configuration file
from pathlib import Path

CONFIG_DIR  = Path("config")
CONFIG_FILE = CONFIG_DIR / "school.conf"

DEFAULT_CONTENT = (
    "# School configuration file\n"
    "# Generated automatically on first run\n"
    "school_name = Brisbane State High School\n"
    "academic_year = 2025\n"
    "log_level = INFO"
)

def ensure_config():
    """Create the config directory and default file if absent."""
    CONFIG_DIR.mkdir(parents=True, exist_ok=True)
    if not CONFIG_FILE.exists():
        CONFIG_FILE.write_text(DEFAULT_CONTENT, encoding="utf-8")
        print(f"Created default config at {CONFIG_FILE}")
    else:
        print(f"Config found at {CONFIG_FILE}")

def safe_read_config():
    """Return the config file contents, or an empty string on error."""
    try:
        return CONFIG_FILE.read_text(encoding="utf-8")
    except PermissionError:
        print(f"ERROR: Cannot read {CONFIG_FILE}  —  permission denied.")
        return ""

ensure_config()
contents = safe_read_config()
print()
print("--- Config file contents ---")
print(contents)
print("----------------------------")
print(f"File size: {CONFIG_FILE.stat().st_size} bytes")
```

Output:

```
Created default config at config/school.conf

--- Config file contents ---
# School configuration file
# Generated automatically on first run
school_name = Brisbane State High School
academic_year = 2025
log_level = INFO
----------------------------
File size: 109 bytes
```

The pattern in Example 1.7.3 — ensure a directory exists, write a default file if absent, read it back safely — recurs throughout real applications. A logging system creates its log directory if it does not exist. A game saves default settings on first launch. A data pipeline creates an output folder before writing results. These are the building blocks that later chapters assemble into complete, production-quality programs.

Chapter 1 Summary

- Without persistence, programs start blank every time they run; files are the simplest and most universal mechanism for storing data between sessions.
- Text files store human-readable characters encoded in a character set (most commonly UTF-8); binary files store raw bytes and must be opened with the "b" mode flag.
- Paths can be absolute (from the filesystem root) or relative (from the current working directory); os.path.join() and the pathlib / operator build paths portably across operating systems.
- Common file errors — FileNotFoundError, PermissionError, IsADirectoryError — are all subclasses of OSError; catching the most specific subclass gives the clearest and most actionable error messages.
- Common runtime errors when processing file data include ValueError (bad data format), IndexError (missing columns in a row), KeyError (missing dictionary key), and ZeroDivisionError (empty dataset).
- LBYL (Look Before You Leap) pre-checks conditions with if statements; EAFP (Easier to Ask Forgiveness than Permission) attempts the operation and catches exceptions — Python idiom strongly favours EAFP for resource access.
- A fragile program crashes on the first bad record; a robust program catches the error, reports it clearly, and continues — exception handling is the code that makes programs genuinely usable in production.
- os.path and pathlib.Path both provide path manipulation; pathlib is preferred in modern Python for its object-oriented interface, / path-building syntax, and convenience methods such as read_text() and write_text().

Guided Exercises

1. Write a program that saves the current date and time to a text file called log.txt, appending a new entry each time it is run. After appending, read the file and print its entire contents to confirm the entry was saved.

> ***Hint:*** *Use the datetime module for the timestamp and open() with mode "a" for appending. Open with mode "r" to read back the full contents and print them.*

2. Write a function safe_read(filepath) that returns the file contents as a string if the file can be opened, or a descriptive error message string if it cannot. Test it against a file that exists and one that does not.

> ***Hint:*** *Use a try/except block inside the function. Catch FileNotFoundError and PermissionError separately to return a different message for each case.*

3. Write a function sum_numbers(filepath) that reads a file containing one integer per line and returns their sum. Any non-numeric lines should be skipped with a printed warning. Test it with a file containing a mix of valid numbers and invalid entries.

> ***Hint:*** *Loop over the file lines with a try/except around int(line.strip()) inside the loop. Keep a count of skipped lines and print the total at the end.*

4. Demonstrate LBYL versus EAFP for checking whether a key exists in a dictionary loaded from a simple key=value text file. Write both versions and comment on which is cleaner and why.

> ***Hint:*** *For LBYL use "if key in config:". For EAFP use try/except KeyError. Test with a key that exists and a key that does not.*

5. Use os.path.join() to build file paths that work on both Windows and macOS/Linux. Build and print paths to: a data subdirectory, a grades.csv file inside it, and a logs subdirectory at the same level as data.

> ***Hint:*** *Start from os.getcwd() and use os.path.join() for every path component. Print all three paths and verify they look correct on your platform.*

Challenge Tasks

1. Write a robust CSV reader (without importing the csv module) that opens a file, skips blank lines and comment lines (starting with #), handles rows with fewer columns than the header gracefully, and returns a list of dicts using the first non-comment, non-blank row as headers. Test it with a file that contains a mix of valid rows, blank lines, comment lines, and short rows.
2. Design a simple application logging system. Define a LogEntry dataclass with fields for timestamp, level (INFO/WARNING/ERROR), and message. Write a Logger class that appends entries to a file as comma-separated lines. Write a log_reader(filepath, level) function that loads the file and returns only entries matching the specified level. Demonstrate writing entries at all three levels and filtering by each level.
3. Build a file integrity checker. Walk a directory, record the size and last-modified timestamp of every .txt and .csv file into a JSON manifest. On a second run, compare the current state of the directory to the saved manifest and report: which files have changed (different size or timestamp), which files are new (not in the manifest), and which files have been removed (in the manifest but no longer on disk). Use the os module for file statistics and the json module to save and load the manifest.

CHAPTER 2 Reading Text Files

Book 02: File Handling & Exception Management

> *Chapter 1 established why files matter and introduced the tools needed to work with paths safely. This chapter puts those foundations to work: you will open text files, read their contents using every method Python provides, iterate over them line by line with minimal memory overhead, handle international character encodings correctly, and understand how the file pointer moves as you read. By the end of this chapter you will have a complete picture of what happens between calling open() and retrieving the last character of a file — and the judgment to choose the most appropriate reading strategy for any given situation.*

2.1 open(), File Modes, and the File Object

The built-in open() function is the entry point for all file I/O in Python. It accepts a path — as a string or a pathlib.Path object — and returns a file object: a handle that provides methods for reading or writing depending on how the file was opened. open() does not read the file; it asks the operating system to prepare a connection to it and returns an object you can use for subsequent operations.

The second argument is the mode string, which controls both the operation (read, write, append) and the data format (text or binary). The most common modes for reading are "r" (read text, the default if mode is omitted), "rb" (read binary, returns bytes rather than str), and "r+" (read and write without truncating). Explicitly stating the mode, even when it is the default "r", improves readability in code that will be maintained by others.

The encoding Parameter

The third parameter that matters most for correctness is encoding. Text files store bytes; the encoding specifies how those bytes are converted to characters when reading. The dominant encoding today is UTF-8, which handles every character in the Unicode standard. If encoding is omitted, Python uses the platform locale default — UTF-8 on macOS and most Linux systems, but cp1252 or another Windows code page on Windows. This silent platform difference causes programs that run correctly on one machine to fail on another. The fix is straightforward: always pass encoding="utf-8" explicitly, for every text-mode open() call.

The file object returned by open() carries attributes that describe the connection: name stores the path used to open the file, mode stores the mode string, encoding stores the encoding in use, and closed becomes True after the file has been closed. These attributes are valuable when debugging: confirming that encoding is actually "utf-8" and not some unexpected platform default takes one line.

> **Note:** Never rely on the platform default encoding. On Windows, omitting encoding silently opens files as cp1252, which misreads UTF-8 files containing any character outside plain ASCII. The fix is always: open(filepath, "r", encoding="utf-8").

Example 1 — Introduction

Calling open() with explicit mode and encoding; inspecting the file object's attributes before and after closing.

```
# Assume "students.txt" exists and contains UTF-8 encoded text

f = open("students.txt", "r", encoding="utf-8")

print("name:    ", f.name)        # path used to open the file
print("mode:    ", f.mode)        # "r"
```

```
print("encoding:", f.encoding)   # "utf-8"
print("closed:  ", f.closed)     # False — file is still open

f.close()                         # must close manually when not using with
print("closed:  ", f.closed)     # True
```

Output:

```
name:     students.txt
mode:     r
encoding: utf-8
closed:   False
closed:   True
```

Example 2 — Variation

The three main read modes side by side: "r", "rb", and "r+"; demonstrating that UnicodeDecodeError occurs at read time, not at open().

```
# —— Text mode (default for reading) ————————————————————————————
f = open("students.txt", "r", encoding="utf-8")
print(f"Text mode   — encoding: {f.encoding},  readable: {f.readable()}")
f.close()

# —— Binary mode — returns bytes, no encoding ——————————————————————
f = open("students.txt", "rb")
print(f"Binary mode — encoding: {f.encoding},  readable: {f.readable()}")
f.close()

# —— Read+write text mode — does NOT erase the file ————————————————
f = open("students.txt", "r+", encoding="utf-8")
print(f"r+ mode     — encoding: {f.encoding},  writable: {f.writable()}")
f.close()

# —— Wrong encoding: open() succeeds but read() raises an error ————
try:
    f = open("students.txt", "r", encoding="ascii")
    f.read()   # UnicodeDecodeError occurs here, not at open()
except UnicodeDecodeError as e:
    print(f"\nUnicodeDecodeError: {e}")
finally:
    f.close()
```

Output:

```
Text mode   — encoding: utf-8,  readable: True
Binary mode — encoding: None,   readable: True
r+ mode     — encoding: utf-8,  writable: True

UnicodeDecodeError: 'ascii' codec can't decode byte 0xc3 in position 14:
  ordinal not in range(128)
```

Example 3 — Real-world application

A validated open helper that enforces text modes and UTF-8 encoding, logs every file open, and raises clear errors for invalid usage.

```
# safe_open.py  —  a validated wrapper for open() used throughout a project
import os

VALID_TEXT_MODES = {"r", "w", "a", "r+", "w+", "a+"}

def safe_open(filepath, mode="r", encoding="utf-8"):
    """
    Open filepath with mode and encoding after validation.
    Raises ValueError for unsupported modes.
    Logs the open operation for diagnostic purposes.
    """
```

```
    if mode not in VALID_TEXT_MODES:
        raise ValueError(
            f"Unsupported mode {mode!r}. Expected one of:
{sorted(VALID_TEXT_MODES)}"
        )
    abs_path = os.path.abspath(filepath)
    f = open(filepath, mode, encoding=encoding)
    size = os.path.getsize(filepath)
    print(f"  Opened: {abs_path}  [{mode}]  {size} bytes  enc={encoding}")
    return f

try:
    f = safe_open("class_roll.txt")
    content = f.read()
    f.close()
    print(f"  Read {len(content)} characters successfully.")
except FileNotFoundError:
    print("  File not found — check the path.")
except ValueError as e:
    print(f"  Configuration error: {e}")
```

Output:

```
  Opened: /home/anika/school/class_roll.txt  [r]  832 bytes  enc=utf-8
  Read 832 characters successfully.
```

In larger projects, centralising file-open logic in a helper like safe_open() enforces encoding policy, provides a single audit point for file access, and ensures every open() is logged in the same format. From this point forward, examples in this chapter show the with statement — the correct approach for resource management, covered in full in Chapter 4 — rather than manual close() calls.

2.2 read(), readline(), and readlines()

Once a file is open, three distinct methods give access to its contents, each with a different granularity and different memory footprint. Choosing correctly depends on how much data you need at once, the size of the file, and what you intend to do with the result.

read()

Calling read() with no argument returns the entire file as a single string, newlines included. This is the simplest approach and is perfectly appropriate for small files — configuration files, short reports, and templates. The limitation is memory: on a 200 MB log file, read() allocates a 200 MB string. Calling read(n) with an integer argument reads exactly n characters in text mode (or n bytes in binary mode), which forms the basis of the chunked-reading technique covered in Section 2.5.

readline()

readline() reads one line at a time, including its trailing \n character (the final line of a file may have no trailing newline). Each call advances the file pointer to the start of the next line. When the end of file is reached, readline() returns an empty string — the standard sentinel for a while loop. Strip the result with .strip() or .rstrip("\n") to remove the trailing newline before processing the content.

readlines()

readlines() reads the entire file and returns a list of strings, one per line, each including its \n. It is memory-equivalent to read() since the full file is loaded at once, but the result is pre-split into lines. This is useful when you need random access to specific lines by index, need to know the total line count before processing begins, or intend to process the file multiple times. For a single sequential pass, the for-loop iterator in Section 2.3 is more efficient.

> **Note:** readline() returns an empty string at end-of-file. A blank line in the file returns "\n" — one newline character, not an empty string. The walrus-operator form "while line := f.readline():" correctly stops on empty string and continues on blank lines.

Example 1 — Introduction

Demonstrating read(), readline(), and readlines() on the same small file, with repr() to show the newline characters explicitly.

```
# File "haiku.txt" contains three lines:
#   Old pond—
#   a frog jumps in,
#   sound of water.

# — read(): entire file as one string ————————————————————————
with open("haiku.txt", "r", encoding="utf-8") as f:
    content = f.read()
print("read():")
print(repr(content))   # \n characters are visible

# — readline(): one line per call ————————————————————————————
with open("haiku.txt", "r", encoding="utf-8") as f:
    print("\nreadline():")
    line = f.readline()
    while line:              # empty string = end of file
        print(repr(line))
        line = f.readline()

# — readlines(): all lines as a list —————————————————————————
with open("haiku.txt", "r", encoding="utf-8") as f:
    all_lines = f.readlines()
print("\nreadlines():")
print(all_lines)
print(f"Line count: {len(all_lines)}")
```

Output:

```
read():
'Old pond\u2014\na frog jumps in,\nsound of water.'

readline():
'Old pond\u2014\n'
'a frog jumps in,\n'
'sound of water.'

readlines():
['Old pond\u2014\n', 'a frog jumps in,\n', 'sound of water.']
Line count: 3
```

Example 2 — Variation

Using read(n) for partial reads and the walrus-operator form of the readline() loop.

```
# — read(n): read a fixed number of characters at a time ————————
with open("haiku.txt", "r", encoding="utf-8") as f:
    chunk1 = f.read(8)    # first 8 characters
    chunk2 = f.read(10)   # next 10 characters
    rest   = f.read()     # remainder of the file

print(f"chunk1: {chunk1!r}")
print(f"chunk2: {chunk2!r}")
print(f"rest:   {rest!r}")

# — readline() with walrus operator (Python 3.8+) ——————————————
print("\nreadline() walrus form:")
with open("haiku.txt", "r", encoding="utf-8") as f:
    while line := f.readline():
```

```
        print(line.rstrip())   # rstrip() removes the trailing \n
```

Output:

```
chunk1: 'Old pond'
chunk2: '\u2014\na frog j'
rest:   'umps in,\nsound of water.'

readline() walrus form:
Old pond—
a frog jumps in,
sound of water.
```

Example 3 — Real-world application

A mark-sheet reader using readlines() to allow indexed access to specific lines and report a chosen student's results by ID.

```
# marksheet_reader.py  —  random-access line lookup using readlines()
# File: marks.txt format: StudentID,Name,Maths,English,Science

def load_marksheet(filepath):
    """Return (header_list, data_rows_list) or (None, []) on error."""
    try:
        with open(filepath, "r", encoding="utf-8") as f:
            lines = f.readlines()
    except FileNotFoundError:
        print(f"ERROR: {filepath!r} not found.")
        return None, []

    if not lines:
        return None, []

    header = lines[0].strip().split(",")
    rows   = [line.strip().split(",") for line in lines[1:] if line.strip()]
    return header, rows

def find_student(rows, student_id):
    """Return the first row whose first column matches student_id."""
    for row in rows:
        if row and row[0] == student_id:
            return row
    return None

header, rows = load_marksheet("marks.txt")
if header:
    print(f"Loaded {len(rows)} record(s). Columns: {header}")
    student = find_student(rows, "10044")
    if student:
        print()
        for col, val in zip(header, student):
            print(f"  {col:<14} {val}")
    else:
        print("Student ID not found.")
```

Output:

```
Loaded 4 record(s). Columns: ['StudentID', 'Name', 'Maths', 'English',
'Science']

  StudentID      10044
  Name           Priya Nair
  Maths          95
  English        88
  Science        92
```

Use readlines() when the line index matters or when you need to pass the line list to multiple functions. For a single sequential scan — the overwhelmingly common case — the for-loop iterator in Section 2.3 is both cleaner and kinder to memory.

2.3 Iterating Over a File Line by Line

A file object opened in text mode is itself an iterator: it implements the iterator protocol (see Book 01, Chapter 8) and can be used directly in a for loop. Writing "for line in f:" yields one line at a time, each including its trailing \n, advancing through the file with every iteration. This is Python's idiomatic way to read a text file and is the correct first choice for any sequential processing task.

The memory advantage is significant. Rather than loading all lines into a list before the loop starts, the iterator pulls one line from the OS read buffer at a time. On a log file with two million entries, readlines() would allocate the entire file in memory; the for-loop iterator holds only the current line. For the majority of file processing tasks — searching, filtering, parsing, aggregating — no line after the current one is needed, so there is no reason to hold all of them simultaneously.

Cleaning and Filtering Lines

Each line from the iterator includes its trailing \n. Calling line.strip() removes leading and trailing whitespace including the newline; line.rstrip("\n") removes only the newline, preserving intentional leading whitespace. Blank lines in the file are yielded as "\n" and can be skipped with: if not line.strip(): continue. Comment lines prefixed with # are equally simple: if line.strip().startswith("#"): continue. Placing both guards at the top of the loop produces clean, defensive iteration that handles the file formats encountered in practice.

> **Note:** Do not mix the for-loop iterator with readline() calls on the same open file object. Python uses an internal read-ahead buffer for the iterator, and interleaving readline() with the iterator can cause lines to be skipped or doubled. Choose one approach per with block and use it exclusively.

Example 1 — Introduction

The basic for-loop iteration pattern: iterating a CSV file, stripping newlines, printing each line.

```
# File: enrolments.csv
# StudentID,Name,Course
# 10042,Anika Patel,Digital Technologies
# 10043,Liam Torres,Mathematics
# 10044,Priya Nair,Science

with open("enrolments.csv", "r", encoding="utf-8") as f:
    for line in f:
        clean = line.strip()    # removes \n and any trailing spaces
        print(repr(clean))
```

Output:

```
'StudentID,Name,Course'
'10042,Anika Patel,Digital Technologies'
'10043,Liam Torres,Mathematics'
'10044,Priya Nair,Science'
```

Example 2 — Variation

Skipping blank lines and comment lines; counting valid records; using enumerate() to track line numbers.

```
# File: semester_data.txt (mix of data, blanks, and # comments)
# # Semester 2 results - Year 10
# # Generated: 2025-08-14
# Anika Patel,88,A
```

```
#
# Liam Torres,72,B
# # Top result follows
# Priya Nair,95,A+
# Sam Wong,81,B+

processed = 0

with open("semester_data.txt", "r", encoding="utf-8") as f:
    for lineno, line in enumerate(f, 1):
        stripped = line.strip()
        if not stripped:                # blank line
            continue
        if stripped.startswith("#"):    # comment line
            continue
        parts = stripped.split(",")
        if len(parts) < 3:
            print(f"  Line {lineno}: too few columns — skipped")
            continue
        name, score, grade = parts[0], parts[1], parts[2]
        print(f"  {name:<20} {score:>4}  {grade}")
        processed += 1

print(f"\nProcessed {processed} record(s).")
```

Output:

```
  Anika Patel            88   A
  Liam Torres             72   B
  Priya Nair              95   A+
  Sam Wong                81   B+

Processed 4 record(s).
```

Example 3 — Real-world application

An attendance register reader for St Lucia State High School that iterates line by line, parses class sections, and produces a structured summary.

```
# attendance_reader.py  —  parse a multi-class attendance register
# File format (attendance.txt):
#   # Attendance Register  —  St Lucia State High School
#   # Period: Term 3, Week 4
#   CLASS=10A
#   Anika Patel,PRESENT
#   Liam Torres,ABSENT
#   Maya Chen,PRESENT
#   CLASS=10B
#   Sam Wong,PRESENT
#   Priya Nair,LATE

def parse_attendance(filepath):
    """
    Return dict mapping class name to list of (student, status) tuples.
    Skips blank and # comment lines; reports malformed data lines.
    """
    attendance = {}
    current_class = None
    header_lines  = 0

    try:
        with open(filepath, "r", encoding="utf-8") as f:
            for lineno, line in enumerate(f, 1):
                stripped = line.strip()
                if not stripped or stripped.startswith("#"):
                    header_lines += 1
                    continue
                if stripped.startswith("CLASS="):
```

```
                current_class = stripped[6:]
                attendance[current_class] = []
            elif current_class and "," in stripped:
                name, _, status = stripped.partition(",")
                attendance[current_class].append((name.strip(),
status.strip()))
            else:
                print(f"  Line {lineno}: unrecognised format — skipped")
    except FileNotFoundError:
        print(f"ERROR: {filepath!r} not found.")
        return {}

    print(f"({header_lines} header/blank line(s) skipped)")
    return attendance

def summarise(attendance):
    for cls, records in attendance.items():
        present = sum(1 for _, s in records if s == "PRESENT")
        print(f"\n  {cls}  ({len(records)} students, {present} present)")
        for name, status in records:
            note_str = "" if status == "PRESENT" else f"  ** {status}"
            print(f"    {name:<22}{note_str}")

data = parse_attendance("attendance.txt")
summarise(data)
```

Output:

```
(2 header/blank line(s) skipped)

  10A  (3 students, 2 present)
    Anika Patel
    Liam Torres           ** ABSENT
    Maya Chen

  10B  (2 students, 1 present)
    Sam Wong
    Priya Nair            ** LATE
```

The for-loop iterator is the workhorse of text file reading. Using enumerate(f, 1) to carry the line number through the loop at zero extra cost is a habit worth forming early — it makes every error message in a file-processing program immediately actionable.

2.4 Encoding: UTF-8, ASCII, and the encoding Parameter

Every text file on disk is a sequence of bytes. An encoding defines the mapping between those bytes and the characters they represent. Choosing the wrong encoding does not always produce an immediate error — sometimes it silently substitutes wrong characters, corrupting data in a way that may not be discovered until the output is examined carefully. When it does raise an error, Python raises UnicodeDecodeError at read time rather than at open(), which can be misleading if you are not expecting it.

ASCII and UTF-8

ASCII uses 7 bits per character and defines 128 code points: the English alphabet, digits, common punctuation, and control characters. UTF-8 is a superset: its first 128 code points are byte-for-byte identical to ASCII, so every valid ASCII file is also a valid UTF-8 file. For any character outside those 128 — accented letters, Greek, Cyrillic, Chinese, Japanese, Korean, emoji — UTF-8 uses two to four bytes. A decoder expecting ASCII will raise UnicodeDecodeError on the very first multi-byte sequence it encounters.

The errors Parameter

The errors parameter of open() specifies what to do when a byte sequence cannot be decoded with the given encoding. The default, "strict", raises UnicodeDecodeError immediately. Setting errors="ignore" silently discards any undecoded byte, which can produce garbled text without warning. Setting errors="replace" substitutes the Unicode replacement character � wherever a byte fails to decode, making the problem visible without halting the program. A fourth option, errors="backslashreplace", represents problematic bytes as Python escape sequences — useful when diagnosing encoding issues. In production code, "strict" is almost always correct: failing loudly is far preferable to silently delivering incorrect data.

Legacy Encodings

Files originating from older Australian government systems, legacy databases, or pre-2010 Windows software may use latin-1 (iso-8859-1) or cp1252. Both assign different characters to bytes in the range 0x80–0xFF. Opening such a file with encoding="utf-8" typically raises UnicodeDecodeError somewhere in that byte range. A reliable fallback strategy is to attempt UTF-8 first and, on failure, retry with encoding="latin-1". Because latin-1 maps every possible byte value to a valid character, it never raises UnicodeDecodeError — making it the encoding of last resort for files of unknown provenance.

> **Note:** UnicodeDecodeError reports the byte position of the problem, not the line number. To locate an encoding error by line, open in binary mode ("rb") and attempt line.decode("utf-8") inside a try/except for each line. This gives you the exact line number without losing the context of what was around the bad byte.

Example 1 — Introduction

Reading a UTF-8 file containing accented characters correctly, then triggering UnicodeDecodeError by specifying the wrong encoding.

```
# File: students_intl.txt (saved as UTF-8)
# Contents (three student names with accented characters):
#   Nguyễn Thị Hương
#   José Ramírez
#   Astrid Müller

# ── Correct encoding ──────────────────────────────────────────────
print("UTF-8 (correct):")
with open("students_intl.txt", "r", encoding="utf-8") as f:
    for line in f:
        print(" ", line.strip())

# ── Wrong encoding triggers UnicodeDecodeError at read time ───────
print("\nASCII (wrong):")
try:
    with open("students_intl.txt", "r", encoding="ascii") as f:
        f.read()   # the error occurs here, not at open()
except UnicodeDecodeError as e:
    print(f"  UnicodeDecodeError: {e}")
    print("  Diagnosis: file contains non-ASCII characters.")
    print("  Fix:       use encoding=\"utf-8\" instead.")
```

Output:

```
UTF-8 (correct):
  Nguyễn Thị Hương
  José Ramírez
  Astrid Müller

ASCII (wrong):
  UnicodeDecodeError: 'ascii' codec can't decode byte 0xe1 in position 4:
  ordinal not in range(128)
  Diagnosis: file contains non-ASCII characters.
  Fix:       use encoding="utf-8" instead.
```

Example 2 — Variation

Demonstrating the effect of errors="strict", "ignore", and "replace" on a file containing a byte that is invalid in UTF-8.

```
# Write a file that contains a byte invalid under UTF-8 (0xe9 in isolation)
with open("corrupt.txt", "wb") as f:
    f.write(b"Student: Andr\xe9 Martin\nSchool: Brisbane\n")

# — strict (default): stops immediately ——————————————————————
try:
    with open("corrupt.txt", "r", encoding="utf-8", errors="strict") as f:
        print("strict:  ", repr(f.read()))
except UnicodeDecodeError:
    print("strict:   UnicodeDecodeError raised – cannot decode byte 0xe9")

# — ignore: silently drops the undecodable byte ————————————————
with open("corrupt.txt", "r", encoding="utf-8", errors="ignore") as f:
    print("ignore:  ", repr(f.read()))

# — replace: substitutes \ufffd (Unicode replacement character) ———
with open("corrupt.txt", "r", encoding="utf-8", errors="replace") as f:
    print("replace: ", repr(f.read()))
```

Output:

```
strict:   UnicodeDecodeError raised – cannot decode byte 0xe9
ignore:   'Student: Andr Martin\nSchool: Brisbane\n'
replace:  'Student: Andr�Martin\nSchool: Brisbane\n'
```

Example 3 — Real-world application

A name-file reader that tries UTF-8 first, falls back to latin-1 on failure, flags non-ASCII characters, and reports which encoding was used.

```
# name_reader.py  –  handle student name files from mixed legacy systems

def read_names(filepath):
    """
    Try UTF-8 first; fall back to latin-1 if UnicodeDecodeError occurs.
    Returns (names_list, encoding_used, error_message).
    """
    for encoding in ("utf-8", "latin-1"):
        try:
            with open(filepath, "r", encoding=encoding) as f:
                names = [line.strip() for line in f if line.strip()]
            return names, encoding, None
        except FileNotFoundError:
            return [], None, f"File not found: {filepath!r}"
        except UnicodeDecodeError:
            continue   # try the next encoding
    return [], None, "Could not decode with utf-8 or latin-1"

def print_name_report(filepath):
    names, enc, err = read_names(filepath)
    if err:
        print(f"ERROR: {err}")
        return
    print(f"File: {filepath}  (decoded as {enc})")
    print(f"  {len(names)} name(s):")
    for name in names:
        flag = "  ← non-ASCII" if any(ord(c) > 127 for c in name) else ""
        print(f"    {name}{flag}")
    print()

print_name_report("students_intl.txt")    # UTF-8 file
print_name_report("students_legacy.txt")   # latin-1 file
```

Output:

```
File: students_intl.txt  (decoded as utf-8)
```

```
  3 name(s):
    Nguyễn Thị Hương  ← non-ASCII
    José Ramírez  ← non-ASCII
    Astrid Müller  ← non-ASCII

File: students_legacy.txt  (decoded as latin-1)
  2 name(s):
    Françoise Dupont  ← non-ASCII
    Gómez Herrera  ← non-ASCII
```

The UTF-8-first, latin-1-fallback pattern is a practical solution to the encoding diversity found in educational and government data files in Australia. Flagging non-ASCII characters in the output makes unexpected encoding issues visible during testing rather than silently present in production.

2.5 Reading Large Files Efficiently: Chunked Reads

For most school-scale data — class rolls, grade sheets, weekly timetables — any of the reading methods covered so far is appropriate because the files are small. Real-world programs regularly encounter much larger files: server access logs that accumulate hundreds of megabytes in a day, scientific data exports in the gigabyte range, or database dumps too large to hold in RAM. Calling read() on such files allocates a string as large as the file itself, which exhausts memory on any ordinary machine.

The solution is chunked reading: requesting a fixed number of characters or bytes at a time, processing each piece before asking for the next. In text mode, read(size) reads up to size characters; in binary mode it reads up to size bytes. Both return an empty string or empty bytes object when the end of file is reached, which serves as the loop termination condition. The chunk size is a tuning parameter: too small means many system calls; too large means excessive memory. For text files, values between 4 KB and 64 KB are typical.

Chunked reads in text mode have one important limitation: a chunk boundary can fall in the middle of a line. If your processing requires complete lines, use the for-loop iterator (Section 2.3) rather than explicit chunked reads, because the iterator handles buffering and line assembly internally. Explicit chunked reads are most suitable for operations that work on bytes or characters without regard to line structure: counting, hashing, searching for substrings, or streaming data to another destination.

Note: In text mode, read(n) reads n characters, which may correspond to more than n bytes for UTF-8 files with multi-byte characters. For precise byte-level control, open the file in binary mode ("rb") and use read(n) on the resulting binary file object.

Example 1 — Introduction

Reading a text file in 1 KB chunks and counting total characters, demonstrating the loop pattern.

```
CHUNK_SIZE = 1024   # 1 KB per read call

def count_chars(filepath):
    """Count total characters using chunked reads — never loads whole file."""
    total = 0
    with open(filepath, "r", encoding="utf-8") as f:
        while True:
            chunk = f.read(CHUNK_SIZE)
            if not chunk:   # empty string = end of file
                break
            total += len(chunk)
    return total

chars = count_chars("access_log.txt")
print(f"Total characters: {chars:,}")
```

Output:
```
Total characters: 2,847,392
```

Example 2 — Variation

Counting newline bytes in a large file using binary chunked reads — faster than text-mode iteration for purely byte-level operations.

```
CHUNK_SIZE = 65536   # 64 KB — larger chunks reduce system-call overhead

def count_lines_binary(filepath):
    """
    Count lines by counting \n bytes in binary mode.
    Avoids text decoding overhead — fastest for pure line counting.
    """
    line_count = 0
    with open(filepath, "rb") as f:
        while True:
            chunk = f.read(CHUNK_SIZE)
            if not chunk:
                break
            line_count += chunk.count(b"\n")
    return line_count

import time

start = time.perf_counter()
n_text = sum(1 for _ in open("access_log.txt", "r", encoding="utf-8"))
ms_text = (time.perf_counter() - start) * 1000

start = time.perf_counter()
n_bin = count_lines_binary("access_log.txt")
ms_bin = (time.perf_counter() - start) * 1000

print(f"Text-mode iterator: {n_text:,} lines  in {ms_text:.1f} ms")
print(f"Binary chunked:     {n_bin:,} lines  in {ms_bin:.1f} ms")
```

Output:
```
Text-mode iterator: 48,271 lines  in 38.4 ms
Binary chunked:     48,271 lines  in 9.2 ms
```

Example 3 — Real-world application

A log-file keyword scanner using the line iterator, with a configurable result cap to handle very large files gracefully.

```
# log_scanner.py  —  memory-efficient keyword search through a large log

def scan_log(filepath, keyword, max_results=20):
    """
    Find lines in filepath containing keyword (case-insensitive).
    Uses the line iterator rather than read() to avoid loading the full file.
    Returns list of (line_number, text) tuples.
    """
    keyword_lower = keyword.lower()
    results       = []
    lines_scanned = 0

    try:
        with open(filepath, "r", encoding="utf-8", errors="replace") as f:
            for lineno, line in enumerate(f, 1):
                lines_scanned += 1
                if keyword_lower in line.lower():
                    results.append((lineno, line.rstrip()))
                    if len(results) >= max_results:
                        print(f"  (result cap of {max_results} reached)")
```

```
                    break
        except FileNotFoundError:
            print(f"ERROR: {filepath!r} not found.")
            return []

        print(f"Scanned {lines_scanned:,} lines. Found {len(results)} match(es).")
        return results

hits = scan_log("access_log.txt", "ERROR", max_results=5)
print()
for lineno, text in hits:
    print(f"  Line {lineno:>6}: {text[:70]}")
```

Output:

```
Scanned 48,271 lines. Found 5 match(es).
  (result cap of 5 reached)

  Line    842: 2025-08-14 09:14:22 ERROR Failed to connect to database
  Line   1204: 2025-08-14 10:02:55 ERROR Timeout reading config file
  Line   3871: 2025-08-14 14:38:01 ERROR Disk quota exceeded on /data
  Line   5622: 2025-08-14 16:10:17 ERROR Unhandled exception in worker
  Line   9103: 2025-08-15 08:44:32 ERROR Failed to connect to database
```

The combination of a configurable result cap and the line iterator gives Section 2.5.3 the efficiency of chunked processing with the convenience of line-oriented output. For operations that truly require byte-level granularity — file format parsing, checksum computation, binary search — the explicit read(size) chunked loop in the first two examples is the appropriate approach.

2.6 File Position: tell() and seek()

Every open file maintains an internal cursor called the file pointer. It records the byte position of the next character (or byte) to be read. Every read operation advances the pointer by the amount of data consumed. When the pointer reaches the end of the file, further reads return an empty string. The file pointer is transparent during normal sequential reading, but two methods — tell() and seek() — give direct control over it.

tell()

tell() returns the current pointer position as an integer. In binary mode this is an exact byte offset from the start of the file. In text mode with UTF-8 encoding, the value Python returns is an opaque internal value — it encodes additional state needed to handle multi-byte characters correctly and should not be interpreted as a simple byte count. tell() values in text mode are valid only as arguments to seek() on the same file object opened with the same encoding; storing them as byte offsets for later use in a different context is unreliable.

seek()

seek(offset, whence) moves the file pointer. The whence argument specifies what offset is relative to: 0 means the start of the file (the default), 1 means the current position, and 2 means the end of the file. In text mode, only seek(0) to rewind to the start, and seek(pos) with a value previously returned by tell(), are guaranteed to work correctly on all platforms. seek(0, 2) — which jumps to the end of the file — is reliable in binary mode and is a standard technique for determining file size without a separate stat call.

> **Note:** In text mode, seek(n, 1) or seek(n, 2) with a non-zero n is not portable across platforms and encoding combinations. For any file position work beyond "rewind to start", use binary mode to guarantee consistent behaviour.

Example 1 — Introduction

Using tell() to observe the pointer moving through a file and seek(0) to rewind for a second read.

```
with open("haiku.txt", "r", encoding="utf-8") as f:
    print("Initial position:", f.tell())

    line1 = f.readline()
    print(f"After line 1: pos={f.tell()},  text={line1.strip()!r}")

    line2 = f.readline()
    print(f"After line 2: pos={f.tell()},  text={line2.strip()!r}")

    f.seek(0)    # rewind to the beginning
    print(f"\nAfter seek(0): pos={f.tell()}")

    first_again = f.readline()
    print(f"Re-read first line: {first_again.strip()!r}")
```

Output:

```
Initial position: 0
After line 1: pos=11,  text='Old pond—'
After line 2: pos=30,  text='a frog jumps in,'

After seek(0): pos=0
Re-read first line: 'Old pond—'
```

Example 2 — Variation

Using seek(0, 2) in binary mode to determine file size, then rewinding to read the header row.

```
# Binary mode gives reliable seek() at any position

with open("enrolments.csv", "rb") as f:
    # Jump to end to measure file size without reading the content
    f.seek(0, 2)          # 2 = SEEK_END
    file_size = f.tell()  # byte offset from start = total bytes
    print(f"File size: {file_size} bytes")

    # Rewind and read the header row
    f.seek(0)
    header = f.readline().decode("utf-8").strip()
    print(f"Header: {header!r}")

    # Save position, read row 1, restore position
    saved = f.tell()
    row1  = f.readline().decode("utf-8").strip()
    print(f"Row 1:  {row1!r}")

    f.seek(saved)
    row1b = f.readline().decode("utf-8").strip()
    print(f"Row 1 re-read from saved pos: {row1b!r}")
```

Output:

```
File size: 97 bytes
Header: 'StudentID,Name,Course'
Row 1:  '10042,Anika Patel,Digital Technologies'
Row 1 re-read from saved pos: '10042,Anika Patel,Digital Technologies'
```

Example 3 — Real-world application

A smart reader that uses file size (via seek/tell) to choose between read() and line iteration automatically, without a separate stat call.

```
# smart_reader.py  —  select reading strategy based on file size

SIZE_THRESHOLD = 256 * 1024   # 256 KB
```

```
def smart_read_lines(filepath):
    """
    For small files: use read() then splitlines().
    For large files: use the line iterator.
    Returns (lines_list, strategy_used).
    """
    try:
        # Measure size efficiently using seek/tell in binary mode
        with open(filepath, "rb") as fb:
            fb.seek(0, 2)
            size = fb.tell()

        if size <= SIZE_THRESHOLD:
            strategy = f"read() [{size} bytes <= threshold]"
            with open(filepath, "r", encoding="utf-8") as f:
                lines = [l for l in f.read().splitlines() if l.strip()]
        else:
            strategy = f"iterator [{size:,} bytes > threshold]"
            lines = []
            with open(filepath, "r", encoding="utf-8") as f:
                for line in f:
                    if line.strip():
                        lines.append(line.rstrip())

        return lines, strategy

    except FileNotFoundError:
        return [], "error — file not found"

for fname in ["config.txt", "access_log.txt"]:
    lines, strat = smart_read_lines(fname)
    print(f"{fname}: {strat}")
    print(f"  Lines: {len(lines):,}\n")
```

Output:

```
config.txt: read() [142 bytes <= threshold]
  Lines: 6

access_log.txt: iterator [2,847,392 bytes > threshold]
  Lines: 48,271
```

The seek/tell pattern for measuring file size without a separate stat call is a minor but clean optimisation: it opens the file once and uses the connection it already has rather than making a second OS call. For larger programs that open many files, this kind of attention to unnecessary round-trips accumulates into meaningfully faster code.

2.7 Real-world Patterns: Configuration, Log, and Data Files

The preceding six sections have established the complete toolkit for reading text files. This section brings those techniques together in three self-contained, reusable functions that address the file types encountered most frequently in practice: key=value configuration files, timestamped log files, and delimited data files. Each function combines open() with explicit encoding, for-loop iteration, blank and comment line skipping, per-line error handling, and the exception handling patterns introduced in Chapter 1.

Configuration Files

Configuration files store human-editable program settings. The simplest format is one key=value pair per line, with blank lines and # comment lines ignored. This format requires no imported module, works in any text editor, and is immediately legible to non-programmers. Python's configparser module handles more structured INI-style configs with named sections; for flat settings files the hand-written parser below is sufficient and keeps dependencies to zero.

Log Files

Log files record timestamped events, each tagged with a severity level. A widely used format is: TIMESTAMP LEVEL MESSAGE on a single line, where LEVEL is DEBUG, INFO, WARNING, or ERROR. Reading and filtering logs is routine in any system that generates them. The essential skills are splitting each line into its components reliably, treating malformed lines without crashing, and filtering by level efficiently.

Structured Data Files

Structured data files follow a consistent per-line schema, commonly comma- or tab-delimited. This chapter's final example combines everything: encoding detection, comment and blank line skipping, per-record error handling with line numbers, and a formatted report. The csv module (Chapter 5) handles CSV robustly in production — including quoted fields with embedded commas, different dialects, and Unicode edge cases. Understanding the manual approach first reveals exactly what the module handles on your behalf.

Example 1 — Introduction

A key=value configuration reader that returns a dict, merging parsed values with caller-supplied defaults.

```
# config_reader.py  —  parse a simple flat configuration file
# File: school.conf
# # Brisbane State High School — Application Configuration
# school_name = Brisbane State High School
# academic_year = 2025
# log_dir = /var/log/school_app
# max_enrolments = 1800

def read_config(filepath, defaults=None):
    """
    Parse key=value pairs; skip blank and # comment lines.
    Lines without "=" are skipped with a printed warning.
    Returned dict is the defaults dict updated with file values.
    """
    config = dict(defaults) if defaults else {}

    try:
        with open(filepath, "r", encoding="utf-8") as f:
            for lineno, line in enumerate(f, 1):
                stripped = line.strip()
                if not stripped or stripped.startswith("#"):
                    continue
                if "=" not in stripped:
                    print(f"  Warning: line {lineno} has no '=' — skipped:
{stripped!r}")
                    continue
                key, _, value = stripped.partition("=")
                config[key.strip()] = value.strip()
    except FileNotFoundError:
        print(f"  Config {filepath!r} not found — using defaults.")

    return config

DEFAULTS = {"debug_mode": "false", "log_dir": "logs", "max_enrolments": "500"}
cfg = read_config("school.conf", defaults=DEFAULTS)

print("Configuration loaded:")
for key, val in cfg.items():
    print(f"  {key:<20} = {val}")
```

Output:

```
Configuration loaded:
```

```
debug_mode          = false
log_dir             = /var/log/school_app
max_enrolments      = 1800
school_name         = Brisbane State High School
academic_year       = 2025
```

Example 2 — Variation

A log-file reader that parses TIMESTAMP LEVEL MESSAGE lines and returns only entries matching a specified severity level.

```
# log_reader.py  —  parse and filter a timestamped event log
# File: app.log  format: 2025-08-14 09:14:22 ERROR message text

from datetime import datetime

KNOWN_LEVELS = {"DEBUG", "INFO", "WARNING", "ERROR"}

def parse_log(filepath, filter_level=None):
    """
    Read log file; return list of (datetime, level, message) tuples.
    Pass filter_level="ERROR" to retrieve only error entries.
    Malformed lines are counted but do not raise an exception.
    """
    entries, skipped = [], 0

    try:
        with open(filepath, "r", encoding="utf-8") as f:
            for line in f:
                parts = line.strip().split(" ", 3)
                if len(parts) < 4 or parts[2] not in KNOWN_LEVELS:
                    skipped += 1
                    continue
                date_s, time_s, level, message = parts
                if filter_level and level != filter_level:
                    continue
                try:
                    ts = datetime.strptime(f"{date_s} {time_s}", "%Y-%m-%d %H:
%M:%S")
                except ValueError:
                    skipped += 1
                    continue
                entries.append((ts, level, message))
    except FileNotFoundError:
        print(f"ERROR: {filepath!r} not found.")

    if skipped:
        print(f"  ({skipped} malformed line(s) skipped)")
    return entries

errors = parse_log("app.log", filter_level="ERROR")
print(f"Found {len(errors)} ERROR entry/entries:")
for ts, level, msg in errors:
    print(f"  [{ts:%d %b %Y %H:%M}]  {msg}")
```

Output:

```
Found 3 ERROR entry/entries:
  [14 Aug 2025 09:14]  Failed to connect to database
  [14 Aug 2025 10:02]  Timeout reading config file
  [15 Aug 2025 08:44]  Failed to connect to database
```

Example 3 — Real-world application

A complete student marks reader combining UTF-8/latin-1 detection, comment skipping, per-record validation, and a formatted report.

```
# marks_report.py  —  robust reader for a delimited marks file
```

```
# File: marks.txt  format: StudentID,Name,Subject,Score
# (may contain blank lines, # comments, and non-ASCII names)

def load_marks(filepath):
    """
    Try UTF-8 then latin-1; parse StudentID,Name,Subject,Score rows.
    Returns (records_list, error_log_list).
    """
    records, error_log = [], []

    for encoding in ("utf-8", "latin-1"):
        try:
            with open(filepath, "r", encoding=encoding) as f:
                raw = f.readlines()
            break
        except FileNotFoundError:
            return [], [f"File not found: {filepath!r}"]
        except UnicodeDecodeError:
            continue
    else:
        return [], ["Cannot decode with utf-8 or latin-1"]

    for i, line in enumerate(raw, 1):
        stripped = line.strip()
        if not stripped or stripped.startswith("#"):
            continue
        parts = stripped.split(",", 3)
        if len(parts) < 4:
            error_log.append(f"Line {i}: too few columns")
            continue
        try:
            score = float(parts[3].strip())
        except ValueError:
            error_log.append(f"Line {i}: invalid score {parts[3].strip()!r}")
            continue
        records.append({"id": parts[0].strip(), "name": parts[1].strip(),
                        "subject": parts[2].strip(), "score": score})
    return records, error_log

def print_report(records, error_log):
    bar = "=" * 54
    print(bar)
    print(f"  MARKS REPORT   ({len(records)} valid record(s))")
    print(bar)
    if records:
        for r in records:
            print(f'  {r["id"]}  {r["name"]:<20} {r["subject"]:<12}
{r["score"]:.1f}')
        avg = sum(r["score"] for r in records) / len(records)
        print("-" * 54)
        print(f"  Class average: {avg:.2f}")
    if error_log:
        print(f"\n  Data warnings ({len(error_log)}):")
        for e in error_log:
            print(f"    - {e}")
    print(bar)

records, errors = load_marks("marks.txt")
print_report(records, errors)
```

Output:

```
======================================================
  MARKS REPORT   (4 valid record(s))
======================================================
  10042  Anika Patel          Mathematics  88.0
  10043  Liam Torres          English      72.5
  10044  Priya Nair           Science      95.0
  10045  Sam Wong             Physics      81.0
```

```
--------------------------------------------------------
  Class average: 84.12

  Data warnings (2):
    - Line 3: invalid score 'N/A'
    - Line 7: too few columns
========================================================
```

These three patterns — config reader, log filter, marks report — are templates you will return to repeatedly. Each builds correctly on what came before it in this chapter: explicit encoding, line iteration, blank and comment skipping, granular exception handling, and clean output formatting. Chapter 3 turns to writing and appending, and Chapter 5 replaces the manual CSV splitting here with the robust csv module.

Chapter 2 Summary

- open(filepath, mode, encoding) establishes a file connection and returns a file object; always specify both mode and encoding explicitly — never rely on platform defaults, which differ between Windows, macOS, and Linux.
- read() returns the entire file as one string; read(n) reads n characters at a time; readline() returns one line including \n; readlines() returns a list of all lines. Each suits different use cases with different memory implications.
- The file object is an iterator: "for line in f:" is the idiomatic, memory-efficient approach to sequential line processing, yielding one line at a time without loading the entire file into memory.
- UTF-8 is a superset of ASCII and the correct default encoding; always pass encoding="utf-8". The errors parameter controls behaviour on decoding failure: "strict" raises immediately (recommended), "ignore" drops bad bytes, "replace" substitutes �.
- For files too large to load into memory, read() with a fixed size argument reads in chunks; the for-loop iterator is preferred when line-complete processing is needed; binary chunked reads are fastest for byte-level operations.
- tell() returns the current file pointer position; seek(0) rewinds; seek(0, 2) jumps to end (reliable in binary mode). In text mode, only seek(0) and seek() with a prior tell() return value are portable.
- Combining blank-line skipping, comment-line filtering, per-record exception handling, and encoding detection produces functions that process real-world data files reliably without crashing on the first anomaly.
- Three core patterns: key=value config reader (partition on "=", skip blanks/comments), log filter (split with maxsplit=3, filter by level, parse timestamp), structured data reader (split on delimiter, validate each field individually, report errors with line numbers).

Guided Exercises

1. Write a function word_count(filepath) that returns the total number of words in a text file. Handle FileNotFoundError by returning -1 and printing a clear message. Test it on at least two files of different sizes.

> ***Hint:*** *Open in text mode and iterate line by line. Call line.split() (no argument) to split on any whitespace and accumulate the lengths. Wrap in try/except for FileNotFoundError.*

2. Write a function find_lines(filepath, keyword) that returns a list of all lines containing keyword (case-insensitive), each stripped of its trailing newline. Return an empty list and print the error if the file cannot be opened.

> ***Hint:*** *Use "for line in f:" and check "keyword.lower() in line.lower()". Collect matches with line.rstrip("\n") and return the list after the with block.*

3. Write read_config(filepath) that parses a key=value text file and returns a dict. Ignore blank lines and # comment lines. Print a warning for any line that does not contain "=", then skip it. Test with a file that contains a mix of valid entries, blank lines, comments, and one invalid line.

Hint: Use line.partition("=") to split on the first "=" only, preserving "=" characters in values. Strip both key and value with .strip() before storing in the dict.

4. Open a text file, use read(200) to read the first 200 characters, record the position with tell(), then use seek(0) to rewind. Read the same 200 characters again and verify they are identical. In a separate binary-mode open, use seek(0, 2) and tell() to report the file's total size in bytes.

Hint: Two separate with blocks: the first in text mode ("r") for read/tell/seek/re-read; the second in binary mode ("rb") for the seek(0, 2) + tell() size measurement.

5. Write safe_read_utf8(filepath) that reads a file as UTF-8. If UnicodeDecodeError occurs, re-read the file with errors="replace" and print a warning. Return the file contents as a string in both cases, and print a confirmation message indicating which path was taken.

Hint: Try the first open() in a try/except UnicodeDecodeError block. In the except branch, open again with the same path but errors="replace". Print a different message from each branch so the caller can see which was used.

Challenge Tasks

1. Write a tail(filepath, n) function that returns the last n lines of a text file as a list of strings (stripped of trailing newlines), without reading the entire file into memory when the file is large. Use binary mode with seek() to jump near the end of the file and work backwards to find the last n newline characters. Handle files with fewer than n lines by returning all lines. Test with n=5, n=50, and with a file that has fewer lines than n.

2. Write a log_summary(filepath) function that reads a structured log file (format: YYYY-MM-DD HH:MM:SS LEVEL MESSAGE) and returns a dict mapping each level (DEBUG, INFO, WARNING, ERROR) to a nested dict containing "count" (int) and "recent" (list of the 3 most recent messages at that level, newest first). Malformed lines should be counted in a separate "malformed" key but must not crash the function. After calling log_summary(), print a formatted table showing level, count, and the most recent message for each level found.

3. Build a multi-file keyword search tool. Given a directory path and a search term, open every .txt and .log file in that directory (not subdirectories), find all lines containing the term (case-insensitive), and write a report to a new file called search_results.txt. Each hit should appear as: FILENAME LINE_NUMBER LINE_CONTENT. The report must begin with a header section showing the search term, directory, date/time, total files scanned, and total hits. Handle UnicodeDecodeError on individual files by logging a warning line in the report and continuing to the next file. Use pathlib.Path.iterdir() to find files.

CHAPTER 3 Writing and Appending to Files

Book 02: File Handling & Exception Management

> *Chapter 2 covered reading in full: every method Python provides, the encoding mechanics, and the strategies that keep large files from exhausting memory. This chapter turns to the other side of the transaction — putting data into files. You will write new files and overwrite existing ones, append entries to growing logs, use writelines() for efficient batch output, understand how Python's write buffer interacts with the OS, create files and directories safely, format output for human and machine readers alike, and build the log rotation and reporting patterns that reappear throughout every serious Python project.*

3.1 Write Mode and Append Mode

Opening a file for writing requires choosing between two modes, and the difference between them is consequential. Write mode ("w") opens the file for writing and immediately truncates it to zero length, erasing all existing content. If the file does not yet exist, Python creates it. This mode is the correct choice whenever you are producing a fresh output each time the program runs — a generated report, an exported data file, or a configuration file written from scratch.

Append mode ("a") opens the file for writing but moves the file pointer to the end of any existing content, so every write call adds to what is already there. If the file does not exist, Python creates it just as write mode does. Append mode is the correct choice for any data that accumulates over time: event logs, audit trails, score histories, and session records. The critical distinction is that append mode never reads or erases existing content — it can only add to the end.

Additional Mode Variants

Two further variants combine reading and writing. Mode "w+" opens for reading and writing, truncating the file to zero length first. Mode "a+" opens for reading and appending: existing content is preserved, new writes always go to the end, but reads can be performed after a seek(0). In practice, w+ and a+ are used rarely — most programs either read a file or write one, not both simultaneously. Chapter 4 shows how the with statement interacts with all of these modes, and Chapter 2 Section 2.1 covers the full mode table.

One behaviour worth noting explicitly: opening a file with mode "w" destroys its contents before any write() call is made. There is no recovery if you accidentally open the wrong file in write mode. Defensive code checks the target path before opening for writing, particularly when the path comes from user input or a configuration file rather than a hard-coded string.

> **Note:** Opening an existing file with mode "w" silently erases it before your first write() call. If you need to add to an existing file, always use "a". If you are unsure whether a target path is correct, check with os.path.exists() or pathlib.Path.exists() before opening in write mode.

Example 1 — Introduction

Demonstrating that mode "w" creates a file and that opening it a second time with "w" erases the previous content.

```
import os

# — First write: creates the file ——————————————————————
with open("output.txt", "w", encoding="utf-8") as f:
    f.write("Line one\n")
```

```
    f.write("Line two\n")

print("After first write:")
print(open("output.txt", encoding="utf-8").read())

# ── Second write with "w": silently erases everything ────────────────
with open("output.txt", "w", encoding="utf-8") as f:
    f.write("Fresh content only\n")

print("After second write (w mode erased previous content):")
print(open("output.txt", encoding="utf-8").read())
```

Output:

```
After first write:
Line one
Line two

After second write (w mode erased previous content):
Fresh content only
```

Example 2 — Variation

Append mode preserving existing content across multiple runs; comparing file size before and after each append.

```
import os
from datetime import datetime

LOG_FILE = "session_log.txt"

def log_session(message):
    """Append a timestamped entry to the session log."""
    timestamp = datetime.now().strftime("%Y-%m-%d %H:%M:%S")
    with open(LOG_FILE, "a", encoding="utf-8") as f:
        f.write(f"{timestamp}  {message}\n")

# Simulate three separate program runs appending to the same log
for msg in ["Program started", "User logged in: anika", "Saved report.csv"]:",
    size_before = os.path.getsize(LOG_FILE) if os.path.exists(LOG_FILE) else 0
    log_session(msg)
    size_after = os.path.getsize(LOG_FILE)
    print(f"  +{size_after - size_before:3d} bytes  —  {msg}")

print("\nFull log:")
print(open(LOG_FILE, encoding="utf-8").read())
```

Output:

```
  + 46 bytes  —  Program started
  + 49 bytes  —  User logged in: anika
  + 47 bytes  —  Saved report.csv

Full log:
2025-08-14 10:22:01  Program started
2025-08-14 10:22:01  User logged in: anika
2025-08-14 10:22:01  Saved report.csv
```

Example 3 — Real-world application

A grade export function that writes a fresh CSV report each run ("w") and separately appends an audit entry to a permanent change log ("a").

```
# grade_export.py  —  write mode for report, append mode for audit log
import os
from datetime import datetime

REPORT_FILE = "grade_report.csv"
```

```
AUDIT_FILE  = "audit.log"

STUDENT_GRADES = [
    ("10042", "Anika Patel",  "Mathematics", 88),
    ("10043", "Liam Torres",  "English",     72),
    ("10044", "Priya Nair",   "Science",     95),
    ("10045", "Sam Wong",     "Physics",     81),
]

def export_grades(grades, report_path, audit_path):
    # Write mode: always produces a fresh report
    with open(report_path, "w", encoding="utf-8") as f:
        f.write("StudentID,Name,Subject,Score\n")   # header row
        for sid, name, subject, score in grades:
            f.write(f"{sid},{name},{subject},{score}\n")
    print(f"Report written: {report_path}  ({len(grades)} record(s))")

    # Append mode: permanent record of every export
    timestamp = datetime.now().strftime("%Y-%m-%d %H:%M:%S")
    with open(audit_path, "a", encoding="utf-8") as f:
        f.write(f"{timestamp}  Exported {len(grades)} grades to {report_path}\
n")
    print(f"Audit entry appended: {audit_path}")

export_grades(STUDENT_GRADES, REPORT_FILE, AUDIT_FILE)

print("\n--- Report contents ---")
print(open(REPORT_FILE, encoding="utf-8").read())
print("--- Audit log ---")
print(open(AUDIT_FILE, encoding="utf-8").read())
```

Output:

```
Report written: grade_report.csv  (4 record(s))
Audit entry appended: audit.log

--- Report contents ---
StudentID,Name,Subject,Score
10042,Anika Patel,Mathematics,88
10043,Liam Torres,English,72
10044,Priya Nair,Science,95
10045,Sam Wong,Physics,81

--- Audit log ---
2025-08-14 10:22:04  Exported 4 grades to grade_report.csv
```

The pattern in Example 3.1.3 appears in almost every data-processing application: a regenerated output file for the current results, and a permanent append-only log for accountability. These two files serve completely different purposes, and each mode is chosen deliberately to match that purpose.

3.2 write() and writelines()

Two methods write data to an open text file. write(string) writes a single string and returns the number of characters written. It does not append a newline automatically — if you want each write() call to produce a new line, you must include \n explicitly at the end of the string. writelines(iterable) accepts any iterable of strings and writes each one to the file in sequence, again without inserting newlines between items. The distinction between the two is primarily one of convenience: write() for single strings, writelines() for sequences.

Newlines Are Your Responsibility

A common mistake when switching from print() to write() is forgetting that write() produces no line terminator. print("hello") outputs "hello\n"; f.write("hello") outputs "hello" with no newline. Every line in a file must include its own \n, which you supply either by writing it explicitly in the string, or by using an f-string or format call that includes it. When using writelines(), the same rule applies to every string in the iterable: each must carry its own \n if the output should be line-separated.

Return Value

write() returns an integer — the number of characters written. In normal use this is equal to len(string), but in certain edge cases involving buffering or write errors it may differ. Checking the return value is rarely necessary in day-to-day code but is relevant when writing to network sockets or non-standard file objects where partial writes can occur. For ordinary disk files in Python, write() either writes the complete string or raises an exception; a partial write without an exception does not occur.

> **Note:** writelines() does not add newlines between items — the name is slightly misleading. It writes each string in the iterable verbatim. If your strings do not end with "\n", the entire output will be on a single line. Always include "\n" at the end of each string passed to writelines().

Example 1 — Introduction

write() and writelines() on the same data; showing that neither adds newlines automatically.

```
words = ["Brisbane", "Melbourne", "Sydney", "Adelaide"]

# ── write(): one call per string ──────────────────────────
with open("cities_write.txt", "w", encoding="utf-8") as f:
    for word in words:
        chars = f.write(word + "\n")  # must add \n explicitly
        print(f"  write() returned: {chars}")

# ── writelines(): one call for the whole sequence ─────────
with open("cities_wl.txt", "w", encoding="utf-8") as f:
    f.writelines(word + "\n" for word in words)  # \n in each item

# ── What happens without \n ───────────────────────────────
with open("cities_noeol.txt", "w", encoding="utf-8") as f:
    f.writelines(words)   # no newlines — all on one line

print("\ncities_write.txt:", repr(open("cities_write.txt", encoding="utf-
8").read()))
print("cities_noeol.txt:", repr(open("cities_noeol.txt", encoding="utf-
8").read()))
```

Output:

```
  write() returned: 9
  write() returned: 10
  write() returned: 7
  write() returned: 9

cities_write.txt: 'Brisbane\nMelbourne\nSydney\nAdelaide\n'
cities_noeol.txt: 'BrisbaneMelbourneSydneyAdelaide'
```

Example 2 — Variation

Using writelines() with a generator expression to write a filtered, formatted sequence efficiently.

```
# Student records  —  write only students who passed (score >= 50)
students = [
    ("Anika Patel",  88),
    ("Liam Torres",  42),   # fail
    ("Priya Nair",   95),
    ("Sam Wong",     81),
    ("Maya Chen",    38),   # fail
]
```

```
passed = [(name, score) for name, score in students if score >= 50]

with open("passed.txt", "w", encoding="utf-8") as f:
    # writelines with a generator — no intermediate list built
    f.writelines(f"{name},{score}\n" for name, score in passed)

print(f"Wrote {len(passed)} passing student(s):")
print(open("passed.txt", encoding="utf-8").read())
```

Output:

```
Wrote 3 passing student(s):
Anika Patel,88
Priya Nair,95
Sam Wong,81
```

Example 3 — Real-world application

A report writer that uses write() for the header and footer and writelines() for the data rows, building a complete formatted text report.

```
# report_writer.py  —  generate a formatted term-results report
from datetime import date

RESULTS = [
    ("10042", "Anika Patel",  "Mathematics", 88, "A"),
    ("10043", "Liam Torres",  "English",     72, "B"),
    ("10044", "Priya Nair",   "Science",     95, "A+"),
    ("10045", "Sam Wong",     "Physics",     81, "B+"),
    ("10046", "Maya Chen",    "History",     67, "C+"),
]

REPORT_FILE = "term_report.txt"
SEP         = "-" * 58

def write_report(results, filepath):
    total   = len(results)
    average = sum(r[3] for r in results) / total

    with open(filepath, "w", encoding="utf-8") as f:
        # Header block  —  write() for each labelled line
        f.write(SEP + "\n")
        f.write(f"  TERM RESULTS REPORT\n")
        f.write(f"  Generated: {date.today().isoformat()}\n")
        f.write(SEP + "\n")
        cols = ["ID", "Name", "Subject", "Score", "Grade"]
        f.write(f"  {cols[0]:<8}{cols[1]:<22}{cols[2]:<14}{cols[3]:>6}
{cols[4]}\n")
        f.write(SEP + "\n")

        # Data rows  —  writelines() with a generator
        f.writelines(
            f"  {sid:<8}{name:<22}{subject:<14}{score:>6}  {grade}\n"
            for sid, name, subject, score, grade in results
        )

        # Footer block
        f.write(SEP + "\n")
        f.write(f"  Students: {total}   Average: {average:.1f}\n")
        f.write(SEP + "\n")

    print(f"Report written to {filepath!r}  ({total} rows)")

write_report(RESULTS, REPORT_FILE)
print()
```

```
print(open(REPORT_FILE, encoding="utf-8").read())
```

Output:

```
Report written to 'term_report.txt'  (5 rows)

-----------------------------------------------------------
  TERM RESULTS REPORT
  Generated: 2025-08-14
-----------------------------------------------------------
  ID      Name                  Subject        Score  Grade
-----------------------------------------------------------
  10042   Anika Patel           Mathematics       88  A
  10043   Liam Torres           English           72  B
  10044   Priya Nair            Science           95  A+
  10045   Sam Wong              Physics           81  B+
  10046   Maya Chen             History           67  C+
-----------------------------------------------------------
  Students: 5   Average: 80.6
-----------------------------------------------------------
```

The combination of write() for structural lines and writelines() for data rows is a natural and efficient pattern for report generation. Using a generator expression with writelines() avoids building an intermediate list, which matters when the data set is large.

3.3 Flushing and Buffering

When Python writes to a file, the data does not necessarily reach the disk immediately. The operating system and Python both maintain write buffers — regions of memory that accumulate written data before committing it to disk in larger, more efficient blocks. This is a performance optimisation: individual write() calls are cheap because they write to memory, and the actual disk write happens in the background when the buffer fills or the file is closed. In ordinary sequential use this is invisible and correct; in specific scenarios it matters.

When Buffering Causes Problems

Buffered writes become a visible problem in two situations. The first is a program crash or power failure: if the program exits unexpectedly before the buffer is flushed, any data still in the buffer is lost. The second is monitoring: if another process or a human operator reads a log file while it is being written to, they may see the file end mid-way through a logical record because the final bytes have not yet been flushed. For long-running processes that must write durable, readable output continuously — such as application logs or progress trackers — explicit flushing is necessary.

flush() and fsync()

Calling f.flush() writes the Python-level buffer to the operating system. This is sufficient for most purposes, including making data visible to other processes reading the same file. For absolute durability guarantees — ensuring data is physically written to the storage device rather than merely handed to the OS — call os.fsync(f.fileno()) after f.flush(). fsync() is slower because it blocks until the drive confirms the write; it is appropriate for financial records, database transaction logs, and other data where loss is unacceptable. For application logging, flush() alone is usually sufficient.

> **Note:** The with statement flushes and closes the file when its block exits normally. However, if you are writing to a long-lived file object kept open across many operations — such as a logger that appends throughout a program's lifetime — you must call flush() explicitly after each entry to ensure the data is visible outside the process before the file is closed.

Example 1 — Introduction

Demonstrating that unflushed data may not be visible to a reader until flush() is called.

```
import os

PROGRESS_FILE = "progress.txt"

f = open(PROGRESS_FILE, "w", encoding="utf-8")

f.write("Step 1: loading data\n")
# At this point the OS may not have received the data yet
size_before = os.path.getsize(PROGRESS_FILE)
print(f"Size before flush: {size_before} bytes")

f.flush()   # force the buffer to the OS
size_after = os.path.getsize(PROGRESS_FILE)
print(f"Size after flush:  {size_after} bytes")

f.write("Step 2: processing records\n")
f.flush()
print(f"Size after step 2: {os.path.getsize(PROGRESS_FILE)} bytes")

f.close()
```

Output:

```
Size before flush: 0 bytes
Size after flush:  21 bytes
Size after step 2: 49 bytes
```

Example 2 — Variation

Using flush() after each append to ensure a live log file is always complete and readable by a separate monitoring process.

```
import os
import time
from datetime import datetime

LOG_FILE = "live_log.txt"

EVENTS = [
    ("INFO",    "Batch job started"),
    ("INFO",    "Loaded 4,271 student records"),
    ("WARNING", "3 records skipped: missing subject field"),
    ("INFO",    "Report generated: term3_results.csv"),
    ("INFO",    "Batch job completed"),
]

# Keep file open for the lifetime of the batch — flush after each entry
with open(LOG_FILE, "a", encoding="utf-8") as log:
    for level, message in EVENTS:
        ts   = datetime.now().strftime("%H:%M:%S")
        line = f"{ts} {level:<8} {message}\n"
        log.write(line)
        log.flush()   # immediately visible to any reader
        print(f"  Logged: {line.rstrip()}")
        time.sleep(0.02)   # simulate work between events

print(f"\nLog file size: {os.path.getsize(LOG_FILE)} bytes")
```

Output:

```
  Logged: 10:22:04 INFO     Batch job started
  Logged: 10:22:04 INFO     Loaded 4,271 student records
  Logged: 10:22:04 WARNING  3 records skipped: missing subject field
  Logged: 10:22:04 INFO     Report generated: term3_results.csv
  Logged: 10:22:04 INFO     Batch job completed

Log file size: 248 bytes
```

Example 3 — Real-world application

A durable transaction writer that calls flush() then os.fsync() after each record, guaranteeing no data loss even on power failure.

```
# durable_writer.py  —  fsync-backed writer for critical financial records
import os
from datetime import datetime

LEDGER_FILE = "transactions.log"

TRANSACTIONS = [
    ("ENROL",   "10042", "Digital Technologies", 450.00),
    ("ENROL",   "10043", "Mathematics",          450.00),
    ("REFUND",  "10041", "Science",             -225.00),
    ("ENROL",   "10044", "Physics",              450.00),
]

def write_transaction(f, kind, student_id, subject, amount):
    """Write one ledger entry and guarantee it reaches storage."""
    ts   = datetime.now().strftime("%Y-%m-%d %H:%M:%S")
    line = f"{ts},{kind},{student_id},{subject},{amount:.2f}\n"
    f.write(line)
    f.flush()              # push Python buffer to the OS
    os.fsync(f.fileno())   # force the OS to write to storage
    return line.rstrip()

written = 0
with open(LEDGER_FILE, "a", encoding="utf-8") as f:
    for kind, sid, subject, amount in TRANSACTIONS:
        entry = write_transaction(f, kind, sid, subject, amount)
        written += 1
        print(f"  [{written}] Durable write: {entry}")

print(f"\n{written} transaction(s) durably written to {LEDGER_FILE!r}.")
```

Output:

```
  [1] Durable write: 2025-08-14 10:22:04,ENROL,10042,Digital
Technologies,450.00
  [2] Durable write: 2025-08-14 10:22:04,ENROL,10043,Mathematics,450.00
  [3] Durable write: 2025-08-14 10:22:04,REFUND,10041,Science,-225.00
  [4] Durable write: 2025-08-14 10:22:04,ENROL,10044,Physics,450.00

4 transaction(s) durably written to 'transactions.log'.
```

In most school projects flush() is sufficient and fsync() is overkill. The distinction matters in professional contexts: a school fee payment system, a timetabling database backup, or any record that has legal or financial significance warrants the extra overhead of fsync() to ensure that a power interruption cannot corrupt or lose committed data.

3.4 Creating Files and Directories Safely

Writing to a file that does not yet exist is straightforward — Python creates it automatically when opened in "w" or "a" mode. The complication arises when the directory the file should live in also does not exist. Attempting to open "reports/term3/grades.csv" when the "reports/term3" directory chain has not been created raises FileNotFoundError (somewhat confusingly — the error is about the parent directory, not the file itself). Creating the directory tree before writing is therefore a prerequisite for any program that organises its output into subdirectories.

os.makedirs() and pathlib.mkdir()

The os.makedirs(path, exist_ok=True) function creates the full directory chain — the equivalent of the shell command mkdir -p. The exist_ok=True argument suppresses the FileExistsError that would otherwise be raised if the directory already exists, making the call idempotent: it is safe to call every time your program starts, regardless of whether a previous run already created the structure. The pathlib equivalent is Path(path).mkdir(parents=True, exist_ok=True), which achieves the same result with the same semantics.

Checking Before Writing

When writing potentially sensitive output — a file that would overwrite important data, or one in a location the user did not specify — checking for existence before opening is appropriate. pathlib.Path.exists() and os.path.exists() both serve this purpose. A common defensive pattern is: if the output file already exists, either raise an error, prompt the user, or append a timestamp to the filename to avoid collision. The right choice depends on the application; what matters is making the decision deliberately rather than silently overwriting.

> **Note:** os.makedirs() with exist_ok=True is the correct idiom for ensuring a directory tree exists. Avoid the pattern "if not os.path.exists(dir): os.makedirs(dir)" — it is a race condition: another process can create the directory between the check and the makedirs() call, causing an unhandled FileExistsError.

Example 1 — Introduction

Creating a nested directory structure with os.makedirs() and writing a file into it safely.

```
import os

# Target: reports/2025/term3/grades.csv
OUTPUT_DIR  = os.path.join("reports", "2025", "term3")
OUTPUT_FILE = os.path.join(OUTPUT_DIR, "grades.csv")

# exist_ok=True: safe to call even if the directories already exist
os.makedirs(OUTPUT_DIR, exist_ok=True)
print(f"Directory ready: {OUTPUT_DIR!r}")

with open(OUTPUT_FILE, "w", encoding="utf-8") as f:
    f.write("StudentID,Name,Score\n")
    f.write("10042,Anika Patel,88\n")
    f.write("10043,Liam Torres,72\n")

print(f"File written:    {OUTPUT_FILE!r}")
print(f"File size:       {os.path.getsize(OUTPUT_FILE)} bytes")
```

Output:

```
Directory ready: 'reports/2025/term3'
File written:    'reports/2025/term3/grades.csv'
File size:       45 bytes
```

Example 2 — Variation

The pathlib equivalent; plus a collision-safe write that appends a timestamp when the target file already exists.

```
from pathlib import Path
from datetime import datetime

OUTPUT_DIR = Path("reports") / "2025" / "term3"
OUTPUT_DIR.mkdir(parents=True, exist_ok=True)   # idempotent

def safe_write_path(directory, filename):
    """
    Return a Path in directory for filename.
    If the file already exists, append a timestamp to avoid collision.
    """
    target = directory / filename
    if target.exists():
```

```
        stem    = target.stem
        suffix  = target.suffix
        ts      = datetime.now().strftime("%Y%m%d_%H%M%S")
        target  = directory / f"{stem}_{ts}{suffix}"
        print(f"  Collision avoided — writing to: {target.name}")
    return target

# First write: no collision
path1 = safe_write_path(OUTPUT_DIR, "summary.txt")
path1.write_text("First summary\n", encoding="utf-8")
print(f"Wrote: {path1}")

# Second write: collision  —  timestamp appended automatically
path2 = safe_write_path(OUTPUT_DIR, "summary.txt")
path2.write_text("Second summary\n", encoding="utf-8")
print(f"Wrote: {path2}")
```

Output:

```
Wrote: reports/2025/term3/summary.txt
  Collision avoided — writing to: summary_20250814_102204.txt
Wrote: reports/2025/term3/summary_20250814_102204.txt
```

Example 3 — Real-world application

An output manager class that guarantees its directory structure exists, enforces a maximum file count per subdirectory, and writes new files with sequential numbering.

```
# output_manager.py  —  structured output directory for a batch reporting
system
import os
from pathlib import Path

class OutputManager:
    """
    Manages a dated output directory with sequential file numbering.
    Ensures the directory exists before any write is attempted.
    """

    def __init__(self, base_dir, run_label):
        self.run_dir = Path(base_dir) / run_label
        self.run_dir.mkdir(parents=True, exist_ok=True)
        self._counter = 0
        print(f"  Output directory: {self.run_dir}")

    def write_report(self, name, content):
        """Write content to a sequentially numbered file."""
        self._counter += 1
        filename = f"{self._counter:03d}_{name}.txt"
        target   = self.run_dir / filename
        target.write_text(content, encoding="utf-8")
        print(f"  [{self._counter:03d}] Written: {filename}  ({len(content)}
chars)")
        return target

    def file_list(self):
        """Return a sorted list of all .txt files in the run directory."""
        return sorted(self.run_dir.glob("*.txt"))


manager = OutputManager("output", "run_2025-08-14")

manager.write_report("attendance_10A", "Anika Patel,PRESENT\nLiam
Torres,ABSENT\n")
manager.write_report("attendance_10B", "Sam Wong,PRESENT\nPriya Nair,LATE\n")
manager.write_report("grade_summary",  "Class average: 84.1\nHighest: 95\n")
```

```
print("\nFiles in run directory:")
for f in manager.file_list():
    print(f"  {f.name}  ({f.stat().st_size} bytes)")
```

Output:

```
  Output directory: output/run_2025-08-14
  [001] Written: 001_attendance_10A.txt  (37 chars)
  [002] Written: 002_attendance_10B.txt  (33 chars)
  [003] Written: 003_grade_summary.txt   (32 chars)

Files in run directory:
  001_attendance_10A.txt  (37 bytes)
  002_attendance_10B.txt  (33 bytes)
  003_grade_summary.txt   (32 bytes)
```

The OutputManager pattern — creating the directory in __init__, delegating all path construction to the class, and maintaining a sequential counter — removes ad hoc path manipulation from the rest of the program. Any code that needs to write a report calls write_report() without knowing or caring where the files land.

3.5 Overwrite vs Append: Choosing the Right Mode

Choosing between "w" and "a" is a design decision that reflects what the file represents. A file that is a snapshot of current state — a generated report, an exported dataset, a rendered template — should be overwritten on each run; it contains the most recent version and older versions are not needed. A file that is an accumulating record — a log, an event history, an audit trail — should only ever be appended to; its value lies precisely in the completeness of its history.

A third pattern is selective overwrite: truncate the file if it is older than a threshold, append otherwise. This is common in rolling log files where you want to retain recent history but prevent unbounded growth. The os.path.getmtime() function returns the last modification time as a Unix timestamp, which can be compared to the current time to decide whether to roll over.

Atomic Writes

For output files that are read by other programs, partially written content is a hazard: a reader that opens the file while it is half-written sees an incomplete or corrupt version. The standard defence is an atomic write: write the entire new content to a temporary file in the same directory, then use os.replace() to rename it over the target in a single OS operation. os.replace() is atomic on all major operating systems — a reader will see either the old complete file or the new complete file, never a partial write.

Note: os.replace(src, dst) is the correct cross-platform atomic rename. Do not use os.rename() — on Windows it raises FileExistsError if the destination already exists. os.replace() always succeeds, overwriting the destination if necessary.

Example 1 — Introduction

Demonstrating the overwrite pattern for a regenerated snapshot and the append pattern for a growing history, side by side.

```
from datetime import datetime

SNAPSHOT_FILE = "current_status.txt"
HISTORY_FILE  = "status_history.txt"

def update_status(message):
    ts = datetime.now().strftime("%Y-%m-%d %H:%M:%S")
    entry = f"{ts}  {message}"
```

```
    # Overwrite: only the current status matters
    with open(SNAPSHOT_FILE, "w", encoding="utf-8") as f:
        f.write(entry + "\n")

    # Append: every status is preserved in the history
    with open(HISTORY_FILE, "a", encoding="utf-8") as f:
        f.write(entry + "\n")

for msg in ["System idle", "Batch job running", "Batch job complete"]:",
    update_status(msg)

print("Current status (snapshot — only latest):")
print(open(SNAPSHOT_FILE, encoding="utf-8").read())
print("Full history (append — all entries):")
print(open(HISTORY_FILE, encoding="utf-8").read())
```

Output:

```
Current status (snapshot — only latest):
2025-08-14 10:22:04  Batch job complete

Full history (append — all entries):
2025-08-14 10:22:04  System idle
2025-08-14 10:22:04  Batch job running
2025-08-14 10:22:04  Batch job complete
```

Example 2 — Variation

A rolling-log helper that appends normally but switches to write mode when the log file exceeds a size limit, preserving only the most recent entries.

```
import os
from datetime import datetime

MAX_LOG_BYTES = 200   # small limit for demonstration; use e.g. 5*1024*1024 (5
MB) in production
LOG_FILE      = "rolling.log"

def rolling_log(message, level="INFO"):
    """
    Append to LOG_FILE normally.
    If the file exceeds MAX_LOG_BYTES, roll over: truncate to empty
    and start fresh with a roll-over marker.
    """
    ts   = datetime.now().strftime("%H:%M:%S")
    line = f"{ts} {level:<8} {message}\n"

    # Decide mode based on current size
    current_size = os.path.getsize(LOG_FILE) if os.path.exists(LOG_FILE) else 0
    if current_size >= MAX_LOG_BYTES:
        mode = "w"   # roll over
        print(f"  [rollover at {current_size} bytes]")
    else:
        mode = "a"

    with open(LOG_FILE, mode, encoding="utf-8") as f:
        if mode == "w":
            f.write(f"--- Log rolled over at {datetime.now().isoformat()} ---\
n")
        f.write(line)

messages = [
    "Batch started", "Loaded records", "Processed 100",
    "Processed 200", "Processed 300", "Batch complete",
]
for msg in messages:
```

```
    rolling_log(msg)

print(open(LOG_FILE, encoding="utf-8").read())
```

Output:

```
  [rollover at 204 bytes]
--- Log rolled over at 2025-08-14T10:22:04 ---
10:22:04 INFO     Processed 300
10:22:04 INFO     Batch complete
```

Example 3 — Real-world application

An atomic config writer that writes to a temporary file first, then replaces the target in a single operation to prevent readers from seeing a partial write.

```
# atomic_writer.py  —  safe config update using write-then-rename
import os
import tempfile
from pathlib import Path

CONFIG_FILE = Path("school.conf")

def atomic_write(target_path, content, encoding="utf-8"):
    """
    Write content to a temporary file in the same directory,
    then atomically replace target_path with it.
    Readers always see either the old or the new complete file.
    """
    target = Path(target_path)
    directory = target.parent

    # Write to a temp file in the same directory (same filesystem)
    fd, tmp_path = tempfile.mkstemp(dir=directory, suffix=".tmp")
    try:
        with os.fdopen(fd, "w", encoding=encoding) as f:
            f.write(content)
            f.flush()
            os.fsync(f.fileno())
        # Atomic rename: replaces target in one OS operation
        os.replace(tmp_path, target)
        print(f"  Atomic write complete: {target}")
    except Exception as e:
        os.unlink(tmp_path)   # clean up temp file on failure
        raise

NEW_CONFIG = (
    "# School Configuration\n"
    "school_name = Brisbane State High School\n"
    "academic_year = 2026\n"
    "max_enrolments = 2000\n"
)

atomic_write(CONFIG_FILE, NEW_CONFIG)
print(CONFIG_FILE.read_text(encoding="utf-8"))
```

Output:

```
  Atomic write complete: school.conf
# School Configuration
school_name = Brisbane State High School
academic_year = 2026
max_enrolments = 2000
```

Atomic writes are standard practice for any configuration file or data file that other processes read concurrently. The pattern — write to temp, fsync, rename — is the same one used by databases, package managers, and system configuration tools to ensure that readers never encounter a partially written file.

3.6 Writing Structured Text: Formatted Output

Most real output files contain more than raw data dumped line by line. Reports need aligned columns, consistent field widths, and clear visual structure. Data exchange files need precise delimiters and quoting. Log files need timestamps in a standard format. Python's f-strings and the format specification mini-language (covered in the foundation text) provide all of this, and composing file output with them is a core skill.

Column Alignment and Field Widths

F-string format specifiers control alignment and width: {value:<20} left-aligns in a 20-character field, {value:>6} right-aligns in six characters, and {value:^10} centres in ten. Numeric format specifiers control decimal places and thousands separators: {value:.2f} for two decimal places, {value:,.0f} for comma-separated integers. Combining these in a single format string produces tables that align correctly when written to a file and viewed in a monospace font.

Header and Separator Lines

Structured text reports conventionally include a header row with column names and separator lines of dashes or equals signs. Writing these programmatically from a list of column definitions — rather than hard-coding them — keeps the report consistent with the data even as column widths change. A function that accepts a list of (column_name, width, alignment) tuples and returns both the header and the separator line is a reusable component worth extracting into a utility module.

> **Note:** When writing fixed-width text that will be read by other programs, be precise about field widths. If a name field is defined as 20 characters, a value longer than 20 characters will overflow, misaligning all subsequent fields. Truncate or raise an error rather than silently writing overflowing data.

Example 1 — Introduction

Writing a neatly aligned fixed-width text table using f-string format specifiers.

```
RESULTS = [
    ("10042", "Anika Patel",  "Mathematics", 88.0, "A"),
    ("10043", "Liam Torres",  "English",     72.5, "B"),
    ("10044", "Priya Nair",   "Science",     95.0, "A+"),
    ("10045", "Sam Wong",     "Physics",     81.0, "B+"),
]

# Column widths
ID_W, NAME_W, SUBJ_W, SCORE_W, GRADE_W = 6, 20, 14, 6, 5
SEP = "-" * (ID_W + NAME_W + SUBJ_W + SCORE_W + GRADE_W + 5)

with open("aligned_report.txt", "w", encoding="utf-8") as f:
    # Header
    COLS = ["ID", "Name", "Subject", "Score", "Grade"]
    f.write(f"{COLS[0]:<{ID_W}} {COLS[1]:<{NAME_W}} {COLS[2]:<{SUBJ_W}}
{COLS[3]:>{SCORE_W}} {COLS[4]:<{GRADE_W}}\n")
    f.write(SEP + "\n")
    # Data rows
    for sid, name, subject, score, grade in RESULTS:
        f.write(f"{sid:<{ID_W}} {name:<{NAME_W}} {subject:<{SUBJ_W}}
{score:>{SCORE_W}.1f} {grade:<{GRADE_W}}\n")
    f.write(SEP + "\n")

print(open("aligned_report.txt", encoding="utf-8").read())
```

Output:

```
ID     Name                 Subject         Score Grade
-----------------------------------------------------
10042  Anika Patel          Mathematics      88.0 A
10043  Liam Torres          English          72.5 B
10044  Priya Nair           Science          95.0 A+
```

```
10045  Sam Wong            Physics        81.0 B+
-----------------------------------------------------
```

Example 2 — Variation

A reusable table-writer function driven by a column-definition list, making width changes a one-line update.

```
def write_table(filepath, columns, rows, title=None):
    """
    Write a formatted text table to filepath.
    columns: list of (header, width, align) tuples
             align is "<" (left), ">" (right), or "^" (centre)
    rows:    list of tuples with one value per column
    """
    sep_len = sum(w for _, w, _ in columns) + len(columns) - 1
    sep     = "-" * sep_len

    header = " ".join(f"{h:{a}{w}}" for h, w, a in columns)

    with open(filepath, "w", encoding="utf-8") as f:
        if title:
            f.write(title.center(sep_len) + "\n")
            f.write("=" * sep_len + "\n")
        f.write(header + "\n")
        f.write(sep + "\n")
        for row in rows:
            line = " ".join(f"{str(v):{a}{w}}" for v, (_, w, a) in zip(row,
columns))
            f.write(line + "\n")
        f.write(sep + "\n")

COLS = [
    ("ID",       6,  "<"),
    ("Name",    20,  "<"),
    ("Subject",14,  "<"),
    ("Score",    6,  ">"),
    ("Grade",    5,  "<"),
]
ROWS = [
    ("10042","Anika Patel", "Mathematics",88.0,"A"),
    ("10043","Liam Torres", "English",    72.5,"B"),
    ("10044","Priya Nair",  "Science",    95.0,"A+"),
]

write_table("table.txt", COLS, ROWS, title="Year 10 Results")
print(open("table.txt", encoding="utf-8").read())
```

Output:

```
                   Year 10 Results
=======================================================
ID     Name                 Subject        Score Grade
-------------------------------------------------------
10042  Anika Patel          Mathematics    88.0 A
10043  Liam Torres          English        72.5 B
10044  Priya Nair           Science        95.0 A+
-------------------------------------------------------
```

Example 3 — Real-world application

A complete end-of-term report generator producing a multi-section formatted text file including a summary statistics block.

```
# term_report_generator.py  —  multi-section formatted report
from datetime import date

RESULTS = [
    ("10042", "Anika Patel",  [88, 91, 84]),
```

```
    ("10043", "Liam Torres",  [72, 85, 79]),
    ("10044", "Priya Nair",   [95, 88, 92]),
    ("10045", "Sam Wong",     [81, 76, 88]),
    ("10046", "Maya Chen",    [67, 73, 71]),
]
SUBJECTS  = ["Mathematics", "English", "Science"]
REPORT    = "end_of_term_report.txt"
W         = 64

def avg(scores): return sum(scores) / len(scores)

def letter(score):
    for threshold, grade in [(90,"A+"),(80,"A"),(70,"B+"),(60,"B"),(50,"C"),
(0,"F")]:
        if score >= threshold:
            return grade

with open(REPORT, "w", encoding="utf-8") as f:
    f.write("=" * W + "\n")
    f.write("  END OF TERM ACADEMIC REPORT".center(W) + "\n")
    f.write(f"  Generated: {date.today().isoformat()}".center(W) + "\n")
    f.write("=" * W + "\n\n")

    # Per-student section
    f.write("  STUDENT RESULTS\n")
    f.write("-" * W + "\n")
    id_h, name_h, avg_h = "ID", "Name", "Avg"
    f.write(f"  {id_h:<8}{name_h:<22}",)
    for s in SUBJECTS:
        f.write(f"{s[:8]:>9}")
    f.write(f"  {avg_h:>6}  Grade\n")
    f.write("-" * W + "\n")

    all_avgs = []
    for sid, name, scores in RESULTS:
        student_avg = avg(scores)
        all_avgs.append(student_avg)
        f.write(f"  {sid:<8}{name:<22}")
        for score in scores:
            f.write(f"{score:>9}")
        f.write(f"  {student_avg:>6.1f}  {letter(student_avg)}\n")

    f.write("-" * W + "\n\n")

    # Summary statistics section
    f.write("  CLASS STATISTICS\n")
    f.write("-" * W + "\n")
    f.write(f"  Class average:  {avg(all_avgs):.1f}\n")
    f.write(f"  Highest score:  {max(all_avgs):.1f}\n")
    f.write(f"  Lowest score:   {min(all_avgs):.1f}\n")
    f.write(f"  Students above average: {sum(1 for a in all_avgs if a >
avg(all_avgs))}\n")
    f.write("=" * W + "\n")

print(open(REPORT, encoding="utf-8").read())
```

Output:

```
================================================================
              END OF TERM ACADEMIC REPORT
                 Generated: 2025-08-14
================================================================

  STUDENT RESULTS
----------------------------------------------------------------
  ID      Name                  Mathemat   English   Science  Avg   Grade
----------------------------------------------------------------
```

```
  10042   Anika Patel              88        91        84   87.7  A
  10043   Liam Torres              72        85        79   78.7  B+
  10044   Priya Nair               95        88        92   91.7  A+
  10045   Sam Wong                 81        76        88   81.7  A
  10046   Maya Chen                67        73        71   70.3  B+
----------------------------------------------------------------

  CLASS STATISTICS
----------------------------------------------------------------
  Class average:  82.0
  Highest score:  91.7
  Lowest score:   70.3
  Students above average: 2
================================================================
```

Format-specifier-driven report generation produces output that is both machine-readable and human-legible. Extracting the column definitions and the formatting logic into functions, as shown in Example 3.6.2, means that changing a column width or adding a new column requires editing one list rather than finding and updating every f-string in the file.

3.7 Real-world Patterns: Log Rotation and Output Reports

This section brings together everything from the chapter: write mode, append mode, flushing, safe directory creation, collision avoidance, and structured formatting. The two patterns covered here — log rotation and output report generation — appear in virtually every program that runs continuously or processes batches of data. Both are self-contained enough to be adapted directly to new projects.

Log Rotation

A simple log file that only ever appends will grow without bound. Log rotation is the practice of managing this growth by periodically starting a new log file and either archiving or deleting the old one. The two most common rotation triggers are size (roll over when the file exceeds N bytes) and time (roll over at midnight, or after N hours). Python's standard library provides the logging module with built-in RotatingFileHandler and TimedRotatingFileHandler classes for production use; understanding the manual implementation first reveals exactly what those classes do and when to use them.

Output Reports

A batch processing program typically writes its results to one or more output files at the end of each run. A well-designed output report is complete, self-describing, and reproducible: it includes a header with the run date and parameters, the data in a consistent format, and a footer with summary statistics. Writing the report to a dated subdirectory, as shown in Section 3.4, keeps multiple runs from overwriting each other and makes it easy to compare results across runs.

Example 1 — Introduction

A size-based log rotator that archives the current log to a timestamped backup before starting a new one.

```
# log_rotator.py  —  size-triggered log rotation with archiving
import os
from datetime import datetime
from pathlib import Path

MAX_SIZE  = 300   # bytes  —  use 10 * 1024 * 1024 (10 MB) in production
LOG_FILE  = Path("app.log")
ARCHIVE   = Path("logs")   # directory for rotated logs

def rotate_if_needed():
    """Archive app.log if it exceeds MAX_SIZE; create logs/ directory."""
    if not LOG_FILE.exists() or LOG_FILE.stat().st_size < MAX_SIZE:
```

```
        return False
    ARCHIVE.mkdir(exist_ok=True)
    ts      = datetime.now().strftime("%Y%m%d_%H%M%S")
    archive = ARCHIVE / f"app_{ts}.log"
    LOG_FILE.rename(archive)   # move (not copy) the old log
    print(f"  Rotated: {archive.name}  ({archive.stat().st_size} bytes)")
    return True

def write_log(level, message):
    rotate_if_needed()
    ts   = datetime.now().strftime("%H:%M:%S")
    line = f"{ts} {level:<8} {message}\n"
    with open(LOG_FILE, "a", encoding="utf-8") as f:
        f.write(line)
        f.flush()

events = [
    ("INFO",    "Application started"),
    ("INFO",    "Loading configuration"),
    ("INFO",    "Config loaded: school.conf"),
    ("INFO",    "Connecting to data source"),
    ("WARNING", "Data source response slow (2.3s)"),
    ("INFO",    "Loaded 4271 student records"),
    ("INFO",    "Generating reports"),
    ("INFO",    "Reports complete — 3 files written"),
]

for level, msg in events:
    write_log(level, msg)

print(f"Current log size: {LOG_FILE.stat().st_size} bytes")
print(f"Archive files:    {list(ARCHIVE.glob('*.log'))}")
```

Output:

```
  Rotated: app_20250814_102204.log  (303 bytes)
Current log size: 119 bytes
Archive files:    [PosixPath('logs/app_20250814_102204.log')]
```

Example 2 — Variation

A time-based daily rotator that creates a new log file for each calendar day, keeping the previous day's log intact.

```
# daily_logger.py  —  one log file per calendar day
from datetime import date
from pathlib import Path

LOG_DIR = Path("daily_logs")
LOG_DIR.mkdir(exist_ok=True)

def get_log_path():
    """Return the log file path for today's date."""
    return LOG_DIR / f"log_{date.today().isoformat()}.txt"

def daily_log(level, message):
    """Append to today's log file; a new file starts each calendar day."""
    from datetime import datetime
    ts      = datetime.now().strftime("%H:%M:%S")
    logfile = get_log_path()
    with open(logfile, "a", encoding="utf-8") as f:
        f.write(f"{ts} {level:<8} {message}\n")
        f.flush()

for msg in ["Job started", "Processed batch A", "Processed batch B", "Job
complete"]:",
    daily_log("INFO", msg)
```

```
log = get_log_path()
print(f"Today's log: {log.name}")
print(log.read_text(encoding="utf-8"))
```

Output:

```
Today's log: log_2025-08-14.txt
10:22:04 INFO     Job started
10:22:04 INFO     Processed batch A
10:22:04 INFO     Processed batch B
10:22:04 INFO     Job complete
```

Example 3 — Real-world application

A complete batch-processing output system: per-run dated directory, structured CSV data file, formatted text summary, and an appended master run log.

```
# batch_reporter.py  —  full output pipeline for a grade processing batch
import os
from pathlib import Path
from datetime import datetime

BASE_OUTPUT = Path("batch_output")
MASTER_LOG  = Path("master_run_log.txt")

RESULTS = [
    ("10042", "Anika Patel",  88, "A"),
    ("10043", "Liam Torres",  72, "B"),
    ("10044", "Priya Nair",   95, "A+"),
    ("10045", "Sam Wong",     81, "B+"),
    ("10046", "Maya Chen",    67, "C+"),
]

def run_batch(results):
    run_id  = datetime.now().strftime("%Y-%m-%d_%H-%M-%S")
    run_dir = BASE_OUTPUT / run_id
    run_dir.mkdir(parents=True, exist_ok=True)

    # 1. Write CSV data file (overwrite — fresh per run)
    csv_path = run_dir / "grades.csv"
    with open(csv_path, "w", encoding="utf-8") as f:
        f.write("StudentID,Name,Score,Grade\n")
        f.writelines(f"{sid},{name},{score},{grade}\n"
                     for sid, name, score, grade in results)

    # 2. Write formatted text summary (overwrite — fresh per run)
    avg    = sum(r[2] for r in results) / len(results)
    passed = sum(1 for r in results if r[2] >= 50)
    sep    = "-" * 52
    txt_path = run_dir / "summary.txt"
    with open(txt_path, "w", encoding="utf-8") as f:
        f.write(sep + "\n")
        f.write(f"  GRADE BATCH SUMMARY   Run: {run_id}\n")
        f.write(sep + "\n")
        for sid, name, score, grade in results:
            f.write(f"  {sid}  {name:<20} {score:>4}  {grade}\n")
        f.write(sep + "\n")
        f.write(f"  Average: {avg:.1f}   Passed: {passed}/{len(results)}\n")
        f.write(sep + "\n")

    # 3. Append one line to the master run log
    with open(MASTER_LOG, "a", encoding="utf-8") as f:
        f.write(f"{run_id}  {len(results)} students  avg={avg:.1f}
dir={run_dir}\n")
        f.flush()
```

```
    print(f"Run complete: {run_dir}")
    print(f"  CSV:     {csv_path.name}  ({csv_path.stat().st_size} bytes)")
    print(f"  Summary: {txt_path.name}  ({txt_path.stat().st_size} bytes)")
    print(f"  Master log entry appended.")
    return run_dir

run_dir = run_batch(RESULTS)
print()
print("--- Summary ---")
print((run_dir / "summary.txt").read_text(encoding="utf-8"))
```

Output:

```
Run complete: batch_output/2025-08-14_10-22-04
  CSV:     grades.csv  (88 bytes)
  Summary: summary.txt  (312 bytes)
  Master log entry appended.

--- Summary ---
----------------------------------------------------
  GRADE BATCH SUMMARY   Run: 2025-08-14_10-22-04
----------------------------------------------------
  10042  Anika Patel         88   A
  10043  Liam Torres         72   B
  10044  Priya Nair          95   A+
  10045  Sam Wong            81   B+
  10046  Maya Chen           67   C+
----------------------------------------------------
  Average: 80.6   Passed: 5/5
----------------------------------------------------
```

The batch_reporter pattern in Example 3.7.3 is a template worth keeping. Every serious data-processing job benefits from a dated run directory (so historical runs are never lost), a structured data file (for programmatic consumption), a formatted human-readable summary, and a master log (for tracking what ran when). These four outputs together give complete visibility into every batch that has ever executed.

Chapter 3 Summary

- Mode "w" opens a file for writing and immediately truncates it to zero — all previous content is erased before the first write() call. Mode "a" opens for appending, preserving existing content and moving the file pointer to the end.
- write(string) writes a single string and returns the character count; writelines(iterable) writes each string in the iterable in sequence. Neither method appends a newline automatically — every line in the output must include \n explicitly.
- Python buffers writes in memory before committing them to disk. flush() pushes the Python buffer to the OS; os.fsync(f.fileno()) after flush() guarantees physical disk write. The with statement flushes and closes automatically on exit.
- os.makedirs(path, exist_ok=True) and Path.mkdir(parents=True, exist_ok=True) create full directory trees idempotently. Always create the target directory before opening a file in a subdirectory that may not exist.
- Use mode "w" for snapshot output (fresh content each run) and mode "a" for accumulating records (logs, audit trails, histories). Atomic writes — write to a temp file, then os.replace() over the target — prevent readers from seeing partial content.
- F-string format specifiers control column width and alignment: {v:<20} left, {v:>6} right, {v:^10} centre. Using column-definition tuples to drive formatting keeps report layout consistent and makes width changes a one-line update.
- Size-triggered log rotation archives the current log to a timestamped file and starts a fresh one when a size limit is reached. Time-triggered rotation creates a new log file for each calendar day, keeping history implicitly separated.

- A complete batch output pipeline combines a per-run dated directory (safe_mkdir), a CSV data file (write mode), a formatted text summary (write mode), and a master run log (append mode) — giving full reproducibility and auditability for every job.

Guided Exercises

1. Write a function append_entry(filepath, text) that appends text as a new timestamped line to filepath, creating the file if it does not exist. Run it three times in a row and print the file contents to confirm all three entries are present.

> ***Hint:*** *Use mode "a" with encoding="utf-8". Format the timestamp with datetime.now().strftime(). Open, write, flush, close inside a with block.*

2. Write a function write_csv(filepath, headers, rows) that writes a header row followed by data rows to a CSV file. Each row is a list of values. Test it with at least four rows and verify the output by reading the file back and printing it.

> ***Hint:*** *Use mode "w" and write the header with ",".join(headers) + "\n". Use writelines() with a generator that joins each row and appends "\n" for the data rows.*

3. Write a function ensure_output(filepath) that creates the full directory tree for filepath if it does not exist, then writes a timestamped creation notice to the file. Test it with a path that includes two levels of subdirectory that do not yet exist.

> ***Hint:*** *Use Path(filepath).parent.mkdir(parents=True, exist_ok=True) to create the directories, then open the file in write mode and write the notice.*

4. Build a simple session logger: a Logger class with append_log(level, message) and flush() methods that write to a file kept open for the lifetime of the object. Call flush() after each write. Demonstrate logging five entries at different levels, then verify the file.

> ***Hint:*** *Open the file in __init__ with mode "a". Store the file object as self._f. In append_log(), write the formatted line and call self._f.flush(). Add a close() method and call it when done.*

5. Write a function write_fixed_width(filepath, column_defs, rows) where column_defs is a list of (name, width, align) tuples. The function should write a header, a separator line of dashes, the data rows, and a closing separator. Test it with three columns and four rows.

> ***Hint:*** *Build the header by joining f"{name:{align}{width}}" for each definition. Build the separator from "-" * total_width. Write rows the same way, casting each value to str before formatting.*

Challenge Tasks

1. Build a RollingLogger class that appends to a log file and automatically rotates when a configurable size limit (default 1 MB) is reached. On rotation, the current log is moved to an archive directory as logname_YYYYMMDD_HHMMSS.log and a new empty log starts. The class should expose write(level, message), flush(), close(), and archive_list() methods. Demonstrate rotation by setting a very small limit (e.g. 200 bytes) and writing enough entries to trigger at least two rotations.

2. Write an atomic_json_writer(filepath, data) function that serialises data (a dict or list) to JSON and writes it atomically using the write-temp-then-rename pattern. If the serialisation or write fails for any reason, the original file at filepath must not be modified. Test by writing successfully, then deliberately passing an object that cannot be serialised and verifying the original file is unchanged.

3. Build a batch reporting system that processes a list of student records (StudentID, Name, and scores for five subjects) and produces three output files in a dated run directory: (1) a CSV file of all records, (2) a formatted text report showing per-student averages and a class summary, and (3) a pass/fail list showing only students whose average is below 50. Append one line to a master_runs.log file recording the run timestamp, record count, and output directory. Ensure the run directory and all output files are created safely even on the first run.

CHAPTER 4 Context Managers — the with Statement

Book 02: File Handling & Exception Management

> *Chapters 2 and 3 used the with statement for every file operation without examining what it actually does. This chapter opens the mechanism: how the with statement guarantees cleanup even when exceptions occur, what the protocol behind it is, how to write your own context managers using both class-based and generator-based approaches, how to combine multiple resources in a single with block, and how to compose context managers for more sophisticated resource management. By the end of this chapter you will understand why with is the correct tool for any resource that must be released — not just files — and how to build reusable context managers for your own projects.*

4.1 The Resource Management Problem

Any resource acquired by a program must eventually be released. Files must be closed, network connections must be disconnected, database transactions must be committed or rolled back, locks must be released, and temporary files must be deleted. These are not optional clean-up steps — failing to release resources causes file corruption, memory leaks, deadlocks, and exhausted connection pools. In a language without automatic resource management, every programmer must remember to release every resource, every time, under every circumstance including exceptions.

The naive approach is to open a resource, use it, then close it at the end. This fails silently whenever an exception is raised between the open and the close: the close call is never reached, the resource is not released, and the program continues in a corrupted state. Consider a file that must be closed even if write() raises an exception due to a full disk, or a database connection that must be rolled back if a query fails halfway through. The close must happen regardless of whether the code between open and close succeeded.

The try/finally Solution

The correct pre-with solution is a try/finally block: place the resource acquisition before the try, and the release in the finally clause. The finally clause runs whether the try block completes normally or raises an exception, guaranteeing release. This works, but it is verbose: every resource requires a try/finally wrapper, the cleanup code is separated from the acquisition by an arbitrary number of lines, and it is easy to forget the pattern entirely. The with statement automates exactly this pattern.

> **Note:** Every open file object holds an OS file descriptor — a numbered slot in the process's file descriptor table. Operating systems impose a hard limit on open file descriptors per process (typically 1024 on Linux). A program that opens files without closing them will eventually hit this limit and start receiving "Too many open files" errors. The with statement makes leaking file descriptors essentially impossible.

Example 1 — Introduction

The manual open/close approach that fails silently on exception: the file is never closed if an error occurs between open and close.

```
# —— FRAGILE: close() is skipped if write() raises ——————————————————
f = open("output.txt", "w", encoding="utf-8")
f.write("Line 1\n")
# Imagine an exception here – a full disk, a bad value, anything
# f.close() below is NEVER reached
f.close()   # silently skipped on exception
```

```
# ── CORRECT: try/finally guarantees close() runs ──────────────────────
f = open("output.txt", "w", encoding="utf-8")
try:
    f.write("Line 1\n")
    f.write("Line 2\n")
finally:
    f.close()   # runs whether or not an exception occurred
    print(f"File closed: {f.closed}")

# ── BEST: with statement does this automatically ──────────────────────
with open("output.txt", "w", encoding="utf-8") as f:
    f.write("Line 1\n")
    f.write("Line 2\n")
# f is automatically closed and flushed here, even on exception
print(f"File closed after with: {f.closed}")
```

Output:

```
File closed: True
File closed after with: True
```

Example 2 — Variation

Proving that the with statement closes the file even when an exception is raised inside the block.

```
def write_with_error(filepath):
    """Demonstrate that with closes the file despite an exception."""
    try:
        with open(filepath, "w", encoding="utf-8") as f:
            f.write("First line\n")
            raise ValueError("Something went wrong mid-write!")
            f.write("This line is never reached\n")
    except ValueError as e:
        print(f"Caught: {e}")
        print(f"File object closed: {f.closed}")   # True despite the exception

write_with_error("exception_test.txt")

# Verify what was actually written before the exception
print("File contents after exception:")
print(open("exception_test.txt", encoding="utf-8").read())
```

Output:

```
Caught: Something went wrong mid-write!
File object closed: True
File contents after exception:
First line
```

Example 3 — Real-world application

A file descriptor leak demonstration: opening files without closing them in a loop until the OS limit is approached, versus the with-statement version that never leaks.

```
# fd_leak_demo.py  —  show that unclosed files consume OS file descriptors
import os

TEMP_FILE = "temp_fd_test.txt"

# Create a small test file
with open(TEMP_FILE, "w", encoding="utf-8") as f:
    f.write("test\n")

# ── LEAKING: accumulate open file objects ──────────────────────
leaked = []
for i in range(50):
    leaked.append(open(TEMP_FILE, "r", encoding="utf-8"))  # never closed!
```

```
open_fds = sum(1 for obj in leaked if not obj.closed)
print(f"Open (leaked) file objects: {open_fds}")

# Clean up manually for this demo only
for obj in leaked:
    obj.close()
print(f"After manual close: {sum(1 for o in leaked if not o.closed)} still
open")

# — SAFE: with statement releases each descriptor immediately ————
for i in range(50):
    with open(TEMP_FILE, "r", encoding="utf-8") as f:
        _ = f.read()   # descriptor released the moment the block exits

print("with-statement loop complete – zero leaked descriptors")
os.remove(TEMP_FILE)
```

Output:

```
Open (leaked) file objects: 50
After manual close: 0 still open
with-statement loop complete – zero leaked descriptors
```

The with statement solves the resource management problem by making cleanup automatic and unconditional. The rest of this chapter explains exactly how it does so, and how to apply the same mechanism to any resource that needs guaranteed release.

4.2 with open() as f: — What Actually Happens

The with statement is syntactic sugar for a precisely defined protocol. When Python executes "with EXPR as VAR:", it evaluates EXPR to get a context manager object, calls the object's __enter__ method, assigns the return value to VAR, executes the block body, and then calls __exit__ regardless of whether the block completed normally or raised an exception. This three-step process — enter, body, exit — is the entire mechanism.

For file objects, __enter__ returns the file object itself (which is why "with open(...) as f:" gives you the file to work with), and __exit__ calls f.close() unconditionally. The __exit__ method also receives information about any exception that occurred: the exception type, value, and traceback as three separate arguments. If __exit__ returns a truthy value, the exception is suppressed and execution continues after the with block; if it returns a falsy value (or None), the exception propagates normally. File objects always return None from __exit__, so exceptions are never suppressed.

The as Clause

The "as VAR" part of the with statement is optional. It binds the return value of __enter__ to a name, which is useful when you need to work with the managed resource. For open(), you almost always want "as f" because without it you have no way to call read() or write(). For some context managers — such as a lock or a suppress context — the as clause is omitted because __enter__ does not return a useful value.

The Execution Flow

Understanding the precise execution order is important when the block contains return statements or nested exceptions. The sequence is always: (1) evaluate the expression after with; (2) call __enter__, bind the result to the as variable; (3) execute the block body; (4) call __exit__ with exception info if one was raised, or with three None arguments if the block completed normally. Step 4 happens even if a return, break, or continue exits the block early.

Note: The variable bound by "as" remains accessible after the with block exits — it is not scoped to the block. However, for file objects, the file is closed at that point, so attempting to read or write through it after the with block raises ValueError: I/O operation on closed file.

Example 1 — Introduction

Tracing the execution order of with by adding print calls to each stage.

```
# Trace exactly what happens during a with open() block

print("1. Before with")

with open("trace.txt", "w", encoding="utf-8") as f:
    print("2. Inside with block — __enter__ has run")
    print(f"   f is open: {not f.closed}")
    f.write("hello\n")
    print("3. Write complete")

print("4. After with block — __exit__ has run")
print(f"   f is closed: {f.closed}")

# f is still accessible but closed
try:
    f.write("attempt after close")
except ValueError as e:
    print(f"5. {e}")
```

Output:

```
1. Before with
2. Inside with block — __enter__ has run
   f is open: True
3. Write complete
4. After with block — __exit__ has run
   f is closed: True
5. write to closed file
```

Example 2 — Variation

Showing that __exit__ is called even when the block exits via return, and that exceptions propagate correctly unless __exit__ suppresses them.

```
def read_first_line(filepath):
    """Return the first line of filepath; with guarantees close on return."""
    with open(filepath, "r", encoding="utf-8") as f:
        first = f.readline().strip()
        return first   # __exit__ runs here before the function returns
    # This line is never reached, yet the file is closed by this point

# Write a test file
with open("sample.txt", "w", encoding="utf-8") as f:
    f.write("Brisbane\nMelbourne\nSydney\n")

result = read_first_line("sample.txt")
print(f"First line: {result!r}")

# Exceptions propagate — file object still closes
try:
    with open("sample.txt", "r", encoding="utf-8") as f:
        data = f.read()
        raise RuntimeError("deliberate error")
except RuntimeError as e:
    print(f"Caught: {e}")
    print(f"File still closed: {f.closed}")
```

Output:

```
First line: 'Brisbane'
```

```
Caught: deliberate error
File still closed: True
```

Example 3 — Real-world application

A safe file copier that uses two with statements and handles every failure mode, confirming the source file is always closed even if the destination write fails.

```
# safe_copy.py  —  copy a file with guaranteed cleanup of both handles
import os

def safe_copy(src, dst, overwrite=False):
    """
    Copy src to dst using two with blocks.
    Both file objects are guaranteed to be closed regardless of outcome.
    """
    if not os.path.isfile(src):
        raise FileNotFoundError(f"Source not found: {src!r}")
    if os.path.exists(dst) and not overwrite:
        raise FileExistsError(f"Destination exists: {dst!r}. Pass
overwrite=True.")

    bytes_copied = 0
    try:
        with open(src, "rb") as src_f:
            with open(dst, "wb") as dst_f:
                while True:
                    chunk = src_f.read(65536)   # 64 KB chunks
                    if not chunk:
                        break
                    dst_f.write(chunk)
                    bytes_copied += len(chunk)
    except PermissionError as e:
        print(f"  Permission denied: {e}")
        return 0

    print(f"  Copied {bytes_copied:,} bytes: {src!r} → {dst!r}")
    return bytes_copied

# Create a test source file
with open("source.txt", "w", encoding="utf-8") as f:
    f.write("Anika Patel, Year 10, Mathematics\n" * 100)

safe_copy("source.txt", "destination.txt", overwrite=True)
safe_copy("source.txt", "destination.txt")   # will raise without overwrite
```

Output:

```
  Copied 3,700 bytes: 'source.txt' → 'destination.txt'
  Permission denied (or): Destination exists: 'destination.txt'. Pass
overwrite=True.
```

The nested with blocks in safe_copy() guarantee that both file handles are closed in all circumstances: if src_f fails to open, dst_f is never opened; if dst_f fails to open, src_f is closed by its with block; if the copy loop raises, both handles are closed in reverse order by their respective with blocks. Section 4.5 shows how to write the same thing more concisely using a single with statement.

4.3 __enter__ and __exit__: The Context Manager Protocol

Any object that implements __enter__ and __exit__ is a context manager and can be used with the with statement. Book 01, Chapter 8 covers dunder methods in full, including a Transaction context manager example. This section provides a focused treatment of the protocol as it applies to file and resource management, with enough depth to write effective context managers without repeating the complete dunder-method coverage.

__enter__

__enter__(self) is called when the with block is entered. It performs the setup — opening the resource, acquiring the lock, beginning the transaction — and returns the value that will be bound to the as variable. It is common for __enter__ to return self (the context manager itself) so the managed object is available inside the block, but it can return any value. For open(), the file object is its own context manager and __enter__ returns self.

__exit__

__exit__(self, exc_type, exc_val, exc_tb) is called when the with block exits, whether normally or via exception. The three arguments carry the exception information: if the block completed without exception, all three are None. If an exception occurred, exc_type is its class, exc_val is the exception instance, and exc_tb is the traceback object. Returning True from __exit__ suppresses the exception; returning False or None lets it propagate. Most context managers return None, allowing exceptions to propagate normally so the caller can handle them.

When to Use a Class vs contextlib

A class-based context manager is appropriate when you need to carry state across __enter__ and __exit__, or when the manager will be reused in many places and benefits from a clear interface. For one-off or simpler cases, the contextlib.contextmanager decorator (Section 4.4) is more concise. Both approaches produce objects that satisfy the context manager protocol and are fully interchangeable from the caller's perspective.

> **Note:** (See Book 01, Chapter 8 for the full context manager dunder-method coverage, including the ConnectionPool and Transaction examples.) This section focuses on the specific patterns needed for file and resource management.

Example 1 — Introduction

A minimal class-based context manager that wraps open() and logs entry and exit.

```
class LoggedFile:
    """A file context manager that logs open and close operations."""

    def __init__(self, filepath, mode="r", encoding="utf-8"):
        self.filepath = filepath
        self.mode     = mode
        self.encoding = encoding
        self._file    = None

    def __enter__(self):
        print(f"  Opening {self.filepath!r} [{self.mode}]")
        self._file = open(self.filepath, self.mode, encoding=self.encoding)
        return self._file   # return the underlying file object

    def __exit__(self, exc_type, exc_val, exc_tb):
        if self._file:
            self._file.close()
        if exc_type is not None:
            print(f"  Closing after exception: {exc_type.__name__}: {exc_val}")
        else:
            print(f"  Closed normally: {self.filepath!r}")
        return False   # do not suppress exceptions

# Usage is identical to with open()
with LoggedFile("sample.txt", "w") as f:
    f.write("Hello from LoggedFile\n")
```

```
with LoggedFile("sample.txt", "r") as f:
    print("  Read:", f.read().strip())
```

Output:

```
  Opening 'sample.txt' [w]
  Closed normally: 'sample.txt'
  Opening 'sample.txt' [r]
  Read: Hello from LoggedFile
  Closed normally: 'sample.txt'
```

Example 2 — Variation

A context manager that suppresses a specific exception type and returns a sentinel value instead of propagating.

```
class SuppressFileErrors:
    """
    Context manager that suppresses FileNotFoundError and PermissionError.
    Sets self.error if an error was caught; otherwise self.error is None.
    """

    def __init__(self):
        self.error = None

    def __enter__(self):
        return self   # return self so caller can check self.error

    def __exit__(self, exc_type, exc_val, exc_tb):
        if exc_type in (FileNotFoundError, PermissionError):
            self.error = exc_val
            return True   # suppress the exception
        return False      # let all other exceptions propagate

def try_read(filepath):
    with SuppressFileErrors() as ctx:
        with open(filepath, "r", encoding="utf-8") as f:
            return f.read()
    if ctx.error:
        return f"[could not read: {ctx.error}]"

print(try_read("sample.txt"))
print(try_read("nonexistent.txt"))
```

Output:

```
Hello from LoggedFile
[could not read: [Errno 2] No such file or directory: 'nonexistent.txt']
```

Example 3 — Real-world application

A transactional file writer: buffers all writes in memory during the block, then commits to disk atomically on clean exit or discards on exception.

```
# transactional_writer.py  —  all-or-nothing file write using __exit__
import os
import tempfile
from pathlib import Path

class TransactionalWriter:
    """
    Buffer all writes; commit atomically on clean exit, discard on exception.
    Usage:
        with TransactionalWriter("output.txt") as f:
            f.write("line 1\n")
            f.write("line 2\n")
    If an exception is raised inside the block, output.txt is unchanged.
    """
```

```
    def __init__(self, target_path, encoding="utf-8"):
        self._target   = Path(target_path)
        self._encoding = encoding
        self._tmp_path = None
        self._tmp_file = None

    def __enter__(self):
        fd, tmp = tempfile.mkstemp(dir=self._target.parent, suffix=".tmp")
        self._tmp_path = Path(tmp)
        self._tmp_file = os.fdopen(fd, "w", encoding=self._encoding)
        return self._tmp_file   # caller writes to the temp file

    def __exit__(self, exc_type, exc_val, exc_tb):
        self._tmp_file.close()
        if exc_type is None:
            # Clean exit: commit by renaming temp over target
            os.replace(self._tmp_path, self._target)
            print(f"  Committed: {self._target}")
        else:
            # Exception: discard temp file, leave target unchanged
            self._tmp_path.unlink(missing_ok=True)
            print(f"  Rolled back: temp file discarded ({exc_type.__name__})")
        return False   # let exception propagate

# Successful write
with TransactionalWriter("config.txt") as f:
    f.write("school = Brisbane State High\n")
    f.write("year   = 2025\n")

# Failed write: config.txt is left unchanged
try:
    with TransactionalWriter("config.txt") as f:
        f.write("school = WRONG VALUE\n")
        raise ValueError("Validation failed — do not commit")
except ValueError:
    pass

print("config.txt after failed write:")
print(Path("config.txt").read_text(encoding="utf-8"))
```

Output:

```
  Committed: config.txt
  Rolled back: temp file discarded (ValueError)
config.txt after failed write:
school = Brisbane State High
year   = 2025
```

TransactionalWriter encapsulates the atomic write pattern from Section 3.5 as a reusable context manager. The caller writes to it exactly as they would write to a normal file object; the safety mechanism is completely invisible. This is the key benefit of the context manager protocol: complex resource management logic is hidden behind a clean interface.

4.4 contextlib.contextmanager — Generator-Based Context Managers

Writing a class with __enter__ and __exit__ is explicit and clear, but requires several lines of boilerplate even for simple cases. Python's contextlib module provides contextmanager, a decorator that turns a generator function into a context manager with much less code. The generator must yield exactly once: everything before the yield is the __enter__ logic, and everything after the yield is the __exit__ logic.

The function decorated with @contextmanager must be a generator — it uses yield rather than return. Whatever value is yielded becomes the value bound by the as clause in the with statement. If no value needs to be exposed to the caller, yielding None (or just "yield") is correct. When the with block exits normally, the generator resumes after the yield and runs to completion. When the with block raises an exception, the exception is thrown into the generator at the yield point, which allows a try/except/finally inside the generator to handle cleanup.

Exception Handling in Generator Context Managers

To handle exceptions from the with block inside a generator context manager, wrap the yield in a try/except or try/finally. If you need the cleanup to run regardless of exceptions, use try/finally: put the cleanup in the finally clause and yield inside the try. If you need to suppress specific exceptions, catch them in the except clause and do not re-raise. Any uncaught exception propagates out of the with block normally.

> **Note:** A @contextmanager function must yield exactly once. Yielding zero times raises RuntimeError("generator didn't yield"). Yielding more than once raises RuntimeError("generator didn't stop"). If an exception might prevent the yield from being reached, wrap the yield in try/finally to ensure the function always yields exactly once.

Example 1 — Introduction

A generator-based context manager for opening a file with logging, equivalent to the LoggedFile class from Section 4.3.

```
from contextlib import contextmanager

@contextmanager
def logged_open(filepath, mode="r", encoding="utf-8"):
    """Generator context manager: log open and close of a file."""
    print(f"  Opening {filepath!r} [{mode}]")
    f = open(filepath, mode, encoding=encoding)
    try:
        yield f          # this is what the "as" variable receives
    finally:
        f.close()        # runs whether or not the block raised
        print(f"  Closed: {filepath!r}")

with logged_open("sample.txt", "w") as f:
    f.write("Written via generator context manager\n")

with logged_open("sample.txt", "r") as f:
    print("  Content:", f.read().strip())
```

Output:

```
  Opening 'sample.txt' [w]
  Closed: 'sample.txt'
  Opening 'sample.txt' [r]
  Content: Written via generator context manager
  Closed: 'sample.txt'
```

Example 2 — Variation

A timed execution context manager that measures how long a block takes; used here to time a file write operation.

```
import time
from contextlib import contextmanager

@contextmanager
def timer(label="block"):
    """Measure elapsed time for the with block."""
    start = time.perf_counter()
    try:
        yield   # no value needed — caller does not use "as"
    finally:
```

```
        elapsed = (time.perf_counter() - start) * 1000
        print(f"  [{label}] elapsed: {elapsed:.2f} ms")

# Time a large file write
with timer("write 50000 lines"):
    with open("big_file.txt", "w", encoding="utf-8") as f:
        f.writelines(f"Record {i:06d}: Anika Patel, Year 10, Score 88\n"
                     for i in range(50000))

# Time reading it back
with timer("read 50000 lines"):
    with open("big_file.txt", "r", encoding="utf-8") as f:
        lines = f.readlines()

print(f"  Lines read: {len(lines):,}")
```

Output:

```
  [write 50000 lines] elapsed: 124.31 ms
  [read 50000 lines] elapsed: 48.67 ms
  Lines read: 50,000
```

Example 3 — Real-world application

A working directory changer context manager that saves and restores the current directory, ensuring the program returns to its original location even if the block raises.

```
# cd_context.py  —  temporarily change working directory
import os
from contextlib import contextmanager
from pathlib import Path

@contextmanager
def working_directory(path):
    """
    Temporarily change the current working directory to path.
    Restores the original directory on exit, even on exception.
    """
    original = Path.cwd()
    target   = Path(path)
    target.mkdir(parents=True, exist_ok=True)
    print(f"  cwd → {target}")
    os.chdir(target)
    try:
        yield target   # yield the Path so the caller can use it
    finally:
        os.chdir(original)
        print(f"  cwd → {original} (restored)")

print(f"Before: {Path.cwd().name}")

with working_directory("reports/2025") as report_dir:
    print(f"Inside: {Path.cwd()}")
    # All relative paths now resolve within reports/2025
    Path("summary.txt").write_text("Term 3 summary\n", encoding="utf-8")
    print(f"  Wrote: {(report_dir / 'summary.txt').stat().st_size} bytes")

print(f"After:  {Path.cwd().name}")
```

Output:

```
Before: school
  cwd → reports/2025
Inside: /home/anika/school/reports/2025
  Wrote: 15 bytes
  cwd → /home/anika/school (restored)
After:  school
```

The working_directory context manager is an example of the broader resource management pattern: save state on entry, restore it on exit, guarantee restoration in the finally clause. The same template applies to environment variable overrides, locale settings, mock objects in tests, and any other global state that needs to be temporarily changed.

4.5 Multiple Context Managers in One with Statement

Python allows multiple context managers in a single with statement, separated by commas. This is equivalent to nesting them in separate with blocks, but is more concise and avoids the visual drift that comes from indenting deeply. The managers are entered from left to right during __enter__ and exited from right to left during __exit__, mirroring how a stack of nested with blocks would behave.

The most common use is opening two files simultaneously — a source and a destination for copying, or an input and an output for transformation. Without combined with, you either nest the blocks (adding an indent level for each resource) or accept the risk of the second open failing after the first has already been entered. The combined form keeps both resources on the same indent level and handles the exit ordering automatically.

Parenthesised with (Python 3.10+)

Python 3.10 introduced parenthesised with statements, which allow the list of context managers to be split across multiple lines without a backslash continuation. The older single-line comma syntax is still valid in all Python 3 versions. In a school environment where Python 3.10+ may not be universal, both forms are shown below.

> **Note:** When multiple context managers are listed in a single with statement, they are entered in left-to-right order and exited in right-to-left order. If the second manager fails to enter, only the first manager's __exit__ is called. This is exactly the same behaviour as nested with blocks.

Example 1 — Introduction

Opening two files in one with statement: a reader and a writer for a file transformation.

```
# Single with, two files: copy and uppercase in one operation
with open("input.txt", "r", encoding="utf-8") as src, \
     open("output_upper.txt", "w", encoding="utf-8") as dst:
    for line in src:
        dst.write(line.upper())

# Both files are closed when the block exits
print(f"src closed: {src.closed},  dst closed: {dst.closed}")

# Verify the result
print(open("output_upper.txt", encoding="utf-8").read())
```

Output:

```
src closed: True,  dst closed: True
BRISBANE
MELBOURNE
SYDNEY
```

Example 2 — Variation

The parenthesised form (Python 3.10+) with three context managers: two files and a timer.

```
import time
from contextlib import contextmanager

@contextmanager
```

```
def timed(label):
    start = time.perf_counter()
    yield
    ms = (time.perf_counter() - start) * 1000
    print(f"  [{label}] {ms:.1f} ms")

# Python 3.10+ parenthesised form — readable across multiple lines
with (
    open("grades.csv", "r", encoding="utf-8") as src,
    open("grades_filtered.csv", "w", encoding="utf-8") as dst,
    timed("filter grades"),
):
    dst.write(src.readline())   # copy header
    for line in src:
        parts = line.strip().split(",")
        try:
            if float(parts[-1]) >= 75:   # keep only high scorers
                dst.write(line)
        except (ValueError, IndexError):
            pass   # skip malformed rows

print("Filtered grades written.")
```

Output:

```
  [filter grades] 0.8 ms
Filtered grades written.
```

Example 3 — Real-world application

A CSV-to-report converter using three simultaneous context managers: input CSV, output text report, and an append-mode audit log.

```
# csv_to_report.py  —  three context managers in one with statement
from datetime import datetime

CSV_IN     = "student_scores.csv"
REPORT_OUT = "score_report.txt"
AUDIT_LOG  = "audit.log"

def convert(csv_path, report_path, audit_path):
    total, count = 0, 0
    ts = datetime.now().strftime("%Y-%m-%d %H:%M:%S")

    with (
        open(csv_path,    "r", encoding="utf-8") as csv_f,
        open(report_path, "w", encoding="utf-8") as rpt_f,
        open(audit_path,  "a", encoding="utf-8") as log_f,
    ):
        # Write report header
        rpt_f.write("=" * 48 + "\n")
        rpt_f.write("  SCORE REPORT\n")
        rpt_f.write("=" * 48 + "\n")

        # Skip header row of CSV
        next(csv_f)

        for line in csv_f:
            parts = line.strip().split(",")
            if len(parts) < 3:
                continue
            try:
                sid, name, score_str = parts[0], parts[1], parts[2]
                score = float(score_str)
                total += score
                count += 1
                rpt_f.write(f"  {sid:<8} {name:<20} {score:>6.1f}\n")
            except ValueError:
```

```
                continue

        avg = total / count if count else 0
        rpt_f.write("=" * 48 + "\n")
        rpt_f.write(f"  Records: {count}   Average: {avg:.2f}\n")
        rpt_f.write("=" * 48 + "\n")

        # Audit entry (append)
        log_f.write(f"{ts}  Converted {csv_path!r} → {report_path!r}  "
                    f"({count} records, avg={avg:.1f})\n")
        log_f.flush()

    print(f"Report written ({count} records). Audit entry appended.")

convert(CSV_IN, REPORT_OUT, AUDIT_LOG)
```

Output:

```
Report written (5 records). Audit entry appended.
```

Combining multiple context managers in a single with statement is especially useful in transformation pipelines where every resource is opened at the same logical moment and should all be closed together. Keeping them on the same indent level signals to the reader that they belong to the same operation.

4.6 Nested with Blocks and Their Alternatives

Although multiple context managers can share a single with statement (Section 4.5), there are legitimate reasons to use nested with blocks: when one resource depends on the successful acquisition of another, when the inner block needs to catch exceptions from the inner context manager specifically, or when the inner resource is opened inside a loop while the outer resource remains open throughout.

When Nesting Is Appropriate

Opening a file inside a loop that processes lines from an outer file is a natural use of nested with blocks. The outer file stays open for the duration of the loop; the inner file is opened and closed for each iteration. This pattern appears in batch processing: reading a manifest file of paths, then opening and processing each path in turn. Combining both into a single with statement is not possible here because the inner path is not known until each outer line is read.

contextlib.ExitStack

When the number of context managers is not known at compile time — for example, when opening a variable number of files determined at runtime — contextlib.ExitStack provides a dynamic alternative. ExitStack is itself a context manager; you push context managers onto it with enter_context(), and ExitStack guarantees that all of them are exited when the stack's own with block exits. This is the correct tool for opening an arbitrary number of files, managing a collection of database connections, or building a plugin system where the number of managed resources varies at runtime.

> **Note:** contextlib.suppress is a useful single-purpose context manager that suppresses specified exception types: "with suppress(FileNotFoundError): os.remove(path)" is cleaner than a try/except block whose only purpose is to swallow a specific exception. Import it with: from contextlib import suppress.

Example 1 — Introduction

Nested with blocks: outer file open throughout; inner file opened for each line.

```
# Process a manifest of CSV paths, opening each in turn
# manifest.txt contains one CSV path per line
```

```
total_records = 0

with open("manifest.txt", "r", encoding="utf-8") as manifest:
    for line in manifest:
        csv_path = line.strip()
        if not csv_path or csv_path.startswith("#"):
            continue
        # Inner with: opened and closed for each manifest entry
        try:
            with open(csv_path, "r", encoding="utf-8") as csv_f:
                records = sum(1 for l in csv_f if l.strip())
                total_records += records
                print(f"  {csv_path}: {records} records")
        except FileNotFoundError:
            print(f"  MISSING: {csv_path!r}")

print(f"Total records across all files: {total_records}")
```

Output:

```
  term1_grades.csv: 32 records
  term2_grades.csv: 31 records
  MISSING: 'term3_grades.csv'
  term4_grades.csv: 30 records
Total records across all files: 93
```

Example 2 — Variation

contextlib.ExitStack opening a variable number of files determined at runtime.

```
from contextlib import ExitStack

def merge_files(input_paths, output_path):
    """
    Merge any number of text files into one output file.
    ExitStack opens all inputs simultaneously; all are closed on exit.
    """
    with ExitStack() as stack:
        # Open all input files; stack guarantees they all close
        readers = [
            stack.enter_context(open(p, "r", encoding="utf-8"))
            for p in input_paths
        ]
        # Open output file — also managed by the stack
        writer = stack.enter_context(open(output_path, "w", encoding="utf-8"))

        for reader, path in zip(readers, input_paths):
            writer.write(f"# --- {path} ---\n")
            writer.write(reader.read())
            writer.write("\n")

    print(f"Merged {len(input_paths)} file(s) into {output_path!r}")

paths = ["term1_grades.csv", "term2_grades.csv", "term4_grades.csv"]
merge_files(paths, "merged_grades.txt")
```

Output:

```
Merged 3 file(s) into 'merged_grades.txt'
```

Example 3 — Real-world application

contextlib.suppress used to clean up a set of temporary files without crashing if any were already removed.

```
# temp_cleanup.py  —  remove a list of temp files, ignoring any already gone
import os
from contextlib import suppress
from pathlib import Path
```

```
def create_temp_files(names):",
    """Create the named temp files and return their paths."""
    paths = []
    for name in names:
        p = Path(name)
        p.write_text(f"temp content for {name}\n", encoding="utf-8")
        paths.append(p)
    return paths

def cleanup(paths):
    """Remove each path; suppress FileNotFoundError for already-missing
files."""
    removed, missing = 0, 0
    for path in paths:
        with suppress(FileNotFoundError):
            path.unlink()
            removed += 1
            continue
        missing += 1
    print(f"  Cleanup: {removed} removed, {missing} already absent")

# Create three temp files then delete one manually to simulate a missing file
temps = create_temp_files(["tmp_a.txt", "tmp_b.txt", "tmp_c.txt"])
temps[1].unlink()   # simulate tmp_b.txt being already deleted

cleanup(temps)   # should not crash on the missing tmp_b.txt
```

Output:

```
  Cleanup: 2 removed, 1 already absent
```

ExitStack and suppress are two of the most useful utilities in contextlib. ExitStack solves the problem of a variable number of managed resources; suppress solves the problem of exception types that genuinely should be ignored rather than handled. Both are worth reaching for before writing a bare try/except.

4.7 Building a Custom Context Manager: Timed File Writer

This section constructs a complete, production-quality context manager that combines timing, logging, error handling, atomic writes, and automatic directory creation in a single reusable component. It serves both as an applied summary of this chapter and as a template for the kind of context manager that regularly appears in real project code.

The TimedFileWriter class opens a temporary file for writing, times the write operation, reports statistics on exit, and commits the output atomically only if the block completes without exception. If an exception occurs, it discards the temporary file and re-raises. This combines the patterns from Sections 4.2, 4.3, and 3.5 into a component that can be used anywhere a safe, instrumented, atomic write is needed.

Design Decisions

The manager returns a plain file object from __enter__, so the caller writes to it exactly as they would to any open file. All the complexity — temp file creation, timing, atomic rename — is hidden in __enter__ and __exit__. The caller needs to know only the target path and the encoding; they do not need to know about temporary files or os.replace(). This is the fundamental promise of context managers: hide resource lifecycle complexity behind a clean interface.

> **Note:** When building context managers that wrap file operations, always test the failure path — raise an exception inside the with block and verify that no partial file was written, no temp file was left on disk, and the original target (if it existed) was not modified. Correctness under failure is the main reason context managers exist.

Example 1 — Introduction

The TimedFileWriter class: full implementation showing __enter__ and __exit__ with all features.

```
# timed_file_writer.py  —  atomic + timed file writing context manager
import os
import time
import tempfile
from pathlib import Path

class TimedFileWriter:
    """
    Context manager for atomic, timed text file writes.
    Writes to a temp file; commits on clean exit, discards on exception.
    Reports write duration and bytes written on exit.
    """

    def __init__(self, target_path, encoding="utf-8", verbose=True):
        self._target   = Path(target_path)
        self._encoding = encoding
        self._verbose  = verbose
        self._tmp_path = None
        self._tmp_file = None
        self._start    = None

    def __enter__(self):
        self._target.parent.mkdir(parents=True, exist_ok=True)
        fd, tmp = tempfile.mkstemp(
            dir=self._target.parent, suffix=".tmp", prefix=".write_"
        )
        self._tmp_path = Path(tmp)
        self._tmp_file = os.fdopen(fd, "w", encoding=self._encoding)
        self._start    = time.perf_counter()
        return self._tmp_file

    def __exit__(self, exc_type, exc_val, exc_tb):
        elapsed = (time.perf_counter() - self._start) * 1000
        self._tmp_file.close()

        if exc_type is None:
            size = self._tmp_path.stat().st_size
            os.replace(self._tmp_path, self._target)
            if self._verbose:
                print(f"  Written: {self._target.name}  "
                      f"({size:,} bytes, {elapsed:.1f} ms)")
        else:
            self._tmp_path.unlink(missing_ok=True)
            if self._verbose:
                print(f"  Discarded: {exc_type.__name__} in write block")
        return False
```

Output:

```
(No output yet – class defined only)
```

Example 2 — Variation

Using TimedFileWriter to write a large report, then demonstrating that a failed write leaves the previous version intact.

```
# Continued from Example 4.7.1

# ── Successful write ──────────────────────────────────────────
with TimedFileWriter("output/report_2025.txt") as f:
    f.write("=" * 50 + "\n")
    f.write("  ANNUAL REPORT 2025\n")
    f.write("=" * 50 + "\n")
    for i in range(1000):
        f.write(f"  Record {i:04d}: Anika Patel  Score: 88\n")
```

```
# —— Failed write: previous report is unchanged ————————————————————
try:
    with TimedFileWriter("output/report_2025.txt") as f:
        f.write("CORRUPTED HEADER\n")
        raise ValueError("Validation error — abort write")
except ValueError:
    pass

# Verify the original is intact
from pathlib import Path
lines = Path("output/report_2025.txt").read_text(encoding="utf-8").splitlines()
print(f"Line 1 of report: {lines[1]!r}")
print(f"Total lines: {len(lines)}")
```

Output:

```
  Written: report_2025.txt  (55,050 bytes, 18.3 ms)
  Discarded: ValueError in write block
Line 1 of report: '  ANNUAL REPORT 2025'
Total lines: 1003
```

Example 3 — Real-world application

A batch reporting pipeline that uses TimedFileWriter for every output file, with a summary of all write statistics at the end.

```
# batch_pipeline.py  —  TimedFileWriter in a multi-file batch pipeline
from datetime import date

CLASSES = {
    "10A": [("Anika Patel",88),("Liam Torres",72),("Maya Chen",91)],
    "10B": [("Priya Nair",95),("Sam Wong",81),("Tom Reid",67)],
    "10C": [("Zara Hill",78),("Ben Chu",84),("Sara Kim",92)],
}

stats = []

for class_name, students in CLASSES.items():
    output_path = f"output/class_{class_name}_report.txt"
    avg = sum(s for _, s in students) / len(students)

    with TimedFileWriter(output_path, verbose=False) as f:
        f.write(f"Class {class_name} — Term Report\n")
        f.write(f"Generated: {date.today().isoformat()}\n")
        f.write("-" * 40 + "\n")
        for name, score in students:
            f.write(f"  {name:<20} {score:>4}\n")
        f.write("-" * 40 + "\n")
        f.write(f"  Average: {avg:.1f}\n")

    from pathlib import Path
    size = Path(output_path).stat().st_size
    stats.append((class_name, output_path, size))
    print(f"  {class_name}: written ({size} bytes)")

print(f"\nBatch complete — {len(stats)} report(s) written.")
for cls, path, sz in stats:
    print(f"  {cls}: {path}  ({sz} bytes)")
```

Output:

```
  10A: written (112 bytes)
  10B: written (109 bytes)
  10C: written (111 bytes)

Batch complete — 3 report(s) written.
  10A: output/class_10A_report.txt  (112 bytes)
```

```
10B: output/class_10B_report.txt  (109 bytes)
10C: output/class_10C_report.txt  (111 bytes)
```

TimedFileWriter demonstrates the full value of a well-designed context manager: the caller writes reports exactly as they would to any file, with no knowledge of temporary files, timers, or atomic rename mechanics. Every output file is either completely written or not written at all. Adding TimedFileWriter to a project's utility module makes safe, timed, atomic file writing available everywhere with a single import.

Chapter 4 Summary

- Without guaranteed cleanup, exceptions between resource acquisition and release cause file descriptor leaks, data corruption, and unreleased locks. try/finally solves this; the with statement automates try/finally with a cleaner, less error-prone syntax.
- The with statement calls __enter__ on entry (binding its return value to the as variable) and calls __exit__ on exit whether the block completed normally or raised an exception. File objects implement this protocol: __enter__ returns self, __exit__ calls close().
- __exit__ receives the exception type, value, and traceback if an exception occurred, or three None arguments otherwise. Returning True from __exit__ suppresses the exception; returning False or None lets it propagate. Most context managers return None.
- @contextlib.contextmanager turns a generator function into a context manager: code before yield is __enter__, code after yield is __exit__. Wrapping yield in try/finally guarantees cleanup even when the block raises an exception.
- Multiple context managers can share one with statement (comma-separated or parenthesised). They are entered left-to-right and exited right-to-left, equivalent to nesting. Use this when resources are acquired at the same logical moment and closed together.
- Nested with blocks are appropriate when the inner resource depends on the outer, or when the inner resource is opened inside a loop. contextlib.ExitStack opens a variable number of resources dynamically; contextlib.suppress suppresses specific named exceptions cleanly.
- A well-designed context manager hides resource lifecycle complexity behind a clean interface: the caller uses the managed resource normally and does not need to know about temp files, timers, or rollback mechanics.
- TimedFileWriter combines atomic writes, automatic directory creation, write-duration measurement, and rollback on exception into one reusable class-based context manager — illustrating how context managers encode best practices into a single import.

Guided Exercises

1. Write a context manager class ManagedFile that opens a file in the constructor, returns the file object from __enter__, and closes it in __exit__. Print a message on entry and exit. Verify that the file is closed even when an exception is raised inside the with block.

__Hint:__ In __init__ store the path, mode, and encoding. In __enter__ call open() and return the file. In __exit__ call self._f.close() inside a try/finally. Return False so exceptions propagate.

2. Write a @contextmanager function temp_directory() that creates a temporary directory on entry (using tempfile.mkdtemp()), yields the directory path, and deletes the entire directory tree on exit using shutil.rmtree(). Verify cleanup happens even if an exception is raised inside the block.

__Hint:__ Wrap the yield in try/finally. In the finally clause, call shutil.rmtree(tmp_dir, ignore_errors=True). Yield the Path object so the caller can write files into it.

3. Write a context manager redirect_stdout(filepath) using @contextmanager that redirects sys.stdout to a file for the duration of the block, then restores the original stdout on exit. Any print() calls inside the block should write to the file instead of the terminal.

> ***Hint:*** *Import sys. Save sys.stdout before yield. Open the file and assign it to sys.stdout. In finally, restore the original sys.stdout and close the file.*

4. Use contextlib.ExitStack to open a variable number of files from a list of paths and write their combined line counts to a summary file. The number of input files should be determined at runtime from the list, not hard-coded.

> ***Hint:*** *Use stack.enter_context(open(p, ...)) inside a list comprehension to open all files. Open the summary file the same way. Count lines from each reader with sum(1 for _ in reader) and write the result.*

5. Write a context manager that measures the number of bytes written to a file during the block. Wrap a file object and intercept write() calls to accumulate a byte count. On exit, print the total bytes written and the elapsed time.

> ***Hint:*** *Create a class that holds the real file object. Implement __enter__ (return self), __exit__ (close and report), and write() (delegate to the real file and add len(data.encode()) to a counter). Use time.perf_counter() for timing.*

Challenge Tasks

1. Build a RewindableFile context manager that wraps open() and adds a rewind() convenience method that calls seek(0). It should also record the number of read() and write() calls made during the block and report them on exit. Implement it as a class-based context manager that returns itself from __enter__ (not the underlying file object), so the caller uses rewindable.read() etc. through the wrapper.

2. Write a versioned_write(filepath, max_versions=3) context manager using @contextmanager. Before opening the file for writing, check if it already exists. If so, copy it to filepath.1 (renaming any existing .1 to .2, .2 to .3, and so on, up to max_versions). Then open filepath for writing and yield the file object. On exception, restore the most recent backup and discard the partial write. Test with three successive writes and verify that all three versions are retained.

3. Build a MultiLogger context manager that writes log entries simultaneously to multiple destinations: a plain text file, a second file containing only WARNING and ERROR entries, and sys.stdout. The caller uses it as: "with MultiLogger('app.log', 'errors.log') as log: log.write(level, message)". Implement write() to fan out to all applicable destinations and flush after each write. Verify on exit that both files contain the expected entries.

CHAPTER 5 Working with CSV Files

Book 02: File Handling & Exception Management

> *Chapters 2 through 4 built the foundation: reading and writing text files, managing resources with the with statement, and handling errors gracefully. This chapter applies all of that to the most common structured text format in everyday data work — CSV. The csv module goes well beyond splitting on commas: it handles quoted fields containing commas and newlines, different delimiters, varying quoting strategies, and dialect differences between programs that produce CSV. You will use csv.reader and csv.writer for list-based rows, csv.DictReader and csv.DictWriter for dict-based rows, and custom dialects for the real-world variants that do not follow the textbook format. By the end of this chapter you will be able to read and write any CSV file you are likely to encounter in practice.*

5.1 What Is CSV and When to Use It

CSV stands for Comma-Separated Values. It is a plain text format where each line represents one record and fields within the line are separated by a delimiter — most often a comma. The first line is conventionally a header row naming each field. CSV is not a precisely defined standard: different programs produce subtly different variants, using semicolons or tabs as delimiters, quoting fields differently, and using different line endings. This variation is the source of most CSV-related bugs, and it is the main reason Python provides a dedicated csv module rather than relying on a simple split(",").

CSV's strength is its universality. Spreadsheet programs, databases, government data portals, scientific instruments, and point-of-sale systems all export and import CSV. It requires no library to open (any text editor will do), is human-readable at a glance, and survives being emailed, zipped, and version-controlled without special tooling. Its weakness is that it carries no type information: every value is a string, and the reader must convert numbers, dates, and booleans explicitly. It also has no native support for hierarchical data; for nested structures, JSON (Chapter 6) is more appropriate.

When CSV Is the Right Choice

Use CSV for flat, tabular data that needs to be exchanged with other programs or opened directly in a spreadsheet. Student records, product catalogues, timetable exports, financial transaction lists, and sensor readings are all natural CSV candidates. Avoid CSV when fields contain complex nested structures, when the schema changes frequently, or when the data is consumed exclusively by your own Python code (in which case JSON or a database is more appropriate). The csv module's handling of quoted fields makes it robust enough for production use even with messy real-world data, which Chapter 2's manual split(",") approach could never achieve.

> **Note:** Never parse CSV with raw string splitting. The field "Brisbane, QLD" contains a comma; split(",") would split it into two fields. csv.reader handles quoted fields correctly: "Brisbane, QLD" remains one field. Always use the csv module for any CSV data that may contain quoted fields.

Example 1 — Introduction

Why raw splitting fails on CSV with quoted fields; the csv module handling the same data correctly.

```
# A CSV row where one field contains a comma inside quotes
row = '10042,"Patel, Anika",Mathematics,88'

# — Naive split: WRONG — breaks on the comma inside the name ————————
parts_naive = row.split(",")
```

```
print("Naive split:", parts_naive)
print(f"  Field count: {len(parts_naive)}  (expected 4)")  # gets 5

# —— csv.reader: CORRECT – respects quoting ——————————————————————
import csv, io
reader = csv.reader(io.StringIO(row))
parts_csv = next(reader)
print("\ncsv.reader:", parts_csv)
print(f"  Field count: {len(parts_csv)}  (correct)")
print(f"  Name field:  {parts_csv[1]!r}")
```

Output:

```
Naive split: ['10042', '"Patel', ' Anika"', 'Mathematics', '88']
  Field count: 5  (expected 4)

csv.reader: ['10042', 'Patel, Anika', 'Mathematics', '88']
  Field count: 4  (correct)
  Name field:  'Patel, Anika'
```

Example 2 — Variation

The same problem with a field containing an embedded newline — something split() and readline() cannot handle without csv.

```
import csv, io

# CSV where the address field contains a newline inside quotes
csv_text = '''StudentID,Name,Address
10042,Anika Patel,"12 River Rd
South Brisbane"
10043,Liam Torres,45 Queen St'''

reader = csv.reader(io.StringIO(csv_text))
for row in reader:
    print(row)
```

Output:

```
['StudentID', 'Name', 'Address']
['10042', 'Anika Patel', '12 River Rd\nSouth Brisbane']
['10043', 'Liam Torres', '45 Queen St']
```

Example 3 — Real-world application

Inspecting an unknown CSV file before processing: detect delimiter, count columns and rows, and preview the first three data rows.

```
# csv_inspector.py  —  examine a CSV file before committing to a parse strategy
import csv

def inspect_csv(filepath, sample_rows=3):
    """
    Detect dialect, count rows and columns, preview sample rows.
    Returns a dict of summary information.
    """
    try:
        with open(filepath, "r", encoding="utf-8", newline="") as f:
            sample = f.read(4096)        # read a sample for dialect detection
        dialect = csv.Sniffer().sniff(sample)
        has_header = csv.Sniffer().has_header(sample)
    except csv.Error:
        dialect    = csv.excel          # fall back to standard CSV dialect
        has_header = True

    rows_seen, col_counts, preview = 0, set(), []
    with open(filepath, "r", encoding="utf-8", newline="") as f:
        reader = csv.reader(f, dialect)
```

```
        for row in reader:
            rows_seen += 1
            col_counts.add(len(row))
            if rows_seen <= sample_rows + (1 if has_header else 0):
                preview.append(row)

    info = {
        "rows":       rows_seen,
        "delimiter":  repr(dialect.delimiter),
        "has_header": has_header,
        "col_counts": sorted(col_counts),
        "preview":    preview,
    }
    return info

info = inspect_csv("students.csv")
print(f"Rows:       {info['rows']}")
print(f"Delimiter:  {info['delimiter']}")
print(f"Has header: {info['has_header']}")
print(f"Col counts: {info['col_counts']}")
print("Preview:")
for row in info["preview"]:
    print(f"  {row}")
```

Output:

```
Rows:       5
Delimiter:  ','
Has header: True
Col counts: [4]
Preview:
  ['StudentID', 'Name', 'Subject', 'Score']
  ['10042', 'Anika Patel', 'Mathematics', '88']
  ['10043', 'Liam Torres', 'English', '72']
  ['10044', 'Priya Nair', 'Science', '95']
```

csv.Sniffer().sniff() analyses a sample of text and returns a Dialect object describing the delimiter and quoting style. It is not infallible — particularly on small files or unusual dialects — but it is a useful first step when you receive a CSV file without documentation. When the dialect is known in advance, specifying it explicitly is always preferable to relying on detection.

5.2 csv.reader: Reading Rows as Lists

csv.reader wraps a file object (or any iterable of strings) and yields each row as a list of strings. It is constructed by passing the open file object — not the filename — together with any dialect parameters. The reader is an iterator: it lazily parses one row at a time as you advance through it, so it is memory-efficient for large files. Each field value is always a string; type conversion is the caller's responsibility.

The most important parameter to get right when opening a CSV file is newline. The csv module's documentation explicitly states that the file should be opened with newline="" (an empty string). This suppresses Python's universal newlines translation and lets the csv module handle line endings itself, which is necessary for correct handling of multi-line fields. Omitting newline="" causes incorrect parsing of fields that contain embedded newlines on Windows.

Skipping the Header Row

When a CSV file has a header row, you typically want to skip it before processing data rows. The cleanest idiom is next(reader) to advance past the first row and discard it, or next(reader) assigned to a variable if you need the column names later. Alternatively, csv.DictReader (Section 5.4) handles headers automatically and is the better choice when field names matter more than positional indices.

> **Note:** Always open CSV files with newline="" in the open() call: open(filepath, "r", encoding="utf-8", newline=""). The csv module manages its own line-ending handling. Without newline="", Python's universal newlines mode translates \r\n to \n before the csv module sees the data, which can corrupt multi-line quoted fields.

Example 1 — Introduction

Opening a CSV file with csv.reader and iterating over its rows as lists.

```
import csv

# File: students.csv
# StudentID,Name,Subject,Score
# 10042,Anika Patel,Mathematics,88
# 10043,Liam Torres,English,72
# 10044,Priya Nair,Science,95
# 10045,Sam Wong,Physics,81

with open("students.csv", "r", encoding="utf-8", newline="") as f:
    reader = csv.reader(f)
    header = next(reader)         # consume and store the header row
    print("Header:", header)
    print()
    for row in reader:
        print(row)                # each row is a list of strings
```

Output:

```
Header: ['StudentID', 'Name', 'Subject', 'Score']

['10042', 'Anika Patel', 'Mathematics', '88']
['10043', 'Liam Torres', 'English', '72']
['10044', 'Priya Nair', 'Science', '95']
['10045', 'Sam Wong', 'Physics', '81']
```

Example 2 — Variation

Type-converting fields after reading; handling rows with missing or invalid values gracefully.

```
import csv

def load_scores(filepath):
    """
    Read students.csv; return list of (id, name, subject, score) tuples.
    Skips rows where score is missing or non-numeric.
    """
    records, skipped = [], []

    with open(filepath, "r", encoding="utf-8", newline="") as f:
        reader = csv.reader(f)
        next(reader)   # skip header
        for lineno, row in enumerate(reader, 2):
            if len(row) < 4:
                skipped.append(f"Line {lineno}: only {len(row)} field(s)")
                continue
            try:
                sid, name, subject, score = row[0], row[1], row[2], int(row[3])
                records.append((sid, name, subject, score))
            except ValueError:
                skipped.append(f"Line {lineno}: non-numeric score {row[3]!r}")

    if skipped:
        print(f"Skipped {len(skipped)} row(s):")
        for msg in skipped:
            print(f"  - {msg}")
    return records
```

```
records = load_scores("students.csv")
for sid, name, subject, score in records:
    print(f"  {sid}  {name:<20}  {subject:<14}  {score}")
```

Output:

```
  10042  Anika Patel           Mathematics     88
  10043  Liam Torres           English         72
  10044  Priya Nair            Science         95
  10045  Sam Wong              Physics         81
```

Example 3 — Real-world application

A multi-class grade aggregator that reads several CSV files, merges the records, and produces a combined class summary.

```
# grade_aggregator.py  —  merge multiple CSV grade files into one summary
import csv
from pathlib import Path

CSV_FILES = ["grades_10A.csv", "grades_10B.csv", "grades_10C.csv"]
# Each file: StudentID,Name,Score

def load_csv(filepath):
    """Load (name, score) pairs from a grades CSV file."""
    records = []
    try:
        with open(filepath, "r", encoding="utf-8", newline="") as f:
            reader = csv.reader(f)
            next(reader)   # skip header
            for row in reader:
                if len(row) >= 3:
                    try:
                        records.append((row[1].strip(), int(row[2].strip())))
                    except ValueError:
                        pass
    except FileNotFoundError:
        print(f"  Missing: {filepath}")
    return records

all_records = []
for csv_file in CSV_FILES:
    recs = load_csv(csv_file)
    class_name = Path(csv_file).stem.replace("grades_", "")
    all_records.extend(recs)
    if recs:
        avg = sum(s for _, s in recs) / len(recs)
        print(f"  {class_name}: {len(recs)} students, avg={avg:.1f}")

if all_records:
    overall_avg = sum(s for _, s in all_records) / len(all_records)
    top_score   = max(s for _, s in all_records)
    top_student = next(n for n, s in all_records if s == top_score)
    print(f"\nCombined: {len(all_records)} students")
    print(f"Overall average: {overall_avg:.1f}")
    print(f"Top score: {top_score} ({top_student})")
```

Output:

```
  10A: 4 students, avg=84.8
  10B: 4 students, avg=79.5
  10C: 4 students, avg=82.3

Combined: 12 students
Overall average: 82.2
Top score: 95 (Priya Nair)
```

csv.reader is the right tool when field position is the natural way to access data — when you know that column 0 is always the ID and column 3 is always the score. When the column names are more natural to work with than their indices, csv.DictReader (Section 5.4) is the better choice.

5.3 csv.writer: Writing Rows

csv.writer is the counterpart to csv.reader. It wraps a file object opened for writing and provides a writerow(iterable) method that takes any iterable of values and writes them as a single correctly formatted CSV line. It handles all quoting automatically: if a field value contains the delimiter, a newline, or the quotechar, the writer wraps it in quotes and escapes any embedded quote characters according to the dialect. The result is always valid CSV that csv.reader can read back correctly.

The file must be opened with newline="" for csv.writer, just as for csv.reader. The reason is symmetrical: without newline="", Python's universal newlines mode inserts an extra \r on Windows before the newline the csv module writes, producing \r\r\n instead of \r\n. On Unix this is invisible, but the file will behave incorrectly when opened on Windows. The newline="" argument suppresses this double translation.

writerows()

csv.writer also provides writerows(iterable_of_iterables), which writes multiple rows in a single call. It is equivalent to calling writerow() in a loop but more concise for batch output. Like writerow(), it accepts any iterable of iterables — a list of lists, a list of tuples, or a generator expression. The values within each row are converted to strings by calling str() on them, so integers and floats can be passed directly without pre-converting.

> **Note:** csv.writer converts values to strings with str(). This means float(88.5) becomes "88.5", int(88) becomes "88", and None becomes "None". If you need specific number formatting — e.g. two decimal places — format the value before passing it to writerow(): pass f"{score:.2f}" rather than the raw float.

Example 1 — Introduction

Writing a list of student records to a CSV file with a header row using writerow() and writerows().

```
import csv

HEADER = ["StudentID", "Name", "Subject", "Score"]
RECORDS = [
    ("10042", "Anika Patel",  "Mathematics", 88),
    ("10043", "Liam Torres",  "English",     72),
    ("10044", "Priya Nair",   "Science",     95),
    ("10045", "Sam Wong",     "Physics",     81),
]

with open("output_grades.csv", "w", encoding="utf-8", newline="") as f:
    writer = csv.writer(f)
    writer.writerow(HEADER)       # single header row
    writer.writerows(RECORDS)     # all data rows in one call

# Verify by reading back
print("Written file contents:")
print(open("output_grades.csv", encoding="utf-8").read())
```

Output:

```
Written file contents:
StudentID,Name,Subject,Score
10042,Anika Patel,Mathematics,88
10043,Liam Torres,English,72
10044,Priya Nair,Science,95
10045,Sam Wong,Physics,81
```

Example 2 — Variation

Demonstrating automatic quoting: a name containing a comma is quoted correctly; reading the file back recovers the original value.

```
import csv

# Records where one name contains a comma
RECORDS = [
    ("10042", "Patel, Anika",   "Mathematics", 88),
    ("10043", "Torres, Liam",   "English",     72),
    ("10044", "Nair, Priya",    "Science",     95),
]

with open("quoted_names.csv", "w", encoding="utf-8", newline="") as f:
    writer = csv.writer(f)
    writer.writerow(["StudentID", "Name", "Subject", "Score"])
    writer.writerows(RECORDS)

# Show the raw file to see quoting
raw = open("quoted_names.csv", encoding="utf-8").read()
print("Raw CSV:")
print(raw)

# Read it back — names are restored intact
print("Read back:")
with open("quoted_names.csv", "r", encoding="utf-8", newline="") as f:
    reader = csv.reader(f)
    next(reader)
    for row in reader:
        print(f"  {row}")
```

Output:

```
Raw CSV:
StudentID,Name,Subject,Score
10042,"Patel, Anika",Mathematics,88
10043,"Torres, Liam",English,72
10044,"Nair, Priya",Science,95

Read back:
  ['10042', 'Patel, Anika', 'Mathematics', '88']
  ['10043', 'Torres, Liam', 'English', '72']
  ['10044', 'Nair, Priya', 'Science', '95']
```

Example 3 — Real-world application

A CSV export function that processes a list of student dicts, formats numeric values, and writes a dated output file.

```
# csv_exporter.py  —  produce a dated, formatted CSV export from student data
import csv
from datetime import date
from pathlib import Path

STUDENTS = [
    {"id": "10042", "name": "Anika Patel",  "maths": 88, "english": 91,
"science": 84},
    {"id": "10043", "name": "Liam Torres",  "maths": 72, "english": 85,
"science": 79},
    {"id": "10044", "name": "Priya Nair",   "maths": 95, "english": 88,
"science": 92},
    {"id": "10045", "name": "Sam Wong",     "maths": 81, "english": 76,
"science": 88},
    {"id": "10046", "name": "Maya Chen",    "maths": 67, "english": 73,
"science": 71},
]
```

```
SUBJECTS = ["maths", "english", "science"]

def export_results(students, subjects, output_dir="exports"):
    Path(output_dir).mkdir(exist_ok=True)
    filename = f"results_{date.today().isoformat()}.csv"
    filepath = Path(output_dir) / filename

    header = ["StudentID", "Name"] + [s.capitalize() for s in subjects] +
["Average"]

    with open(filepath, "w", encoding="utf-8", newline="") as f:
        writer = csv.writer(f)
        writer.writerow(header)
        for s in students:
            scores  = [s[subj] for subj in subjects]
            average = sum(scores) / len(scores)
            # Format average to 1 decimal place before passing to writer
            writer.writerow([s["id"], s["name"]] + scores + [f"{average:.1f}"])

    print(f"Exported {len(students)} record(s) to {filepath!r}")
    return filepath

path = export_results(STUDENTS, SUBJECTS)
print()
print(path.read_text(encoding="utf-8"))
```

Output:

```
Exported 5 record(s) to 'exports/results_2025-08-14.csv'

StudentID,Name,Maths,English,Science,Average
10042,Anika Patel,88,91,84,87.7
10043,Liam Torres,72,85,79,78.7
10044,Priya Nair,95,88,92,91.7
10045,Sam Wong,81,76,88,81.7
10046,Maya Chen,67,73,71,70.3
```

csv.writer's automatic quoting means you can pass values with commas, newlines, or quotes without any special handling on your side. This is the core value of the csv module: correctness under all field content, not just the easy cases.

5.4 csv.DictReader: Rows as Dicts with Header Keys

csv.DictReader reads CSV rows as dicts, using the first row (or a caller-supplied list) as the keys. This is the preferred approach when column names are more meaningful than positional indices, or when the column order might change between CSV files from different sources. Accessing row["Score"] is more readable and resilient than row[3], and it continues to work correctly if a new column is inserted before Score.

DictReader takes the same file object and dialect parameters as csv.reader. If the file has a header row, DictReader consumes it automatically and uses it as the dict keys — there is no need to call next(reader) manually. If the file has no header row, pass fieldnames=["col1", "col2", ...] to supply the keys explicitly. The resulting dict for each row preserves insertion order (Python 3.7+), which is the column order from the file.

Handling Missing and Extra Fields

If a data row has fewer fields than the header, the missing keys are set to a configurable restval (default None). If a data row has more fields than the header, the extra values are collected into a list under the key restkey (default None). Both edge cases arise with real-world CSV files; knowing how DictReader handles them avoids surprises when processing data of uncertain quality.

Note: DictReader returns each row as a dict (Python 3.8+: specifically an OrderedDict in older versions, a regular dict in 3.8+). The keys are always strings, as are all values. Type conversion is still the caller's responsibility: row["Score"] is the string "88", not the integer 88.

Example 1 — Introduction

Reading a CSV file with DictReader; accessing fields by name rather than position.

```
import csv

with open("students.csv", "r", encoding="utf-8", newline="") as f:
    reader = csv.DictReader(f)
    print("Fieldnames:", reader.fieldnames)
    print()
    for row in reader:
        # Access by column name — resilient to column reordering
        name  = row["Name"]
        score = int(row["Score"])   # convert string to int
        grade = "Pass" if score >= 50 else "Fail"
        print(f"  {name:<20}  {score:>3}  {grade}")
```

Output:

```
Fieldnames: ['StudentID', 'Name', 'Subject', 'Score']

  Anika Patel            88   Pass
  Liam Torres            72   Pass
  Priya Nair             95   Pass
  Sam Wong               81   Pass
```

Example 2 — Variation

DictReader with an explicit fieldnames list for a headerless CSV file; handling missing fields via restval.

```
import csv

# A CSV file with no header row and one short row
csv_content = """10042,Anika Patel,88
10043,Liam Torres
10044,Priya Nair,95"""

import io
FIELDS = ["StudentID", "Name", "Score"]

reader = csv.DictReader(
    io.StringIO(csv_content),
    fieldnames=FIELDS,
    restval="N/A"   # value used for missing fields
)

for row in reader:
    print(dict(row))   # convert OrderedDict to plain dict for clarity
```

Output:

```
{'StudentID': '10042', 'Name': 'Anika Patel', 'Score': '88'}
{'StudentID': '10043', 'Name': 'Liam Torres', 'Score': 'N/A'}
{'StudentID': '10044', 'Name': 'Priya Nair', 'Score': '95'}
```

Example 3 — Real-world application

A school enrolment loader using DictReader: reads a variable-column CSV, validates required fields, converts types, and returns a list of clean dicts.

```
# enrolment_loader.py  —  robust DictReader-based CSV loader
import csv
```

```
REQUIRED = {"StudentID", "Name", "Year", "Subject"}

def load_enrolments(filepath):
    """
    Load enrolment records from a CSV using DictReader.
    Validates required fields; converts Year to int.
    Returns (records_list, error_list).
    """
    records, errors = [], []

    try:
        with open(filepath, "r", encoding="utf-8", newline="") as f:
            reader = csv.DictReader(f)

            # Check required columns are present in the header
            missing_cols = REQUIRED - set(reader.fieldnames or [])
            if missing_cols:
                return [], [f"Missing columns: {missing_cols}"]

            for lineno, row in enumerate(reader, 2):
                # Check all required fields have non-empty values
                empty = [k for k in REQUIRED if not row.get(k, "").strip()]
                if empty:
                    errors.append(f"Line {lineno}: empty field(s) {empty}")
                    continue
                try:
                    records.append({
                        "id":      row["StudentID"].strip(),
                        "name":    row["Name"].strip(),
                        "year":    int(row["Year"].strip()),
                        "subject": row["Subject"].strip(),
                    })
                except ValueError as e:
                    errors.append(f"Line {lineno}: {e}")

    except FileNotFoundError:
        return [], [f"File not found: {filepath!r}"]

    return records, errors

records, errors = load_enrolments("enrolments.csv")
print(f"Loaded {len(records)} enrolment(s).")
for r in records:
    print(f"  {r['id']}  {r['name']:<20}  Year {r['year']}  {r['subject']}")
if errors:
    print(f"\nWarnings ({len(errors)}):")
    for e in errors:
        print(f"  - {e}")
```

Output:

```
Loaded 4 enrolment(s).
  10042  Anika Patel           Year 10  Digital Technologies
  10043  Liam Torres           Year 10  Mathematics
  10044  Priya Nair            Year 10  Science
  10045  Sam Wong              Year 11  Physics

Warnings (1):
  - Line 5: empty field(s) ['Subject']
```

The column-existence check at the start of load_enrolments() — before any row is processed — catches schema mismatches immediately rather than producing confusing KeyError exceptions on line 2. This is a good example of LBYL (See Book 02, Chapter 1) being appropriate when the check is on data already in memory.

5.5 csv.DictWriter: Writing from Dicts

csv.DictWriter is the writing counterpart to DictReader. You supply a list of field names when constructing the writer; each call to writerow() accepts a dict and writes the values in the order specified by fieldnames. Fields present in the dict but not in fieldnames are ignored (unless extrasaction="raise" is set, which is the default); fields in fieldnames but absent from the dict are written as the value of restval (default empty string).

DictWriter does not write the header row automatically. You must call writer.writeheader() explicitly to write the fieldnames as the first row. This is a deliberate design choice: it allows you to append to an existing CSV file with DictWriter without writing a duplicate header. Always call writeheader() once at the start of a new file.

extrasaction

The extrasaction parameter controls what happens when a dict passed to writerow() contains keys not in fieldnames. The default is "raise", which raises ValueError on any extra key. Setting extrasaction="ignore" silently drops extra keys, which is useful when the source dicts contain metadata fields that should not appear in the CSV output. Choose "raise" during development to catch schema mismatches early, and "ignore" only when you intentionally want to filter the output columns.

> **Note:** DictWriter.writeheader() writes the fieldnames list as the first CSV row. Call it once per file, immediately after constructing the writer. Forgetting it produces a file with no header, which breaks DictReader and confuses any program that reads the file expecting one.

Example 1 — Introduction

Writing a list of student dicts to CSV with DictWriter; using writeheader() and writerow().

```
import csv

STUDENTS = [
    {"StudentID": "10042", "Name": "Anika Patel",  "Score": 88, "Grade": "A"},
    {"StudentID": "10043", "Name": "Liam Torres",  "Score": 72, "Grade": "B"},
    {"StudentID": "10044", "Name": "Priya Nair",   "Score": 95, "Grade": "A+"},
    {"StudentID": "10045", "Name": "Sam Wong",     "Score": 81, "Grade": "B+"},
]

FIELDS = ["StudentID", "Name", "Score", "Grade"]

with open("results_dict.csv", "w", encoding="utf-8", newline="") as f:
    writer = csv.DictWriter(f, fieldnames=FIELDS)
    writer.writeheader()        # write the header row first
    writer.writerows(STUDENTS)  # write all data rows

print(open("results_dict.csv", encoding="utf-8").read())
```

Output:

```
StudentID,Name,Score,Grade
10042,Anika Patel,88,A
10043,Liam Torres,72,B
10044,Priya Nair,95,A+
10045,Sam Wong,81,B+
```

Example 2 — Variation

DictWriter with extrasaction="ignore" to filter out unwanted keys; and with restval to handle missing fields.

```
import csv

# Source dicts have extra keys (e.g. "internal_id") not wanted in export
STUDENTS = [
```

```
    {"StudentID": "10042", "Name": "Anika Patel", "Score": 88,
     "internal_id": "A-001", "enrolled": True},   # extra keys
    {"StudentID": "10043", "Name": "Liam Torres",              # missing Score
     "internal_id": "A-002", "enrolled": True},
]

FIELDS = ["StudentID", "Name", "Score"]

with open("filtered.csv", "w", encoding="utf-8", newline="") as f:
    writer = csv.DictWriter(
        f,
        fieldnames=FIELDS,
        extrasaction="ignore",  # silently drop extra keys
        restval="",             # empty string for missing fields
    )
    writer.writeheader()
    writer.writerows(STUDENTS)

print(open("filtered.csv", encoding="utf-8").read())
```

Output:

```
StudentID,Name,Score
10042,Anika Patel,88
10043,Liam Torres,
```

Example 3 — Real-world application

A CSV round-trip: read a messy input CSV with DictReader, clean and transform the data, and write the clean version with DictWriter.

```
# csv_cleaner.py  —  read, clean, and rewrite a CSV file
import csv

INPUT_FILE  = "messy_enrolments.csv"
OUTPUT_FILE = "clean_enrolments.csv"

# Input columns may include extra whitespace, mixed case, and missing values
OUTPUT_FIELDS = ["StudentID", "Name", "Year", "Subject", "Status"]

def normalise_year(raw):
    """Convert "Year 10", "10", "yr10" etc to plain int 10."""
    digits = "".join(c for c in raw if c.isdigit())
    return int(digits) if digits else None

def normalise_status(raw):
    """Standardise enrolment status strings."""
    mapping = {"enrolled": "Enrolled", "active": "Enrolled",
               "withdrawn": "Withdrawn", "pending": "Pending"}
    return mapping.get(raw.strip().lower(), "Unknown")

cleaned, errors = [], 0

with open(INPUT_FILE, "r", encoding="utf-8", newline="") as fin:
    reader = csv.DictReader(fin)
    for row in reader:
        try:
            year = normalise_year(row.get("Year", "").strip())
            if year is None:
                raise ValueError("cannot parse year")
            cleaned.append({
                "StudentID": row["StudentID"].strip(),
                "Name":      row["Name"].strip().title(),
                "Year":      year,
                "Subject":   row["Subject"].strip().title(),
                "Status":    normalise_status(row.get("Status", "")),
            })
```

```
        except (KeyError, ValueError) as e:
            errors += 1
            print(f"  Skipped row: {e}")

with open(OUTPUT_FILE, "w", encoding="utf-8", newline="") as fout:
    writer = csv.DictWriter(fout, fieldnames=OUTPUT_FIELDS)
    writer.writeheader()
    writer.writerows(cleaned)

print(f"\nCleaned {len(cleaned)} record(s), skipped {errors}.")
print(open(OUTPUT_FILE, encoding="utf-8").read())
```

Output:

```
  Skipped row: cannot parse year

Cleaned 4 record(s), skipped 1.
StudentID,Name,Year,Subject,Status
10042,Anika Patel,10,Digital Technologies,Enrolled
10043,Liam Torres,10,Mathematics,Enrolled
10044,Priya Nair,10,Science,Enrolled
10045,Sam Wong,11,Physics,Pending
```

The read-clean-write round-trip in Example 5.5.3 is one of the most common CSV workflows: transform a source file of uncertain quality into a canonical output file. Using DictReader and DictWriter together makes the schema explicit at every step and makes the transformation logic easy to follow.

5.6 Handling Dialects: Delimiters, Quoting, and Line Endings

The csv module uses the concept of a dialect to bundle all the formatting parameters that control how a CSV file is written and read. A dialect specifies the delimiter, the quotechar, how quoting is applied, the line terminator, and whether whitespace around delimiters is skipped. Python defines two built-in dialects: csv.excel (the Microsoft Excel dialect, with comma delimiter and CRLF line endings) and csv.excel_tab (tab delimiter). Both can be passed by name to csv.reader and csv.writer.

Common Dialect Parameters

The most frequently adjusted parameters are: delimiter (the field separator character, default ","), quotechar (the character used to quote fields containing the delimiter or newlines, default '"'), quoting (one of csv.QUOTE_MINIMAL, csv.QUOTE_ALL, csv.QUOTE_NONNUMERIC, or csv.QUOTE_NONE — controls when fields are quoted), skipinitialspace (if True, strips whitespace after the delimiter), and lineterminator (the line ending written, default "\r\n" for csv.excel). Passing these directly to csv.reader() or csv.writer() overrides the dialect defaults for that object.

Registering Custom Dialects

For a dialect you use repeatedly — for example a semicolon-delimited European CSV or a pipe-delimited export from a specific database — csv.register_dialect("name", ...) registers it under a name that can be passed to reader and writer instead of repeating all the parameters. Registering dialects is particularly useful in larger projects where multiple modules read the same file format and should agree on the parameters without duplication.

> **Note:** Tab-separated values (TSV) files are a common variant of CSV, used by many database tools and the Australian Bureau of Statistics data portal. To read them, pass delimiter="\t" to csv.reader. The file extension is typically .tsv or .txt. All other csv module features — DictReader, DictWriter, quoting — work identically with tab-delimited files.

Example 1 — Introduction

Reading a semicolon-delimited European CSV and a tab-delimited file by specifying the delimiter explicitly.

```
import csv, io

# Semicolon-delimited (common in European locales where , is the decimal
separator)
semi_csv = "StudentID;Name;Score\n10042;Anika Patel;88.5\n10043;Liam
Torres;72.0"

print("Semicolon-delimited:")
reader = csv.reader(io.StringIO(semi_csv), delimiter=";")
for row in reader:
    print(" ", row)

# Tab-delimited
tab_csv = "StudentID\tName\tScore\n10042\tAnika Patel\t88\n10043\tLiam Torres\
t72"

print("\nTab-delimited:")
reader = csv.reader(io.StringIO(tab_csv), delimiter="\t")
for row in reader:
    print(" ", row)
```

Output:

```
Semicolon-delimited:
  ['StudentID', 'Name', 'Score']
  ['10042', 'Anika Patel', '88.5']
  ['10043', 'Liam Torres', '72.0']

Tab-delimited:
  ['StudentID', 'Name', 'Score']
  ['10042', 'Anika Patel', '88']
  ['10043', 'Liam Torres', '72']
```

Example 2 — Variation

Registering a custom dialect for a pipe-delimited database export and using it by name across reader and writer.

```
import csv, io

# Register a reusable dialect for pipe-delimited exports
csv.register_dialect(
    "pipe_delimited",
    delimiter="|",
    quotechar='"',
    quoting=csv.QUOTE_MINIMAL,
    lineterminator="\n",
    skipinitialspace=True,
)

STUDENTS = [
    ["10042", "Anika Patel",  "88"],
    ["10043", "Liam Torres",  "72"],
    ["10044", "Priya Nair",   "95"],
]

# Write using the dialect name
buf = io.StringIO()
writer = csv.writer(buf, dialect="pipe_delimited")
writer.writerow(["StudentID", "Name", "Score"])
writer.writerows(STUDENTS)

raw = buf.getvalue()
print("Pipe-delimited output:")
print(raw)

# Read using the same dialect name
print("Read back:")
```

```
reader = csv.reader(io.StringIO(raw), dialect="pipe_delimited")
for row in reader:
    print(" ", row)
```

Output:

```
Pipe-delimited output:
StudentID|Name|Score
10042|Anika Patel|88
10043|Liam Torres|72
10044|Priya Nair|95

Read back:
  ['StudentID', 'Name', 'Score']
  ['10042', 'Anika Patel', '88']
  ['10043', 'Liam Torres', '72']
  ['10044', 'Priya Nair', '95']
```

Example 3 — Real-world application

A dialect-aware CSV loader that detects delimiter automatically with csv.Sniffer and falls back to explicit parameters if detection fails.

```
# dialect_loader.py  —  robust CSV reader for files of unknown dialect
import csv

def dialect_aware_load(filepath, fallback_delimiter=","):",
    """
    Attempt to detect the CSV dialect with Sniffer.
    Fall back to fallback_delimiter on detection failure.
    Returns (rows_list, dialect_name_str).
    """
    with open(filepath, "r", encoding="utf-8", newline="") as f:
        sample = f.read(8192)

    try:
        dialect  = csv.Sniffer().sniff(sample, delimiters=",;\t|")
        det_name = f"detected: {repr(dialect.delimiter)}"
    except csv.Error:
        dialect  = csv.excel
        # Patch the delimiter if different from comma
        class FallbackDialect(csv.excel):
            delimiter = fallback_delimiter
        dialect  = FallbackDialect
        det_name = f"fallback: {repr(fallback_delimiter)}"

    rows = []
    with open(filepath, "r", encoding="utf-8", newline="") as f:
        reader = csv.reader(f, dialect)
        for row in reader:
            rows.append(row)

    return rows, det_name

for fname in ["students.csv", "students_semi.csv", "students_tab.tsv"]:",
    try:
        rows, dialect_info = dialect_aware_load(fname)
        print(f"{fname}: {dialect_info}  ({len(rows)} rows)")
        for row in rows[:2]:
            print(f"  {row}")
    except FileNotFoundError:
        print(f"{fname}: not found")
```

Output:

```
students.csv: detected: ','  (5 rows)
  ['StudentID', 'Name', 'Subject', 'Score']
  ['10042', 'Anika Patel', 'Mathematics', '88']
students_semi.csv: detected: ';'  (5 rows)
```

```
  ['StudentID', 'Name', 'Subject', 'Score']
  ['10042', 'Anika Patel', 'Mathematics', '88']
students_tab.tsv: detected: '\t'  (5 rows)
  ['StudentID', 'Name', 'Subject', 'Score']
  ['10042', 'Anika Patel', 'Mathematics', '88']
```

Dialect handling is where the csv module proves its worth over manual string splitting. A sniffer-based loader with a sensible fallback handles the majority of real-world CSV variants without requiring the caller to know which format they are dealing with.

5.7 Real-world Patterns: Student Records, Catalogues, and Exports

This section assembles the tools from the chapter into three complete, self-contained programs that cover the most common CSV workflows in educational and business contexts. Each program is designed to be adapted to real projects with minimal modification.

Student Records System

A student records CSV file is the simplest persistent data store for a school application. It typically has a fixed schema (student ID, name, year level, enrolment date, contact details), grows by appending new rows, and is read in full at application startup. The correct approach for this pattern: read with DictReader on startup, modify the in-memory list, write the full list back with DictWriter on shutdown or save. Chapter 10's capstone project builds on this exact foundation.

Product Catalogue

A product catalogue CSV is typically received from an external supplier, converted into an internal representation, filtered, and re-exported in a different format. The conversion pipeline — read, transform, write — is the standard form for ETL (Extract, Transform, Load) work in Python. DictReader and DictWriter are ideal because column names are stable and meaningful, while column order may change between supplier exports.

Batch Export

Batch exports combine multiple in-memory data sources, apply formatting rules, and write a single CSV that a spreadsheet user can open directly. The key considerations are: choose column order deliberately (fieldnames= list), format numeric values before writing, use writeheader() once, and open with newline="" so the file is correct on every platform.

Example 1 — Introduction

A student records manager: load on startup with DictReader, add a new record, save back to disk with DictWriter.

```
# student_records.py  —  load, modify, and save a student records CSV
import csv
from pathlib import Path
from datetime import date

RECORDS_FILE = "student_records.csv"
FIELDS = ["StudentID", "Name", "YearLevel", "EnrolmentDate", "Status"]

def load_records(filepath):
    """Load all student records; return list of dicts."""
    if not Path(filepath).exists():
        return []
    with open(filepath, "r", encoding="utf-8", newline="") as f:
        return list(csv.DictReader(f))

def save_records(filepath, records):
```

```
    """Overwrite filepath with the full records list."""
    with open(filepath, "w", encoding="utf-8", newline="") as f:
        writer = csv.DictWriter(f, fieldnames=FIELDS, extrasaction="ignore")
        writer.writeheader()
        writer.writerows(records)

def add_student(records, student_id, name, year_level):
    """Append a new student record; check for duplicate ID."""
    if any(r["StudentID"] == student_id for r in records):
        print(f"  ID {student_id} already exists.")
        return records
    records.append({
        "StudentID":    student_id,
        "Name":         name,
        "YearLevel":    year_level,
        "EnrolmentDate": date.today().isoformat(),
        "Status":       "Enrolled",
    })
    return records

records = load_records(RECORDS_FILE)
print(f"Loaded {len(records)} existing record(s).")

records = add_student(records, "10047", "Zara Hill", "10")
records = add_student(records, "10048", "Ben Chu",   "11")

save_records(RECORDS_FILE, records)
print(f"Saved {len(records)} record(s) to {RECORDS_FILE!r}.")

print(open(RECORDS_FILE, encoding="utf-8").read())
```

Output:

```
Loaded 4 existing record(s).
Saved 6 record(s) to 'student_records.csv'.
StudentID,Name,YearLevel,EnrolmentDate,Status
10042,Anika Patel,10,2025-02-01,Enrolled
10043,Liam Torres,10,2025-02-01,Enrolled
10044,Priya Nair,10,2025-02-01,Enrolled
10045,Sam Wong,11,2025-02-01,Enrolled
10047,Zara Hill,10,2025-08-14,Enrolled
10048,Ben Chu,11,2025-08-14,Enrolled
```

Example 2 — Variation

A product catalogue transformer: read a supplier CSV with DictReader, apply price markup and category mapping, export a reformatted version with DictWriter.

```
# catalogue_transform.py  —  ETL pipeline for a product catalogue CSV
import csv

INPUT_FILE  = "supplier_catalogue.csv"
OUTPUT_FILE = "internal_catalogue.csv"

# Supplier format: ProductCode,Description,CostPrice,Category
# Internal format: SKU,Name,RRP,Department,Margin

CATEGORY_MAP = {
    "TECH":  "Technology",
    "SPORT": "Sports & Recreation",
    "ART":   "Creative Arts",
}
MARKUP = 1.35   # 35% margin

OUTPUT_FIELDS = ["SKU", "Name", "RRP", "Department", "Margin"]

transformed, errors = [], 0
```

```
with open(INPUT_FILE, "r", encoding="utf-8", newline="") as fin:
    reader = csv.DictReader(fin)
    for row in reader:
        try:
            cost  = float(row["CostPrice"])
            rrp   = cost * MARKUP
            transformed.append({
                "SKU":        row["ProductCode"].strip(),
                "Name":       row["Description"].strip().title(),
                "RRP":        f"{rrp:.2f}",
                "Department": CATEGORY_MAP.get(row["Category"].strip(),
"General"),
                "Margin":     f"{(MARKUP - 1) * 100:.0f}%",
            })
        except (KeyError, ValueError) as e:
            errors += 1
            print(f"  Skipped: {e}")

with open(OUTPUT_FILE, "w", encoding="utf-8", newline="") as fout:
    writer = csv.DictWriter(fout, fieldnames=OUTPUT_FIELDS)
    writer.writeheader()
    writer.writerows(transformed)

print(f"Transformed {len(transformed)} product(s), skipped {errors}.")
print(open(OUTPUT_FILE, encoding="utf-8").read())
```

Output:

```
Transformed 4 product(s), skipped 0.
SKU,Name,RRP,Department,Margin
P001,Wireless Headphones,94.50,Technology,35%
P002,Basketball,40.50,Sports & Recreation,35%
P003,Acrylic Paint Set,27.00,Creative Arts,35%
P004,Scientific Calculator,67.50,Technology,35%
```

Example 3 — Real-world application

A complete end-of-term CSV export: merge grade data from multiple dicts, compute derived columns, and write a spreadsheet-ready output with correctly formatted values.

```
# term_export.py  —  multi-source CSV export ready for spreadsheet use
import csv
from datetime import date
from pathlib import Path

STUDENTS = {
    "10042": {"name": "Anika Patel",  "year": 10},
    "10043": {"name": "Liam Torres",  "year": 10},
    "10044": {"name": "Priya Nair",   "year": 10},
    "10045": {"name": "Sam Wong",     "year": 11},
    "10046": {"name": "Maya Chen",    "year": 11},
}

GRADES = {
    "10042": {"maths": 88, "english": 91, "science": 84},
    "10043": {"maths": 72, "english": 85, "science": 79},
    "10044": {"maths": 95, "english": 88, "science": 92},
    "10045": {"maths": 81, "english": 76, "science": 88},
    "10046": {"maths": 67, "english": 73, "science": 71},
}

SUBJECTS  = ["maths", "english", "science"]
PASS_MARK = 50
OUTPUT    = f"term_export_{date.today().isoformat()}.csv"

FIELDS = ["StudentID", "Name", "Year",
          "Maths", "English", "Science", "Average", "Grade", "Status"]
```

```
def letter_grade(avg):
    for threshold, g in [(90,"A+"),(80,"A"),(70,"B+"),(60,"B"),(50,"C"),
(0,"F")]:
        if avg >= threshold:
            return g

rows = []
for sid, info in STUDENTS.items():
    scores  = GRADES.get(sid, {})
    vals    = [scores.get(s, 0) for s in SUBJECTS]
    avg     = sum(vals) / len(vals)
    rows.append({
        "StudentID": sid,
        "Name":      info["name"],
        "Year":      info["year"],
        "Maths":     scores.get("maths", ""),
        "English":   scores.get("english", ""),
        "Science":   scores.get("science", ""),
        "Average":   f"{avg:.1f}",
        "Grade":     letter_grade(avg),
        "Status":    "Pass" if avg >= PASS_MARK else "Fail",
    })

with open(OUTPUT, "w", encoding="utf-8", newline="") as f:
    writer = csv.DictWriter(f, fieldnames=FIELDS)
    writer.writeheader()
    writer.writerows(rows)

print(f"Exported {len(rows)} record(s) to {OUTPUT!r}")
print(Path(OUTPUT).read_text(encoding="utf-8"))
```

Output:

```
Exported 5 record(s) to 'term_export_2025-08-14.csv'
StudentID,Name,Year,Maths,English,Science,Average,Grade,Status
10042,Anika Patel,10,88,91,84,87.7,A,Pass
10043,Liam Torres,10,72,85,79,78.7,B+,Pass
10044,Priya Nair,10,95,88,92,91.7,A+,Pass
10045,Sam Wong,11,81,76,88,81.7,A,Pass
10046,Maya Chen,11,67,73,71,70.3,B+,Pass
```

The three examples in this section cover the dominant CSV patterns: load-modify-save for a persistent data store, read-transform-write for an ETL pipeline, and multi-source merge-and-export for reporting. Each follows the same structure: open with newline="", use DictReader or DictWriter, format numeric values explicitly before passing to the writer, and validate on read. Chapter 10's capstone project extends the student records pattern from Example 5.7.1 into a full command-line application.

Chapter 5 Summary

- Never parse CSV with raw str.split(","): quoted fields containing commas, newlines, or quote characters will be parsed incorrectly. The csv module handles all of these cases correctly and should always be used for CSV data.
- Always open CSV files with newline="" in the open() call. This suppresses Python's universal newlines translation and lets the csv module manage line endings, which is necessary for correct handling of multi-line quoted fields on all platforms.
- csv.reader yields each row as a list of strings; all values require explicit type conversion. Skip the header row with next(reader) or assign it to a variable; use enumerate(reader, 2) to track line numbers for error reporting.

- csv.writer writes rows from any iterable of values; values are converted to strings via str(). Format numeric values explicitly (e.g. f"{avg:.2f}") before passing them to writerow() if specific formatting is required.
- csv.DictReader yields each row as a dict keyed by the header row; csv.DictWriter writes dicts in the order specified by fieldnames. DictWriter requires an explicit writeheader() call; extrasaction="ignore" silently drops keys not in fieldnames.
- Dialects bundle all formatting parameters (delimiter, quotechar, quoting, lineterminator) into a named object. Use delimiter=";" or delimiter="\t" for non-comma files. csv.register_dialect() saves a custom dialect for reuse across a project.
- csv.Sniffer().sniff() can detect the dialect of an unknown file from a sample; it is a useful first step when the format is undocumented but should be supplemented by a fallback to a known dialect when detection is unreliable.
- The three core CSV patterns are: load-modify-save (DictReader on startup, DictWriter on save, for persistent records), read-transform-write (ETL pipeline with type conversion and field renaming), and multi-source export (merge in-memory data, add derived columns, write a spreadsheet-ready file with writeheader() and writerows()).

Guided Exercises

1. Write a function count_csv_rows(filepath) that returns the number of data rows in a CSV file (excluding the header). Handle FileNotFoundError gracefully. Test it on a file you create.

> ***Hint:*** *Open with newline="", create a csv.reader, skip the header with next(), then use sum(1 for _ in reader) to count. Wrap in try/except for FileNotFoundError.*

2. Write a function csv_to_dicts(filepath) that reads a CSV file and returns a list of dicts using DictReader. Handle missing files and return an empty list with a printed error. Test it by printing each dict on its own line.

> ***Hint:*** *Wrap the open() and list(csv.DictReader(f)) in try/except for FileNotFoundError. Return the list on success and [] on failure.*

3. Create a CSV file of five products (name, price, category) using DictWriter. Then read it back with DictReader and print only the products in a specific category. Remember writeheader() and newline="".

> ***Hint:*** *Define FIELDS = ["Name", "Price", "Category"]. Use DictWriter.writeheader() then writerows(). For the read, use a list comprehension: [r for r in reader if r["Category"] == target].*

4. Write a function merge_csvs(file_list, output_file) that reads multiple CSV files with the same header and writes all rows into a single output file. The header should appear once at the top. Handle missing input files by skipping them with a warning.

> ***Hint:*** *Open the first existing file, copy its header using DictReader.fieldnames. Open the output with DictWriter. Loop over each input file with a nested try/except FileNotFoundError, using writerows() for each.*

5. Write a function filter_and_export(input_file, output_file, min_score) that reads a student grades CSV (StudentID, Name, Score), keeps only rows where Score >= min_score, and writes the filtered rows to output_file. Report how many rows were kept and how many were filtered out.

> ***Hint:*** *Read with DictReader, convert row["Score"] to int inside try/except ValueError. Collect passing rows in a list. Write with DictWriter using the same fieldnames. Print the counts at the end.*

Challenge Tasks

1. Build a CSV database class CsvTable with methods: load() (read the file with DictReader), save() (write all rows with DictWriter), insert(row_dict) (append a row, checking for duplicate primary key),

update(pk_value, updates_dict) (modify matching row in-place), delete(pk_value) (remove matching row), and query(field, value) (return all rows where field == value). The class should accept the filepath, fieldnames, and primary_key_field in its constructor. Demonstrate all methods on a students CSV.
2. Write a dialect_converter(input_file, output_file, input_dialect_params, output_dialect_params) function that reads a CSV in one dialect and writes it in another — for example, converting a semicolon-delimited European CSV to a comma-delimited file. Use csv.Sniffer to detect the input dialect if input_dialect_params is None. Test by converting comma to tab, tab to pipe, and back again, verifying the data is identical after each round-trip.
3. Build a CSV diff tool: given two CSV files with the same header, identify rows that are present in one but not the other (using the first column as a key), rows where the key exists in both files but one or more field values differ, and rows that are identical in both. Write a human-readable diff report to a third file. Handle files with different column orders by normalising to the sorted fieldname order before comparison.

CHAPTER 6 Working with JSON Files

Book 02: File Handling & Exception Management

> *CSV handles flat rows perfectly but cannot represent nested structures, typed values, or heterogeneous collections without awkward workarounds. JSON fills that gap: it is the format of choice for configuration files, API responses, and any data that has hierarchy or mixed types. This chapter covers the complete Python JSON workflow — loading from files and strings, dumping back to disk, the type mapping between Python and JSON, the limits of the default serialiser, and how to extend it for custom objects such as dates and dataclasses. By the end of this chapter you will be able to read, write, validate, and transform any JSON data you encounter, and to design a clean JSON persistence layer for your own applications.*

6.1 What Is JSON and Why Python Loves It

JSON — JavaScript Object Notation — is a lightweight text format for representing structured data. It was derived from JavaScript object literal syntax but is entirely language-independent: every major programming language has a JSON library. A JSON document contains exactly one value, which can be an object (key-value pairs enclosed in curly braces), an array (ordered list enclosed in square brackets), a string (double-quoted), a number (integer or float), a boolean (true or false, lowercase), or null. These six types combine recursively: an object's values can themselves be objects or arrays, enabling arbitrarily deep hierarchies.

Python loves JSON because the mapping between JSON types and Python built-in types is almost perfect. A JSON object becomes a Python dict; a JSON array becomes a Python list; a JSON string becomes a Python str; a JSON number becomes a Python int or float; JSON true and false become Python True and False; and JSON null becomes Python None. This near-one-to-one mapping means that loading a JSON file gives you a plain Python data structure you can work with immediately using the dictionary and list operations you already know.

JSON vs CSV

JSON and CSV are complementary rather than competing. CSV is ideal for flat tabular data — rows with the same fixed columns. JSON is ideal for hierarchical, typed, or heterogeneous data: a student record with nested course enrolments, a configuration file with grouped settings, or an API response containing metadata alongside a data array. JSON also carries type information natively: the value 88 is stored as a number, while "88" is stored as a string, which eliminates the type-conversion step that CSV always requires. For simple flat tables, CSV is more compact and more easily opened in a spreadsheet; for everything else, JSON is more expressive and more reliable.

> **Note:** JSON requires double quotes for all strings and key names. Single quotes, trailing commas, and Python-style None and True are all invalid JSON. json.loads('{"name": 'Anika'}') will raise json.JSONDecodeError. When debugging JSON, always validate it with an online validator or json.loads() in the REPL before attempting to process it programmatically.

Example 1 — Introduction

The six JSON types and their Python equivalents: loading a JSON string and inspecting the result.

```
import json

# A JSON document containing all six value types
json_text = '''
```

```
{
    "student_id": 10042,
    "name": "Anika Patel",
    "enrolled": true,
    "gpa": 6.5,
    "subjects": ["Mathematics", "Science", "English"],
    "emergency_contact": null
}
'''

data = json.loads(json_text)

print(f"Type of data:                {type(data).__name__}")
print(f"student_id  → {type(data["student_id"]).__name__:<8}
{data["student_id"]}")
print(f"name        → {type(data["name"]).__name__:<8} {data["name"]!r}")
print(f"enrolled    → {type(data["enrolled"]).__name__:<8} {data["enrolled"]}")
print(f"gpa         → {type(data["gpa"]).__name__:<8} {data["gpa"]}")
print(f"subjects    → {type(data["subjects"]).__name__:<8} {data["subjects"]}")
print(f"emergency   → {type(data["emergency_contact"]).__name__:<8}
{data["emergency_contact"]}")
```

Output:

```
Type of data:              dict
student_id  → int      10042
name        → str      'Anika Patel'
enrolled    → bool     True
gpa         → float    6.5
subjects    → list     ['Mathematics', 'Science', 'English']
emergency   → NoneType None
```

Example 2 — Variation

A nested JSON structure — a school with multiple classes, each containing students — demonstrating how hierarchy maps to nested Python dicts and lists.

```
import json

school_json = '''
{
    "school": "Brisbane State High School",
    "year": 2025,
    "classes": [
        {
            "name": "10A",
            "students": [
                {"id": "10042", "name": "Anika Patel",  "score": 88},
                {"id": "10043", "name": "Liam Torres",  "score": 72}
            ]
        },
        {
            "name": "10B",
            "students": [
                {"id": "10044", "name": "Priya Nair",   "score": 95},
                {"id": "10045", "name": "Sam Wong",     "score": 81}
            ]
        }
    ]
}
'''

school = json.loads(school_json)
print(f"School: {school['school']}")
print(f"Classes: {len(school['classes'])}")
for cls in school["classes"]:
    scores = [s["score"] for s in cls["students"]]
    avg    = sum(scores) / len(scores)
    print(f"  {cls['name']}: {len(cls['students'])} students, avg={avg:.1f}")
```

Output:
```
School: Brisbane State High School
Classes: 2
  10A: 2 students, avg=80.0
  10B: 2 students, avg=88.0
```

Example 3 — Real-world application

A JSON vs CSV comparison: the same student enrolment data in both formats, showing where JSON's type-awareness and hierarchy make it the better choice.

```
import json, csv, io

# ── CSV representation: types lost, hierarchy impossible ──────────
csv_data = """StudentID,Name,Score,Subjects
10042,Anika Patel,88,"Mathematics,Science"
10043,Liam Torres,72,English
"""

reader = csv.reader(io.StringIO(csv_data))
next(reader)   # skip header
csv_rows = list(reader)
print("CSV row 0:")
print(" ", csv_rows[0])
print(f"  Score type: {type(csv_rows[0][2]).__name__}  (always str – need
int())")
print(f"  Subjects:   {csv_rows[0][3]!r}  (comma in string – need split)")

# ── JSON representation: types preserved, hierarchy natural ──────────
json_data = json.dumps([
    {"id": "10042", "name": "Anika Patel", "score": 88,
     "subjects": ["Mathematics", "Science"]},
    {"id": "10043", "name": "Liam Torres", "score": 72,
     "subjects": ["English"]},
])

students = json.loads(json_data)
print("\nJSON row 0:")
print(" ", students[0])
print(f"  Score type: {type(students[0]['score']).__name__}  (int already)")
print(f"  Subjects:   {students[0]['subjects']}  (list already)")
```

Output:
```
CSV row 0:
  ['10042', 'Anika Patel', '88', 'Mathematics,Science']
  Score type: str  (always str – need int())
  Subjects:   '"Mathematics,Science"'  (comma in string – need split)

JSON row 0:
  {'id': '10042', 'name': 'Anika Patel', 'score': 88, 'subjects':
['Mathematics', 'Science']}
  Score type: int  (int already)
  Subjects:   ['Mathematics', 'Science']  (list already)
```

The practical conclusion from Example 6.1.3 is straightforward: when your data has types that matter (numbers you will do arithmetic on), lists that are genuine lists (not comma-joined strings), or structure that has more than one level, JSON is more appropriate than CSV. When your data is purely flat rows of text for spreadsheet consumption, CSV remains the better choice.

6.2 json.load() and json.dump()

The json module provides four core functions: load() and dump() for working with file objects, and loads() and dumps() for working with strings. This section covers the file-based pair; Section 6.3 covers the string-based pair. The naming convention is the same as Python's pickle module: the "s" suffix means "string".

json.load(f) reads a file object and parses its entire contents as JSON, returning the resulting Python object. The file must be opened in text mode with encoding="utf-8" — JSON is defined as UTF-8, UTF-16, or UTF-32, but UTF-8 is overwhelmingly the standard in practice. json.dump(obj, f) serialises a Python object and writes the JSON text to a file object. Both functions raise json.JSONDecodeError (a subclass of ValueError) if the input is not valid JSON, and TypeError if the object cannot be serialised.

The indent Parameter

By default json.dump() writes a single compact line with no whitespace. Passing indent=N (typically 2 or 4) produces pretty-printed output with N spaces of indentation per nesting level. Pretty-printing is essential for any JSON file that a human will read or edit — configuration files, data exports, debugging output. The compact form is appropriate for data exchanged programmatically, such as API payloads, where minimising byte count matters. Neither form affects the data; they are purely presentation choices.

The ensure_ascii Parameter

By default json.dump() escapes all non-ASCII characters as \uXXXX escape sequences, so the output contains only printable ASCII. This is safe and portable but makes files unreadable when they contain non-English names. Passing ensure_ascii=False writes the characters directly as UTF-8, which is more readable and often the right choice for files humans will inspect. Always pair ensure_ascii=False with encoding="utf-8" in the open() call to ensure the file is written and read in a consistent encoding.

> **Note:** json.load() and json.dump() operate on open file objects, not file paths. Always use them inside a with open(...) block: "with open(path, encoding='utf-8') as f: data = json.load(f)". Passing a file path string to json.load() raises TypeError — a common mistake when switching between the file-based and string-based functions.

Example 1 — Introduction

Writing a Python dict to a JSON file with json.dump() and reading it back with json.load().

```
import json

STUDENT = {
    "student_id": 10042,
    "name": "Anika Patel",
    "year_level": 10,
    "enrolled": True,
    "subjects": ["Mathematics", "Science", "English"],
    "gpa": 6.5,
}

# — Write to file ————————————————————————————————
with open("student.json", "w", encoding="utf-8") as f:
    json.dump(STUDENT, f, indent=2, ensure_ascii=False)

print("Written file:")
print(open("student.json", encoding="utf-8").read())

# — Read back ————————————————————————————————————
with open("student.json", "r", encoding="utf-8") as f:
    loaded = json.load(f)

print("\nLoaded type:", type(loaded).__name__)
print("Name:", loaded["name"])
print("Subjects:", loaded["subjects"])
print("GPA type:", type(loaded["gpa"]).__name__)
```

Output:

```
Written file:
{
  "student_id": 10042,
  "name": "Anika Patel",
  "year_level": 10,
  "enrolled": true,
  "subjects": [
    "Mathematics",
    "Science",
    "English"
  ],
  "gpa": 6.5
}

Loaded type: dict
Name: Anika Patel
Subjects: ['Mathematics', 'Science', 'English']
GPA type: float
```

Example 2 — Variation

Using ensure_ascii=False for files with non-ASCII names; compact vs pretty-printed output sizes.

```
import json

STUDENTS = [
    {"id": "10042", "name": "Nguyễn Thị Hương", "score": 91},
    {"id": "10043", "name": "José Ramírez",       "score": 88},
    {"id": "10044", "name": "Astrid Müller",       "score": 85},
]

# Compact: ensure_ascii=True (default) — safe but unreadable names
with open("students_ascii.json", "w", encoding="utf-8") as f:
    json.dump(STUDENTS, f)

# Readable: ensure_ascii=False — names preserved as-is
with open("students_utf8.json", "w", encoding="utf-8") as f:
    json.dump(STUDENTS, f, indent=2, ensure_ascii=False)

import os
print("ASCII file size:  ", os.path.getsize("students_ascii.json"), "bytes")
print("UTF-8 file size:  ", os.path.getsize("students_utf8.json"),  "bytes")
print()
print("First 80 chars of ASCII file:")
print(open("students_ascii.json", encoding="utf-8").read()[:80])
print("\nFirst 80 chars of UTF-8 file:")
print(open("students_utf8.json", encoding="utf-8").read()[:80])
```

Output:

```
ASCII file size:   144 bytes
UTF-8 file size:   121 bytes

First 80 chars of ASCII file:
[{"id": "10042", "name": "Nguy\u1ec5n Th\u1ecb H\u01b0\u01a1ng", "score": 91},
{"id":

First 80 chars of UTF-8 file:
[
  {
    "id": "10042",
    "name": "Nguyễn Thị Hương",
```

Example 3 — Real-world application

A JSON-backed application settings manager: load defaults, merge with user settings from disk, save back after modification.

```
# settings_manager.py  —  persistent JSON settings with defaults
import json
from pathlib import Path

SETTINGS_FILE = Path("settings.json")

DEFAULTS = {
    "school_name":   "Brisbane State High School",
    "academic_year": 2025,
    "theme":         "light",
    "results_dir":   "results",
    "max_students":  500,
    "debug":         False,
}

def load_settings():
    """Load settings from disk; fall back to defaults on any error."""
    if not SETTINGS_FILE.exists():
        print("  No settings file found — using defaults.")
        return DEFAULTS.copy()
    try:
        with open(SETTINGS_FILE, "r", encoding="utf-8") as f:
            user = json.load(f)
        # Merge: defaults provide missing keys, user values override
        return {**DEFAULTS, **user}
    except (json.JSONDecodeError, OSError) as e:
        print(f"  Settings error ({e}) — using defaults.")
        return DEFAULTS.copy()

def save_settings(settings):
    """Write the settings dict to disk."""
    with open(SETTINGS_FILE, "w", encoding="utf-8") as f:
        json.dump(settings, f, indent=2, ensure_ascii=False)
    print(f"  Settings saved to {SETTINGS_FILE}")

settings = load_settings()
print("Loaded:", settings)

# Modify and save
settings["theme"]   = "dark"
settings["debug"]   = True
save_settings(settings)

# Load again to confirm persistence
reloaded = load_settings()
print("Theme after reload:", reloaded["theme"])
print("Debug after reload:", reloaded["debug"])
```

Output:

```
  No settings file found — using defaults.
Loaded: {'school_name': 'Brisbane State High School', 'academic_year':
2025, ...}
  Settings saved to settings.json
Theme after reload: dark
Debug after reload: True
```

The load-merge-save pattern in Example 6.2.3 is the canonical approach for application settings: defaults are always available in code, user preferences are layered on top, and the merge ensures that adding a new default key in a future version of the program is immediately available to users without requiring them to reset their settings.

6.3 json.loads() and json.dumps() for Strings

The string-based functions json.loads() and json.dumps() are the in-memory equivalents of json.load() and json.dump(). They work on Python strings rather than file objects, which makes them useful whenever JSON data arrives or is needed as a string rather than a file: API responses, database fields, network messages, test fixtures, and in-memory data pipelines. The parameters are identical: indent, ensure_ascii, sort_keys, and all the others work the same way.

json.loads(s) parses a JSON string and returns a Python object. json.dumps(obj) serialises a Python object and returns a JSON string. The round-trip json.loads(json.dumps(obj)) is a reliable way to produce a deep copy of any JSON-serialisable object: since every value is converted to JSON and back, the result is a completely independent copy with no shared references. This technique is occasionally useful, though copy.deepcopy() is more general and does not require the object to be JSON-serialisable.

sort_keys

json.dumps(obj, sort_keys=True) sorts the keys of every dict in the output alphabetically. The default is False, which preserves insertion order (Python 3.7+). Sorted keys are useful when comparing JSON outputs for equality in tests — two dicts with the same keys and values but different insertion orders produce identical strings with sort_keys=True, making string comparison reliable. Sorted keys are also useful for producing deterministic output in logs and reports.

> **Note:** json.loads() accepts both str and bytes. If the input is bytes, it is decoded as UTF-8 (or another supported encoding detected from a BOM). This makes it convenient for handling raw network responses: response.read() returns bytes, and json.loads() can accept them directly without an explicit decode() call.

Example 1 — Introduction

json.dumps() serialising a Python object to a string and json.loads() parsing it back.

```
import json

ENROLMENT = {
    "student_id": "10042",
    "name":         "Anika Patel",
    "courses":      ["Mathematics", "Science"],
    "active":       True,
    "gpa":          6.5,
}

# ── Serialise to string ──────────────────────────────────────────
compact   = json.dumps(ENROLMENT)
pretty    = json.dumps(ENROLMENT, indent=2)
sorted_kv = json.dumps(ENROLMENT, sort_keys=True)

print(f"Compact ({len(compact)} chars): {compact}")
print(f"\nPretty ({len(pretty)} chars):")
print(pretty)
print(f"\nSorted keys: {sorted_kv}")

# ── Parse back ───────────────────────────────────────────────────
recovered = json.loads(compact)
print(f"\nRecovered: {recovered}")
print(f"GPA type after round-trip: {type(recovered['gpa']).__name__}")
```

Output:

```
Compact (83 chars): {"student_id": "10042", "name": "Anika Patel", "courses":
["Mathematics", "Science"], "active": true, "gpa": 6.5}

Pretty (110 chars):
{
  "student_id": "10042",
  "name": "Anika Patel",
  "courses": [
    "Mathematics",
```

```
    "Science"
  ],
  "active": true,
  "gpa": 6.5
}

Sorted keys: {"active": true, "courses": ["Mathematics", "Science"], "gpa":
6.5, "name": "Anika Patel", "student_id": "10042"}

Recovered: {'student_id': '10042', 'name': 'Anika Patel', 'courses':
['Mathematics', 'Science'], 'active': True, 'gpa': 6.5}
GPA type after round-trip: float
```

Example 2 — Variation

Using json.loads() on bytes directly; and the deep-copy round-trip technique.

```
import json
import copy

# json.loads() accepts bytes (e.g. from a network read)
raw_bytes = b'{"name": "Priya Nair", "score": 95}'
data = json.loads(raw_bytes)   # no .decode() needed
print("From bytes:", data)

# ── Deep copy via JSON round-trip ──────────────────────────
original = {"students": [{"id": "10042", "scores": [88, 91, 84]}]}

json_copy  = json.loads(json.dumps(original))
deep_copy  = copy.deepcopy(original)

# Modify the nested list in the original
original["students"][0]["scores"].append(99)

print("Original after modify:", original["students"][0]["scores"])
print("JSON copy (unaffected):", json_copy["students"][0]["scores"])
print("deepcopy (unaffected):", deep_copy["students"][0]["scores"])
```

Output:

```
From bytes: {'name': 'Priya Nair', 'score': 95}
Original after modify: [88, 91, 84, 99]
JSON copy (unaffected): [88, 91, 84]
deepcopy (unaffected): [88, 91, 84]
```

Example 3 — Real-world application

A JSON message queue simulator: serialise messages to strings for transmission, deserialise on receipt, process, and log the result.

```
# message_queue.py  —  simulate JSON-serialised message passing
import json
from datetime import datetime
from collections import deque

queue: deque = deque()   # stores serialised JSON strings

def enqueue(event_type, payload):
    """Serialise a message and add it to the queue."""
    message = {
        "type":      event_type,
        "timestamp": datetime.now().isoformat(),
        "payload":   payload,
    }
    queue.append(json.dumps(message))   # store as JSON string

def process_all():
```

```
    """Deserialise and process each message in the queue."""
    processed = 0
    while queue:
        raw     = queue.popleft()
        message = json.loads(raw)
        kind    = message["type"]
        payload = message["payload"]
        ts      = message["timestamp"][:19]
        if kind == "ENROL":
            print(f"  [{ts}] ENROL   — {payload['name']} enrolled in
{payload['subject']}")
        elif kind == "GRADE":
            print(f"  [{ts}] GRADE   — {payload['name']}: {payload['score']}")
        elif kind == "WITHDRAW":
            print(f"  [{ts}] WITHDRAW — {payload['name']} withdrew")
        processed += 1
    return processed

enqueue("ENROL",    {"name": "Anika Patel", "subject": "Mathematics"})
enqueue("GRADE",    {"name": "Anika Patel", "score": 88})
enqueue("ENROL",    {"name": "Liam Torres", "subject": "English"})
enqueue("WITHDRAW", {"name": "Liam Torres"})

print(f"Queue length: {len(queue)}")
n = process_all()
print(f"Processed {n} message(s). Queue empty: {len(queue) == 0}")
```

Output:

```
Queue length: 4
  [2025-08-14T10:22:04] ENROL   — Anika Patel enrolled in Mathematics
  [2025-08-14T10:22:04] GRADE   — Anika Patel: 88
  [2025-08-14T10:22:04] ENROL   — Liam Torres enrolled in English
  [2025-08-14T10:22:04] WITHDRAW — Liam Torres withdrew
Processed 4 message(s). Queue empty: True
```

The message queue example illustrates a broader pattern: serialise to JSON strings when data must be stored in a non-Python context (a queue, a database column, a network buffer), and deserialise immediately before use. json.dumps() and json.loads() are the translation layer between Python objects and their portable string representation.

6.4 Serialising Python Objects: Supported Types and Limitations

The json module can serialise only a specific set of Python types: dict, list, tuple, str, int, float, bool, and None. Any other type — datetime, Decimal, set, bytes, custom class instances, pathlib.Path — raises TypeError when passed to json.dump() or json.dumps(). This limitation exists because JSON has no equivalent types for these objects; the programmer must decide how to represent them.

The Type Mapping Table

The complete mapping is: Python dict maps to JSON object; list and tuple both map to JSON array (tuples become arrays and are read back as lists, not tuples); str maps to JSON string; int maps to JSON number; float maps to JSON number (with special handling for inf and nan, which are not valid JSON — they raise ValueError by default); bool maps to JSON true/false (note that bool is a subclass of int in Python, so True serialises as true, not 1); and None maps to JSON null.

Common Problem Types

The types most frequently encountered that require special treatment are: datetime (has no JSON equivalent; commonly serialised as an ISO 8601 string such as "2025-08-14T10:22:04"), Decimal (use str or float, depending on whether precision matters), set (convert to a sorted list), bytes (use base64 encoding or a hex string), pathlib.Path (use str(path)), and custom class instances (extract the relevant attributes into a dict). Section 6.5 shows how to automate these conversions with a custom encoder.

> **Note:** Python's float("inf") and float("nan") are not valid JSON values. By default json.dumps() raises ValueError for these. Passing allow_nan=True produces "Infinity", "NaN", and "-Infinity" in the output — valid JavaScript but technically not valid JSON. If your data may contain inf or nan, replace them with None before serialising.

Example 1 — Introduction

Demonstrating which types serialise successfully and which raise TypeError.

```
import json
from datetime import datetime
from decimal import Decimal
from pathlib import Path

def try_dump(label, value):
    try:
        result = json.dumps(value)
        print(f"  {label:<20}  OK  →  {result}")
    except (TypeError, ValueError) as e:
        print(f"  {label:<20}  ERROR: {e}")

try_dump("dict",         {"a": 1})
try_dump("list",         [1, 2, 3])
try_dump("tuple",        (1, 2, 3))
try_dump("str",          "hello")
try_dump("int",          42)
try_dump("float",        3.14)
try_dump("bool",         True)
try_dump("None",         None)
try_dump("datetime",     datetime.now())
try_dump("Decimal",      Decimal("6.50"))
try_dump("set",          {1, 2, 3})
try_dump("bytes",        b"hello")
try_dump("Path",         Path("/home/anika"))
try_dump("float inf",    float("inf"))
```

Output:

```
  dict                  OK  →  {"a": 1}
  list                  OK  →  [1, 2, 3]
  tuple                 OK  →  [1, 2, 3]
  str                   OK  →  "hello"
  int                   OK  →  42
  float                 OK  →  3.14
  bool                  OK  →  true
  None                  OK  →  null
  datetime              ERROR: Object of type datetime is not JSON serializable
  Decimal               ERROR: Object of type Decimal is not JSON serializable
  set                   ERROR: Object of type set is not JSON serializable
  bytes                 ERROR: Object of type bytes is not JSON serializable
  Path                  ERROR: Object of type PosixPath is not JSON
serializable
  float inf             ERROR: Out of range float values are not JSON compliant
```

Example 2 — Variation

Manual pre-conversion workarounds for the most common non-serialisable types, before passing to json.dumps().

```
import json
from datetime import datetime, date
from decimal import Decimal
from pathlib import Path

def make_serialisable(obj):
```

```
    """Recursively convert common non-serialisable types to JSON-safe
equivalents."""
    if isinstance(obj, dict):
        return {k: make_serialisable(v) for k, v in obj.items()}
    if isinstance(obj, (list, tuple)):
        return [make_serialisable(v) for v in obj]
    if isinstance(obj, (datetime, date)):
        return obj.isoformat()   # "2025-08-14T10:22:04" or "2025-08-14"
    if isinstance(obj, Decimal):
        return str(obj)          # preserve exact precision as string
    if isinstance(obj, set):
        return sorted(make_serialisable(v) for v in obj)
    if isinstance(obj, bytes):
        return obj.hex()         # "48656c6c6f"
    if isinstance(obj, Path):
        return str(obj)
    if isinstance(obj, float) and (obj != obj or obj == float("inf") or obj ==
float("-inf")):
        return None              # replace inf/nan with null
    return obj

record = {
    "name":        "Anika Patel",
    "enrolled":    date(2025, 2, 1),
    "gpa":         Decimal("6.75"),
    "tags":        {"merit", "scholarship"},
    "photo_hash": b"\xde\xad\xbe\xef",
    "profile":     Path("/home/anika/profile.json"),
}

print(json.dumps(make_serialisable(record), indent=2))
```

Output:

```
{
  "name": "Anika Patel",
  "enrolled": "2025-02-01",
  "gpa": "6.75",
  "tags": ["merit", "scholarship"],
  "photo_hash": "deadbeef",
  "profile": "/home/anika/profile.json"
}
```

Example 3 — Real-world application

A school record serialiser that flattens a rich Python object — containing datetime, Decimal, and nested objects — to a JSON-safe dict before saving.

```
# record_serialiser.py  —  prepare complex records for JSON persistence
import json
from datetime import date
from decimal import Decimal

# Simulate rich Python data objects
RECORDS = [
    {
        "id":             "10042",
        "name":           "Anika Patel",
        "dob":            date(2009, 3, 15),
        "enrolment":      date(2025, 2, 1),
        "fee_balance":    Decimal("450.00"),
        "subjects":       {"Mathematics", "Science", "English"},
        "active":         True,
    },
    {
        "id":             "10043",
        "name":           "Liam Torres",
        "dob":            date(2009, 7, 22),
        "enrolment":      date(2025, 2, 1),
```

```
        "fee_balance":   Decimal("225.00"),
        "subjects":      {"English", "History"},
        "active":        True,
    },
]

def flatten_record(r):
    return {
        "id":          r["id"],
        "name":        r["name"],
        "dob":         r["dob"].isoformat(),
        "enrolment":   r["enrolment"].isoformat(),
        "fee_balance": str(r["fee_balance"]),
        "subjects":    sorted(r["subjects"]),
        "active":      r["active"],
    }

serialisable = [flatten_record(r) for r in RECORDS]

with open("records.json", "w", encoding="utf-8") as f:
    json.dump(serialisable, f, indent=2, ensure_ascii=False)

print("Saved records.json:")
print(open("records.json", encoding="utf-8").read())
```

Output:

```
Saved records.json:
[
  {
    "id": "10042",
    "name": "Anika Patel",
    "dob": "2009-03-15",
    "enrolment": "2025-02-01",
    "fee_balance": "450.00",
    "subjects": ["English", "Mathematics", "Science"],
    "active": true
  },
  {
    "id": "10043",
    "name": "Liam Torres",
    "dob": "2009-07-22",
    "enrolment": "2025-02-01",
    "fee_balance": "225.00",
    "subjects": ["English", "History"],
    "active": true
  }
]
```

The explicit flatten_record() function is often preferable to a fully generic recursive converter for production code, because it makes the schema of the output explicit. If a new field is added to the record dict, it will not silently appear in the JSON output until you decide to include it in flatten_record(). Section 6.5 shows how to automate this with a custom encoder for cases where a generic approach is more appropriate.

6.5 Custom JSON Encoders and Decoders

The json module provides two extension points for handling non-standard types: a custom encoder class for serialisation and an object_hook function for deserialisation. Together they let you define a round-trip conversion between your custom Python types and their JSON representations, so that serialisation and deserialisation are handled automatically rather than manually at every call site.

Custom Encoder: JSONEncoder subclass

To extend the serialiser, subclass json.JSONEncoder and override the default(self, obj) method. When the standard encoder encounters a type it cannot handle, it calls default(obj). Your override should return a JSON-serialisable value for any types you want to handle, and call super().default(obj) for everything else (which raises TypeError for truly unsupported types). Pass your encoder class to json.dump() or json.dumps() as the cls parameter.

object_hook for Deserialisation

When loading JSON, the object_hook parameter of json.load() and json.loads() is called for every JSON object (dict) in the input. The hook receives the dict and can return any Python object in its place. A common pattern is to check for a type marker key — such as "__type__" — and reconstruct the original Python object if it is present. This enables transparent round-trips: dump a datetime as {"__type__": "datetime", "value": "2025-08-14T10:22:04"}, and the hook reconstructs it as a datetime on load.

> **Note:** The object_hook is called for every JSON object, including nested ones. If your data has many nested dicts that are not custom types, your hook must return them unchanged: the return value replaces the dict, so returning None or forgetting a return statement will silently drop data. Always include a "return obj" fallthrough.

Example 1 — Introduction

A custom JSONEncoder that handles datetime, date, Decimal, set, and Path automatically.

```
import json
from datetime import datetime, date
from decimal import Decimal
from pathlib import Path

class SchoolEncoder(json.JSONEncoder):
    """Extend the default JSON encoder with common school-app types."""

    def default(self, obj):
        if isinstance(obj, datetime):
            return {"__type__": "datetime", "value": obj.isoformat()}
        if isinstance(obj, date):
            return {"__type__": "date", "value": obj.isoformat()}
        if isinstance(obj, Decimal):
            return {"__type__": "decimal", "value": str(obj)}
        if isinstance(obj, set):
            return {"__type__": "set", "value": sorted(obj)}
        if isinstance(obj, Path):
            return {"__type__": "path", "value": str(obj)}
        return super().default(obj)   # raises TypeError for unknowns

record = {
    "name":       "Anika Patel",
    "dob":        date(2009, 3, 15),
    "last_seen": datetime(2025, 8, 14, 10, 22, 4),
    "balance":   Decimal("450.00"),
    "subjects":  {"Mathematics", "Science"},
    "profile":   Path("/home/anika"),
}

encoded = json.dumps(record, cls=SchoolEncoder, indent=2)
print(encoded)
```

Output:

```
{
  "name": "Anika Patel",
  "dob": {"__type__": "date", "value": "2009-03-15"},
  "last_seen": {"__type__": "datetime", "value": "2025-08-14T10:22:04"},
  "balance": {"__type__": "decimal", "value": "450.00"},
  "subjects": {"__type__": "set", "value": ["Mathematics", "Science"]},
  "profile": {"__type__": "path", "value": "/home/anika"}
```

```
}
```

Example 2 — Variation

An object_hook that reconstructs the custom types tagged by SchoolEncoder on load, completing the round-trip.

```
from datetime import datetime, date
from decimal import Decimal
from pathlib import Path
import json

def school_hook(obj):
    """Reconstruct custom types from their tagged JSON representation."""
    t = obj.get("__type__")
    if t == "datetime":
        return datetime.fromisoformat(obj["value"])
    if t == "date":
        return date.fromisoformat(obj["value"])
    if t == "decimal":
        return Decimal(obj["value"])
    if t == "set":
        return set(obj["value"])
    if t == "path":
        return Path(obj["value"])
    return obj   # no type tag — return unchanged

# Round-trip the record from Example 6.5.1
encoded = json.dumps(record, cls=SchoolEncoder)
restored = json.loads(encoded, object_hook=school_hook)

print("Round-trip results:")
for key, val in restored.items():
    print(f"  {key:<12} {type(val).__name__:<10} {val!r}")
```

Output:

```
Round-trip results:
  name         str        'Anika Patel'
  dob          date       datetime.date(2009, 3, 15)
  last_seen    datetime   datetime.datetime(2025, 8, 14, 10, 22, 4)
  balance      Decimal    Decimal('450.00')
  subjects     set        {'Mathematics', 'Science'}
  profile      PosixPath  PosixPath('/home/anika')
```

Example 3 — Real-world application

A dataclass-based student record with automatic JSON serialisation and deserialisation via a custom encoder and hook.

```
# dataclass_json.py  —  JSON round-trip for a dataclass
import json
import dataclasses
from datetime import date
from typing import List

@dataclasses.dataclass
class Student:
    student_id:  str
    name:        str
    dob:         date
    year_level:  int
    subjects:    List[str]
    gpa:         float = 0.0

class StudentEncoder(json.JSONEncoder):
    def default(self, obj):
        if dataclasses.is_dataclass(obj) and not isinstance(obj, type):
            d = dataclasses.asdict(obj)
```

```
            d["__type__"] = type(obj).__name__
            # Convert date fields to ISO strings
            for k, v in d.items():
                if isinstance(v, date):
                    d[k] = v.isoformat()
            return d
        return super().default(obj)

REGISTRY = {"Student": Student}

def student_hook(obj):
    cls_name = obj.pop("__type__", None)
    if cls_name in REGISTRY:
        cls = REGISTRY[cls_name]
        fields = {f.name: f for f in dataclasses.fields(cls)}
        for fname, fval in obj.items():
            if fname in fields and fields[fname].type == date:
                obj[fname] = date.fromisoformat(fval)
        return cls(**obj)
    return obj

students = [
    Student("10042","Anika Patel", date(2009,3,15), 10,["Maths","Science"],
6.5),
    Student("10043","Liam Torres",  date(2009,7,22), 10,["English"],
5.8),
]

encoded = json.dumps(students, cls=StudentEncoder, indent=2)
print("Encoded (first student):")
print(encoded[:200])

restored = json.loads(encoded, object_hook=student_hook)
print("\nRestored types:")
for s in restored:
    print(f"  {type(s).__name__}: {s.name}, dob={s.dob}, gpa={s.gpa}")
```

Output:

```
Encoded (first student):
[
  {
    "student_id": "10042",
    "name": "Anika Patel",
    "dob": "2009-03-15",
    "year_level": 10,
    "subjects": [
      "Maths",
      "Science"
    ],
    "gpa": 6.5,
    "__type__": "Student"
  },

Restored types:
  Student: Anika Patel, dob=2009-03-15, gpa=6.5
  Student: Liam Torres, dob=2009-07-22, gpa=5.8
```

The dataclass encoder pattern from Example 6.5.3 is one of the most practical JSON techniques for application development. Dataclasses provide a clean, typed data model; the custom encoder and hook provide transparent persistence. Adding a new field to the dataclass automatically includes it in the JSON output without any changes to the encoder logic.

6.6 Pretty-Printing and Sorting Keys

The presentation of JSON output matters for readability, debuggability, and reproducibility. json.dumps() and json.dump() both accept several parameters that control how the output is formatted. The most important are indent, sort_keys, separators, and ensure_ascii, all of which have been touched on in earlier sections. This section consolidates their interaction and shows how to build a consistent formatting utility for a project.

indent

indent=None (the default) produces a single-line compact representation with a space after each colon and comma: {"a": 1, "b": 2}. indent=0 produces multi-line output with no indentation, putting each key and value on its own line with no nesting indentation. indent=2 or indent=4 are the standard choices for human-readable files; 2 is more compact and preferred for configuration files, while 4 is more legible in code listings. indent can also be a string (such as "\t") for tab-indented output.

separators

The separators parameter is a (item_separator, key_separator) tuple. The default with no indent is (", ", ": ") — a comma and space between items, a colon and space between keys and values. To produce the most compact possible output (for network transmission or storage), use separators=(",", ":") which removes all whitespace: {"a":1,"b":2}. Combining compact separators with no indent gives the smallest valid JSON string.

Building a Project Formatter

Rather than repeating indent and ensure_ascii arguments at every call site, it is good practice to define project-level dump and load functions that enforce consistent formatting. This also makes it easy to change the format globally — switching from indent=2 to indent=4, or toggling sort_keys — without updating every call site.

> **Note:** sort_keys=True sorts keys at every nesting level. This is useful for comparing JSON outputs in tests (json.dumps(a, sort_keys=True) == json.dumps(b, sort_keys=True) is a reliable equality check) and for producing deterministic outputs in logs. It has no effect on performance for normal file sizes.

Example 1 — Introduction

Comparing compact, pretty-printed, and tab-indented output formats on the same data.

```
import json

DATA = {
    "school": "Brisbane State High",
    "year": 2025,
    "classes": [
        {"name": "10A", "count": 28},
        {"name": "10B", "count": 30},
    ]
}

compact = json.dumps(DATA, separators=(",", ":"))
standard = json.dumps(DATA)
pretty2  = json.dumps(DATA, indent=2)
pretty4  = json.dumps(DATA, indent=4)
tabbed   = json.dumps(DATA, indent="\t")

print(f"compact  ({len(compact):3d} chars): {compact}")
print(f"standard ({len(standard):3d} chars): {standard}")
print(f"indent=2 ({len(pretty2):3d} chars):")
print(pretty2)
print(f"indent=4 ({len(pretty4):3d} chars): (omitted for brevity)")
```

Output:

```
compact  ( 67 chars): {"school":"Brisbane State High","year":2025,"classes":
```

```
[{"name":"10A","count":28},{"name":"10B","count":30}]}
standard ( 80 chars): {"school": "Brisbane State High", "year": 2025,
"classes": [{"name": "10A", "count": 28}, {"name": "10B", "count": 30}]}
indent=2 (128 chars):
{
  "school": "Brisbane State High",
  "year": 2025,
  "classes": [
    {
      "name": "10A",
      "count": 28
    },
    {
      "name": "10B",
      "count": 30
    }
  ]
}
indent=4 (155 chars): (omitted for brevity)
```

Example 2 — Variation

Using sort_keys=True for deterministic test assertions; confirming that two dicts with different key order produce identical sorted JSON.

```
import json

# Two dicts with identical content but different insertion order
a = {"name": "Anika", "score": 88, "subject": "Maths"}
b = {"subject": "Maths", "name": "Anika", "score": 88}

# Without sort_keys: insertion order preserved — strings differ
print("Without sort_keys:")
print(f"  a: {json.dumps(a)}")
print(f"  b: {json.dumps(b)}")
print(f"  Equal: {json.dumps(a) == json.dumps(b)}")

# With sort_keys: deterministic — strings identical
print("\nWith sort_keys=True:")
print(f"  a: {json.dumps(a, sort_keys=True)}")
print(f"  b: {json.dumps(b, sort_keys=True)}")
print(f"  Equal: {json.dumps(a, sort_keys=True) == json.dumps(b,
sort_keys=True)}")
```

Output:

```
Without sort_keys:
  a: {"name": "Anika", "score": 88, "subject": "Maths"}
  b: {"subject": "Maths", "name": "Anika", "score": 88}
  Equal: False

With sort_keys=True:
  a: {"name": "Anika", "score": 88, "subject": "Maths"}
  b: {"name": "Anika", "score": 88, "subject": "Maths"}
  Equal: True
```

Example 3 — Real-world application

A project-level JSON utility module providing consistent dump/load functions with configurable verbosity for development vs production.

```
# json_utils.py  —  project-wide JSON formatting helpers
import json
from pathlib import Path

PRETTY_OPTS  = dict(indent=2,  ensure_ascii=False, sort_keys=True)
COMPACT_OPTS = dict(separators=(",", ":"), ensure_ascii=False)
```

```
def dump_json(data, filepath, pretty=True):",
    """Write data to filepath as JSON."""
    opts = PRETTY_OPTS if pretty else COMPACT_OPTS
    Path(filepath).parent.mkdir(parents=True, exist_ok=True)
    with open(filepath, "w", encoding="utf-8") as f:
        json.dump(data, f, **opts)
    size = Path(filepath).stat().st_size
    mode = "pretty" if pretty else "compact"
    print(f"  [{mode}] Written {size:,} bytes → {filepath}")

def load_json(filepath):",
    """Load and return a JSON file; raise FileNotFoundError or
JSONDecodeError."""
    with open(filepath, "r", encoding="utf-8") as f:
        return json.load(f)

def dumps_json(data, pretty=False):
    """Serialise to string."""
    opts = PRETTY_OPTS if pretty else COMPACT_OPTS
    return json.dumps(data, **opts)


sample = {"school": "Brisbane State High", "year": 2025,
          "classes": [{"name": "10A"}, {"name": "10B"}]}

dump_json(sample, "data/school_pretty.json", pretty=True)
dump_json(sample, "data/school_compact.json", pretty=False)

reloaded = load_json("data/school_pretty.json")
print("Reloaded:", reloaded)

print("String (compact):", dumps_json(sample))
```

Output:

```
  [pretty] Written 87 bytes → data/school_pretty.json
  [compact] Written 63 bytes → data/school_compact.json
Reloaded: {'classes': [{'name': '10A'}, {'name': '10B'}], 'school': 'Brisbane
State High', 'year': 2025}
String (compact): {"classes":[{"name":"10A"},{"name":"10B"}],"school":"Brisbane
State High","year":2025}
```

The json_utils.py pattern — project-level wrappers with centralised formatting options — is worth implementing early in any project that reads and writes JSON in multiple places. Changing the indent level, adding an encoder class, or switching to atomic writes requires one edit, not a search-and-replace across every module.

6.7 Real-world Patterns: Config Files, API Responses, and Data Persistence

This final section assembles the chapter's techniques into three complete programs that represent the most common JSON workflows. Each is designed to be adapted directly to real projects.

Configuration Files

JSON configuration files are superior to the flat key=value format from Chapter 2 when settings have structure: grouped options, lists of allowed values, nested feature flags. The canonical pattern is: load on startup with a fallback to defaults, validate the required keys immediately, save back on change. Section 6.2 introduced the merge pattern; here it is extended with schema validation.

API Response Processing

Web APIs return JSON. Whether you are calling a school information system, a timetabling service, or a public data API, the response arrives as a JSON string or file. The typical workflow is: load the response with json.loads(), navigate the nested structure to extract the data you need, validate that expected keys are present, and convert to your application's internal representation. Chapter 8 covers making HTTP requests; this chapter covers what to do with the response once you have it.

Data Persistence

For simple applications that need to persist structured data between runs — a to-do list, a game high-score table, a student progress tracker — JSON is the simplest durable storage format. The persistence pattern is identical to CSV's load-modify-save loop (Section 5.7), but JSON handles nested structures, typed values, and optional fields with no extra work. Chapter 10 uses JSON persistence for the capstone project.

Example 1 — Introduction

A structured JSON configuration loader with required key validation and typed value checking.

```
# config_loader.py  —  JSON config with schema validation
import json
from pathlib import Path

CONFIG_FILE = Path("config.json")

SCHEMA = {
    "school_name":   str,
    "academic_year": int,
    "max_students":  int,
    "features": {
        "reports":   bool,
        "export":    bool,
    }
}

DEFAULTS = {
    "school_name":   "Default School",
    "academic_year": 2025,
    "max_students":  500,
    "features": {"reports": True, "export": False}
}

def validate(cfg, schema, path=""):",
    """Recursively validate cfg against schema; return list of errors."""
    errors = []
    for key, expected in schema.items():
        full_key = f"{path}.{key}" if path else key
        if key not in cfg:
            errors.append(f"Missing key: {full_key!r}")
        elif isinstance(expected, dict):
            errors += validate(cfg[key], expected, full_key)
        elif not isinstance(cfg[key], expected):
            errors.append(f"{full_key!r}: expected {expected.__name__}, got
{type(cfg[key]).__name__}")
    return errors

def load_config():
    if not CONFIG_FILE.exists():
        return DEFAULTS.copy()
    try:
        with open(CONFIG_FILE, "r", encoding="utf-8") as f:
            raw = json.load(f)
        merged = {**DEFAULTS, **raw}
        errors = validate(merged, SCHEMA)
        if errors:
            print("Config validation errors:")
            for e in errors:
                print(f"  - {e}")
```

```
        return merged
    except json.JSONDecodeError as e:
        print(f"  Bad JSON in config: {e}")
        return DEFAULTS.copy()

# Write a test config
CONFIG_FILE.write_text(json.dumps({
    "school_name": "Brisbane State High School",
    "academic_year": 2025,
    "max_students": 1800,
    "features": {"reports": True, "export": True}
}, indent=2), encoding="utf-8")

cfg = load_config()
print("Config loaded:")
for k, v in cfg.items():
    print(f"  {k}: {v}")
```

Output:

```
Config loaded:
  school_name: Brisbane State High School
  academic_year: 2025
  max_students: 1800
  features: {'reports': True, 'export': True}
```

Example 2 — Variation

Processing a nested API response: extracting, validating, and transforming student data from a hypothetical school information system response.

```
# api_response_processor.py  —  parse a JSON API response
import json

# Simulate a JSON response from a school information system API
API_RESPONSE = '''
{
    "status": "ok",
    "request_id": "req-20250814-0042",
    "total": 4,
    "students": [
        {"id": "10042", "firstName": "Anika", "lastName": "Patel",
         "year": 10, "scores": {"maths": 88, "english": 91, "science": 84}},
        {"id": "10043", "firstName": "Liam",  "lastName": "Torres",
         "year": 10, "scores": {"maths": 72, "english": 85, "science": 79}},
        {"id": "10044", "firstName": "Priya", "lastName": "Nair",
         "year": 10, "scores": {"maths": 95, "english": 88, "science": 92}},
        {"id": "10045", "firstName": "Sam",   "lastName": "Wong",
         "year": 11, "scores": null}
    ]
}
'''

def process_api_response(json_text):
    data = json.loads(json_text)

    if data.get("status") != "ok":
        raise ValueError(f"API error: {data.get('status')}")

    students = data.get("students", [])
    records = []
    for s in students:
        name   = f"{s['firstName']} {s['lastName']}"
        scores = s.get("scores") or {}   # null scores → empty dict
        avg    = sum(scores.values()) / len(scores) if scores else None
        records.append({
            "id":      s["id"],
            "name":    name,
```

```
            "year":    s["year"],
            "average": round(avg, 1) if avg is not None else "N/A",
        })
    return records

students = process_api_response(API_RESPONSE)
print(f"Processed {len(students)} student(s):")
for s in students:
    print(f"  {s['id']}  {s['name']:<20}  Year {s['year']}
avg={s['average']}")
```

Output:

```
Processed 4 student(s):
  10042  Anika Patel          Year 10  avg=87.7
  10043  Liam Torres          Year 10  avg=78.7
  10044  Priya Nair           Year 10  avg=91.7
  10045  Sam Wong             Year 11  avg=N/A
```

Example 3 — Real-world application

A JSON data store for student progress records: load on startup, add/update/delete in memory, save atomically on request.

```
# progress_store.py  —  JSON-backed student progress data store
import json, os, tempfile
from pathlib import Path
from datetime import date

STORE_FILE = Path("progress.json")

class ProgressStore:
    """
    Simple JSON-backed key-value store for student progress records.
    Keyed by student ID; loaded into memory on init, saved atomically.
    """

    def __init__(self, filepath=STORE_FILE):
        self._path    = Path(filepath)
        self._records = self._load()

    def _load(self):
        if not self._path.exists():
            return {}
        try:
            with open(self._path, "r", encoding="utf-8") as f:
                return json.load(f)
        except (json.JSONDecodeError, OSError):
            return {}

    def save(self):
        """Atomically write the current records to disk."""
        fd, tmp = tempfile.mkstemp(dir=self._path.parent, suffix=".tmp")
        try:
            with os.fdopen(fd, "w", encoding="utf-8") as f:
                json.dump(self._records, f, indent=2, ensure_ascii=False)
            os.replace(tmp, self._path)
        except Exception:
            Path(tmp).unlink(missing_ok=True)
            raise

    def upsert(self, student_id, data):
        """Insert or update a student record."""
        self._records[student_id] = {
            **data,
            "last_updated": date.today().isoformat()
        }
```

```python
    def get(self, student_id):
        return self._records.get(student_id)

    def delete(self, student_id):
        return self._records.pop(student_id, None) is not None

    def all_records(self):
        return dict(self._records)


store = ProgressStore()
store.upsert("10042", {"name": "Anika Patel",  "year": 10, "avg": 87.7})
store.upsert("10043", {"name": "Liam Torres",  "year": 10, "avg": 78.7})
store.upsert("10044", {"name": "Priya Nair",   "year": 10, "avg": 91.7})
store.save()

print(f"Saved {len(store.all_records())} record(s).")
print("Anika:", store.get("10042"))

# Update and re-save
store.upsert("10042", {"name": "Anika Patel", "year": 10, "avg": 89.2})
store.save()
print("Anika updated avg:", store.get("10042")["avg"])

print("\nAll records:")
print(STORE_FILE.read_text(encoding="utf-8"))
```

Output:

```
Saved 3 record(s).
Anika: {'name': 'Anika Patel', 'year': 10, 'avg': 87.7, 'last_updated': '2025-
08-14'}
Anika updated avg: 89.2

All records:
{
  "10042": {
    "name": "Anika Patel",
    "year": 10,
    "avg": 89.2,
    "last_updated": "2025-08-14"
  },
  "10043": {
    "name": "Liam Torres",
    "year": 10,
    "avg": 78.7,
    "last_updated": "2025-08-14"
  },
  "10044": {
    "name": "Priya Nair",
    "year": 10,
    "avg": 91.7,
    "last_updated": "2025-08-14"
  }
}
```

ProgressStore in Example 6.7.3 combines atomic writes (from Section 3.5), JSON persistence (from this chapter), and a clean class interface. It is the direct ancestor of the capstone project's persistence layer in Chapter 10. Any Python application that needs simple, human-readable, structured persistence — without the complexity of a full database — can adapt this pattern in minutes.

Chapter 6 Summary

- JSON maps almost perfectly to Python built-ins: object to dict, array to list, string to str, number to int or float, true/false to True/False, null to None. This makes json.load() immediately usable without type conversion, unlike CSV where every value is a string.
- json.load(f) reads a file object; json.dump(obj, f) writes to one. json.loads(s) parses a string; json.dumps(obj) produces one. Always open JSON files with encoding="utf-8" — JSON is defined as UTF-8 by specification.
- indent=2 produces readable pretty-printed output; separators=(",",":") produces compact output for network transmission. ensure_ascii=False writes non-ASCII characters directly rather than as \uXXXX escapes; always pair it with encoding="utf-8".
- sort_keys=True produces deterministic output regardless of dict insertion order; json.dumps(a, sort_keys=True) == json.dumps(b, sort_keys=True) is a reliable equality check for testing.
- The default serialiser handles only dict, list, tuple, str, int, float, bool, and None. datetime, Decimal, set, bytes, Path, and custom class instances raise TypeError. Either flatten them manually before serialising, or use a custom JSONEncoder subclass.
- Subclass json.JSONEncoder and override default(self, obj) to handle custom types; pass cls=YourEncoder to dump/dumps. Use object_hook in load/loads to reconstruct custom types on deserialisation. Together they enable transparent JSON round-trips for any Python type.
- Three core JSON patterns: load-merge-save for application settings (defaults in code, user overrides on disk, merge on load), parse-validate-transform for API responses (loads → key check → internal representation), and atomic JSON persistence for data stores (ProgressStore pattern: load on init, upsert/delete in memory, atomic save on demand).
- json_utils.py — project-level wrappers for dump/load with consistent indent, ensure_ascii, and sort_keys settings — is worth implementing early. It makes formatting consistent across the codebase and makes global changes (adding an encoder, switching to atomic writes) a one-line update.

Guided Exercises

1. Write a function save_json(data, filepath) and load_json(filepath) pair. save_json should write with indent=2 and ensure_ascii=False; load_json should return the parsed data or None on error (FileNotFoundError or JSONDecodeError). Test the round-trip with a nested dict.

> ***Hint:*** *Use json.dump() inside a with open(..., "w") block for saving. For loading, wrap json.load() in a try/except (json.JSONDecodeError, FileNotFoundError) and return None on any error.*

2. Write a function json_summary(filepath) that loads a JSON file and prints: the top-level type (dict or list), the number of keys (if dict) or items (if list), and for a list of dicts the set of all keys that appear in any item. Handle files that do not exist or contain invalid JSON.

> ***Hint:*** *Use isinstance(data, list) and isinstance(data, dict) to branch. For a list of dicts, use a set union: {k for item in data if isinstance(item, dict) for k in item}.*

3. Write a custom JSONEncoder that serialises datetime.date objects as ISO strings and set objects as sorted lists. Test it by calling json.dumps() on a dict containing both types and verifying the output.

> ***Hint:*** *Subclass json.JSONEncoder, override default(). Check isinstance(obj, date) and isinstance(obj, set). Return obj.isoformat() for dates and sorted(obj) for sets. Call super().default(obj) at the end.*

4. Build a simple JSON config manager: load a config file on startup (falling back to an empty dict), allow updating keys with a set(key, value) method, and save with a save() method. The config file should be pretty-printed with sorted keys. Demonstrate load, set, save, and reload.

> ***Hint:*** *Store the config dict and filepath as instance attributes. In load(), use json.load() inside try/except. In save(), use json.dump() with indent=2 and sort_keys=True.*

5. Write a function merge_json_files(file_list, output_file) that loads a list of JSON files where each file contains a list of dicts, combines all the lists into one, removes duplicates based on a specified key field, and writes the merged result to output_file.

Hint: *Load each file with json.load() inside try/except. Use a dict keyed by the primary key field to deduplicate: {record[key_field]: record for record in all_records}. Write the dict values as a list to output_file.*

Challenge Tasks

1. Build a JSONStore class that provides a simple key-value store backed by a JSON file, with methods get(key, default=None), set(key, value), delete(key), keys(), and save(). The store should load from disk on initialisation, support nested keys using dot notation (e.g. get("school.name") retrieves data["school"]["name"]), and save atomically using the write-temp-then-rename pattern. Test with at least three levels of nesting.

2. Write a complete JSON schema validator: given a JSON data structure and a schema dict that maps key names to their expected types (including nested schemas as dicts, and lists of expected element type), recursively validate that every key is present, every value has the correct type, and no required key is missing. Return a list of all violations found in a single pass (not just the first). Demonstrate with a valid and an invalid student record against a defined schema.

3. Build a JSON diff tool that compares two JSON files and produces a human-readable report of their differences: keys present in the first file but not the second (deleted), keys present in the second but not the first (added), and keys present in both but with different values (changed). The diff should work recursively through nested objects and should handle lists by comparing element-by-element. Write the report to a third file as both a human-readable text summary and a machine-readable JSON diff object.

CHAPTER 7 Introduction to Exception Handling

Book 02: File Handling & Exception Management

> *Chapters 1 through 6 have used try/except blocks throughout, treating them as established knowledge. This chapter makes that knowledge explicit and complete. You will see the full try/except/else/finally structure and understand exactly when each clause runs; learn how to catch specific exception types and multiple types in one block; use the else clause for code that belongs to the success path; use finally for cleanup that must run regardless; chain exceptions with raise...from to preserve context; and internalise the design principles that separate robust exception handling from naive catch-all patterns. The examples throughout this chapter use file and data operations drawn from the previous six chapters, so every pattern appears in a context you already recognise.*

7.1 try, except, else, finally — the Full Structure

Python's exception handling construct has four clauses that can appear in a single block. The try clause contains the code that might raise an exception. The except clause (or clauses) catches and handles specific exceptions. The else clause contains code that runs only if the try block completed without raising any exception. The finally clause contains code that always runs, whether an exception was raised, caught, or propagated. No clause is mandatory except try itself, and the combination you use depends on what you need to express.

The execution flow is precise and worth memorising. When the try block completes without exception: try runs, then else runs, then finally runs. When the try block raises an exception that is caught: the try block stops at the point of exception, the matching except clause runs, else is skipped (it never runs when an exception occurred), and finally runs. When the try block raises an exception that is not caught: the try block stops, no except clause matches, else is skipped, finally runs, and then the exception propagates to the caller.

Why All Four Clauses Exist

Each clause has a distinct purpose that cannot be replicated by the others. try isolates risky code. except handles known failure modes. else makes the success path explicit — code in else is guaranteed not to have been reached via an exception, which is important for logic that must only run on clean success. finally guarantees cleanup regardless of outcome. Understanding when to use else vs finally is the key to writing readable, correct exception handling: finally is for cleanup; else is for success-path logic that does not belong in the try block.

> **Note:** Do not put code in the try block that does not need to be there. A common mistake is writing a large try block that wraps unrelated operations together. If only the file open can fail with FileNotFoundError, only the open() call should be in the try block. Code that cannot raise the exceptions you are catching should live outside the try, making the exception scope as narrow as possible.

Example 1 — Introduction

The complete try/except/else/finally structure, showing which clause runs in each scenario.

```
def read_score(filepath):
    """Demonstrate all four clauses in one function."""
    try:
        with open(filepath, "r", encoding="utf-8") as f:
            raw = f.readline().strip()
            score = int(raw)          # ValueError if raw is not numeric
```

```
    except FileNotFoundError:
        print(f"  except: file not found — {filepath!r}")
        return None
    except ValueError:
        print(f"  except: invalid score value — {raw!r}")
        return None
    else:
        # Only reached when try completed without exception
        print(f"  else:   score loaded successfully — {score}")
        return score
    finally:
        # Always reached — even after return in else or except
        print("  finally: cleanup always runs")

print("--- File exists with valid score ---")
read_score("valid_score.txt")   # contains "88"
print()
print("--- File exists with invalid score ---")
read_score("bad_score.txt")     # contains "N/A"
print()
print("--- File does not exist ---")
read_score("missing.txt")
```

Output:

```
--- File exists with valid score ---
  else:   score loaded successfully — 88
  finally: cleanup always runs

--- File exists with invalid score ---
  except: invalid score value — 'N/A'
  finally: cleanup always runs

--- File does not exist ---
  except: file not found — 'missing.txt'
  finally: cleanup always runs
```

Example 2 — Variation

Showing that finally runs even after a return statement in the else clause, and even when no except clause matches (uncaught exception).

```
def divide_from_file(filepath):
    result = None
    try:
        with open(filepath, "r", encoding="utf-8") as f:
            a, b = (int(x) for x in f.read().split())
            result = a / b          # ZeroDivisionError if b == 0
    except FileNotFoundError:
        print("  except: file not found")
    except ValueError:
        print("  except: invalid numbers in file")
    # Note: ZeroDivisionError is NOT caught here — it will propagate
    else:
        print(f"  else:   {a} / {b} = {result:.4f}")
        return result
    finally:
        print("  finally: always executes")

print("--- Valid file: 10 4 ---")
divide_from_file("nums_valid.txt")
print()
print("--- ZeroDivisionError (not caught) ---")
try:
    divide_from_file("nums_zero.txt")  # contains "10 0"
except ZeroDivisionError:
    print("  outer except: caught ZeroDivisionError")
```

Output:

```
--- Valid file: 10 4 ---
```

```
  else:   10 / 4 = 2.5000
  finally: always executes

--- ZeroDivisionError (not caught) ---
  finally: always executes
  outer except: caught ZeroDivisionError
```

Example 3 — Real-world application

A database-style transaction function that uses all four clauses: try to run the operation, except to rollback on failure, else to commit on success, finally to release the connection.

```
# Simulate a record-update operation with transaction semantics

class FakeDB:
    """Minimal stand-in for a database connection."""
    def __init__(self):
        self.data = {"10042": {"name": "Anika Patel", "score": 88}}
        self._committed = False
    def update(self, sid, score):
        if score < 0 or score > 100:
            raise ValueError(f"Score {score} out of range 0-100")
        self.data[sid]["score"] = score
    def commit(self):   self._committed = True
    def rollback(self): self.data["10042"]["score"] = 88
    def close(self):    print("  finally: connection closed")

def update_score(db, student_id, new_score):
    try:
        db.update(student_id, new_score)
    except ValueError as e:
        db.rollback()
        print(f"  except: rollback — {e}")
    except KeyError:
        print(f"  except: student {student_id!r} not found")
    else:
        db.commit()
        print(f"  else:   committed score={new_score} for {student_id}")
    finally:
        db.close()

db = FakeDB()
print("--- Valid update ---")
update_score(db, "10042", 95)
print()
print("--- Invalid score ---")
update_score(db, "10042", 150)
print()
print("--- Unknown student ---")
update_score(db, "99999", 80)
```

Output:

```
--- Valid update ---
  else:   committed score=95 for 10042
  finally: connection closed

--- Invalid score ---
  except: rollback — Score 150 out of range 0-100
  finally: connection closed

--- Unknown student ---
  except: student '99999' not found
  finally: connection closed
```

The transaction pattern — commit in else, rollback in except, release in finally — is the textbook reason the else clause exists. Without else, the commit would have to go inside the try block after the operation, which makes the code misleadingly suggest the commit itself might raise a handled exception.

7.2 Catching Specific Exception Types

Every except clause should name the most specific exception type that accurately describes what it is handling. Catching a broad type — such as Exception — when you only intend to handle one specific failure hides unexpected errors that deserve to be seen. The principle is: catch exactly what you can handle, and let everything else propagate.

Python's built-in exception hierarchy is a tree. At the root is BaseException. Below it are the handful of system-level exceptions (SystemExit, KeyboardInterrupt, GeneratorExit) and Exception, which is the parent of everything raised by normal program errors. Under Exception sit the common types you have already seen: ValueError, TypeError, OSError (and its children FileNotFoundError, PermissionError, IsADirectoryError), IndexError, KeyError, AttributeError, and many more. Catching a parent type catches all its children: catching OSError catches FileNotFoundError; catching Exception catches nearly everything.

The Exception Object

The "as e" syntax in an except clause binds the exception instance to the name e, giving access to its message, arguments, and any custom attributes. For most built-in exceptions, str(e) or repr(e) produces a useful description. The args attribute contains the positional arguments the exception was raised with, and e.__class__.__name__ gives the exception's type name as a string. The exception instance is only accessible within the except block; it is deleted at the end of the block to break reference cycles.

> **Note:** SystemExit, KeyboardInterrupt, and GeneratorExit are direct children of BaseException, not Exception. This means "except Exception:" does not catch them — which is correct. KeyboardInterrupt (Ctrl-C) should propagate so the user can always stop a program. Never write "except BaseException:" unless you specifically intend to catch these system-level signals, and always re-raise them immediately.

Example 1 — Introduction

Catching specific exception types with informative messages for each; using "as e" to inspect the exception object.

```
def load_student(data, student_id):
    """Access a student record by ID; catch specific failure modes."""
    try:
        record = data[student_id]       # KeyError if ID absent
        name   = record["name"]         # KeyError if key absent
        score  = int(record["score"])   # ValueError if not numeric
        rank   = 100 // (100 - score)   # ZeroDivisionError if score == 100
    except KeyError as e:
        print(f"  KeyError:          missing key {e}")
        return None
    except ValueError as e:
        print(f"  ValueError:        {e}")
        return None
    except ZeroDivisionError:
        print(f"  ZeroDivisionError: score is exactly 100 — rank undefined")
        return None
    else:
        return {"name": name, "score": score, "rank": rank}

data = {
    "10042": {"name": "Anika Patel", "score": "88"},
    "10043": {"name": "Liam Torres"},                # missing score
    "10044": {"name": "Priya Nair",  "score": "N/A"},  # bad score
    "10045": {"name": "Sam Wong",    "score": "100"},   # causes ZeroDivision
}

for sid in ["10042", "10043", "10044", "10045", "99999"]:
    result = load_student(data, sid)
```

```
    if result:
        print(f"  {sid}: {result}")
```

Output:

```
  10042: {'name': 'Anika Patel', 'score': 88, 'rank': 8}
  KeyError:          missing key 'score'
  ValueError:        invalid literal for int() with base 10: 'N/A'
  ZeroDivisionError: score is exactly 100 — rank undefined
  KeyError:          missing key '99999'
```

Example 2 — Variation

Using the exception hierarchy: catching OSError catches all its subclasses; inspecting e.__class__.__name__ to identify which subclass was actually raised.

```
import os

def probe_file(path):
    """Attempt to read path; report which OSError subclass was raised."""
    try:
        with open(path, "r", encoding="utf-8") as f:
            content = f.read()
    except OSError as e:
        # One handler catches FileNotFoundError, PermissionError,
        # IsADirectoryError, and any other OSError subclass
        print(f"  {e.__class__.__name__} (errno {e.errno}): {e.strerror}")
        return None
    else:
        return content

# Create test conditions
with open("readable.txt", "w") as f: f.write("hello")
os.makedirs("a_directory", exist_ok=True)

for path in ["readable.txt", "missing.txt", "a_directory"]:
    result = probe_file(path)
    if result is not None:
        print(f"  {path!r}: read {len(result)} char(s)")

# Confirm hierarchy: FileNotFoundError IS an OSError
print(f"\nFileNotFoundError is subclass of OSError:
{issubclass(FileNotFoundError, OSError)}")
```

Output:

```
  'readable.txt': read 5 char(s)
  FileNotFoundError (errno 2): No such file or directory
  IsADirectoryError (errno 21): Is a directory

FileNotFoundError is subclass of OSError: True
```

Example 3 — Real-world application

A CSV data loader that catches different exceptions at different granularities: OSError for file-level failures, ValueError and IndexError for row-level failures.

```
# two_level_handler.py — file-level vs row-level exception handling
import csv

def load_grades(filepath):
    """
    Two-level exception handling:
      Outer: catches file-access errors (OSError)
      Inner: catches per-row data errors (ValueError, IndexError)
    """
    records, row_errors = [], []
    try:
        with open(filepath, "r", encoding="utf-8", newline="") as f:
            reader = csv.reader(f)
```

```
            next(reader)   # skip header
            for lineno, row in enumerate(reader, 2):
                try:
                    sid, name, score = row[0], row[1], int(row[2])
                    records.append({"id": sid, "name": name, "score": score})
                except IndexError:
                    row_errors.append(f"Line {lineno}: too few columns")
                except ValueError as e:
                    row_errors.append(f"Line {lineno}: {e}")
    except FileNotFoundError:
        return None, [f"File not found: {filepath!r}"]
    except PermissionError:
        return None, [f"Permission denied: {filepath!r}"]
    return records, row_errors

records, errors = load_grades("grades.csv")
if records is None:
    print("Fatal error:", errors)
else:
    print(f"Loaded {len(records)} record(s).")
    for r in records:
        print(f"  {r['id']}  {r['name']:<20}  {r['score']}")
    if errors:
        print(f"Row warnings: {errors}")
```

Output:

```
Loaded 3 record(s).
  10042  Anika Patel          88
  10043  Liam Torres          72
  10044  Priya Nair           95
Row warnings: ["Line 5: invalid literal for int() with base 10: 'N/A'"]
```

The two-level structure in Example 7.2.3 — outer file handler, inner row handler — is the correct pattern for any batch processing that must distinguish between “cannot open the file at all” (a fatal error) and “one row is malformed” (a recoverable error). They are different failure modes and deserve different responses.

7.3 Catching Multiple Exception Types

When several exception types all deserve the same response, they can be caught in a single except clause using a parenthesised tuple: except (TypeError, ValueError) as e:. This is preferable to either a separate handler for each type that contains identical code, or catching a broad parent type that would also catch unrelated exceptions. The tuple form catches any of the listed types and binds the matched instance to e.

Ordering matters when multiple except clauses handle different types. Python evaluates them from top to bottom and stops at the first match. If a parent type is listed before a child type, the parent clause will always catch the child’s exceptions and the child clause will never execute. The rule is straightforward: always put more specific types before more general types. If you accidentally place OSError before FileNotFoundError in a chain, the FileNotFoundError handler will never run.

Grouping vs Ordering

The choice between grouping exceptions in a single tuple clause and ordering them in separate clauses comes down to whether you want different behaviour for each type. If the response to both TypeError and ValueError is identical — log the message and skip the record — group them. If FileNotFoundError should produce a different message than PermissionError, use separate clauses. Each except clause can have its own "as e" binding; the tuple form binds whichever type was actually raised.

> **Note:** The syntax "except TypeError, ValueError:" (without parentheses) is a Python 2 syntax that means something different — it catches TypeError and binds the exception to the name ValueError. It is a silent bug in Python 2 and a SyntaxError in Python 3. Always use parentheses for multi-type catches: "except

(TypeError, ValueError):".

Example 1 — Introduction

Grouping two exception types in a single except clause when the response is identical.

```
def parse_record(raw):
    """Parse a "name:score" string. Group TypeError and ValueError."""
    try:
        name, _, score_str = raw.partition(":")
        score = int(score_str.strip())  # ValueError if not numeric
        if not name.strip():
            raise ValueError("name is empty")
        return name.strip(), score
    except (ValueError, AttributeError) as e:
        # ValueError: bad score or empty name
        # AttributeError: raw is not a string (e.g. None)
        print(f"  Skipped {raw!r}: {type(e).__name__}: {e}")
        return None

inputs = [
    "Anika Patel:88",
    "Liam Torres:N/A",  # ValueError
    ":72",              # ValueError (empty name)
    None,               # AttributeError (not a string)
    "Priya Nair:95",
]

results = [r for raw in inputs if (r := parse_record(raw))]
print("Valid records:", results)
```

Output:

```
  Skipped 'Liam Torres:N/A': ValueError: invalid literal for int() with base
10: 'N/A'
  Skipped ':72': ValueError: name is empty
  Skipped None: AttributeError: 'NoneType' object has no attribute 'partition'
Valid records: [('Anika Patel', 88), ('Priya Nair', 95)]
```

Example 2 — Variation

Demonstrating that more-specific types must come before less-specific: OSError before FileNotFoundError causes the specific handler to be unreachable.

```
# ── WRONG order: general before specific ────────────────────────
def probe_wrong(path):
    try:
        open(path)
    except OSError:
        print("  OSError caught (FileNotFoundError handler never reached)")
    except FileNotFoundError:
        print("  FileNotFoundError caught (UNREACHABLE)")

# ── CORRECT order: specific before general ──────────────────────
def probe_correct(path):
    try:
        open(path)
    except FileNotFoundError as e:
        print(f"  FileNotFoundError: {e.strerror}")
    except PermissionError as e:
        print(f"  PermissionError:   {e.strerror}")
    except OSError as e:
        print(f"  Other OSError:     {e}")

print("Wrong order:")
probe_wrong("missing.txt")
print()
print("Correct order:")
probe_correct("missing.txt")
```

Output:
```
Wrong order:
  OSError caught (FileNotFoundError handler never reached)

Correct order:
  FileNotFoundError: No such file or directory
```

Example 3 — Real-world application

A multi-format file loader that tries JSON then CSV parsing, grouping their parse errors and reporting the format that succeeded.

```
# multi_format_loader.py — attempt JSON, fall back to CSV
import json, csv, io

def load_auto(text, source_name="data"):",
    """
    Try to parse text as JSON; if that fails, try CSV.
    Groups json.JSONDecodeError and ValueError as parse failures.
    Returns (format_name, parsed_data) or raises ValueError.
    """
    # ── Attempt JSON ──────────────────────────────────────────
    try:
        data = json.loads(text)
        return "JSON", data
    except (json.JSONDecodeError, ValueError):
        pass   # not JSON — try CSV next

    # ── Attempt CSV ───────────────────────────────────────────
    try:
        reader = csv.DictReader(io.StringIO(text))
        rows   = list(reader)
        if not rows:
            raise ValueError("CSV produced no rows")
        return "CSV", rows
    except (csv.Error, ValueError) as e:
        raise ValueError(f"Could not parse {source_name!r} as JSON or CSV:
{e}")

# Test with JSON input
json_text = '[{"id":"10042","name":"Anika","score":88}]'
fmt, data = load_auto(json_text, "students.json")
print(f"Parsed as {fmt}: {data}")

# Test with CSV input
csv_text = "id,name,score\n10042,Anika,88\n10043,Liam,72"
fmt, data = load_auto(csv_text, "students.csv")
print(f"Parsed as {fmt}: {data}")
```

Output:
```
Parsed as JSON: [{'id': '10042', 'name': 'Anika', 'score': 88}]
Parsed as CSV: [{'id': '10042', 'name': 'Anika', 'score': '88'}, {'id':
'10043', 'name': 'Liam', 'score': '72'}]
```

The auto-detect loader illustrates how grouping parse-error types makes fall-through logic clean. Grouping json.JSONDecodeError and ValueError in the first attempt lets the function move on to CSV without committing to a specific error message, then groups csv.Error and ValueError in the second attempt to produce a unified "could not parse" message if both formats fail.

7.4 The else Clause: Code That Runs Only on Success

The else clause of a try statement runs if and only if the try block completed without raising any exception. This is semantically different from placing the same code at the end of the try block: code inside try is protected by the except clauses, while code in else is not. If code in else raises an exception, it propagates without being caught by the except clauses above it.

The principal use of else is to express the success path separately from the error path. A try block should contain only the operations that can raise the exceptions you are catching. The work that follows — processing the successfully obtained value, logging success, returning the result — belongs in else, because it should only run on clean success and should not be silently swallowed if it itself raises an unexpected exception.

else vs Expanding the try Block

Consider opening a file and then processing its contents. If both the open() and the processing code are inside the try block, and the processing raises an unexpected TypeError, the except FileNotFoundError clause will not catch it and the exception will propagate — which is correct, but potentially confusing to a reader who sees a FileNotFoundError handler next to processing code. Using else makes the intent explicit: try contains only the risky open(); else contains the processing that runs only if the open succeeded.

> **Note:** The else clause is not commonly known among programmers coming from other languages. It is one of Python's more distinctive features. In code reviews, its presence signals that the author understands the precise execution semantics of try/except and is being deliberate about what belongs in each clause.

Example 1 — Introduction

The else clause separating the risky open() from the success-path processing.

```
def count_lines(filepath):
    """Open is in try; line-counting logic is in else."""
    try:
        f = open(filepath, "r", encoding="utf-8")
    except FileNotFoundError:
        print(f"  File not found: {filepath!r}")
        return -1
    else:
        # Only reached when open() succeeded
        with f:
            count = sum(1 for _ in f)
        print(f"  {filepath!r}: {count} line(s)")
        return count

count_lines("grades.csv")   # exists
count_lines("missing.txt")  # does not exist
```

Output:

```
  'grades.csv': 5 line(s)
  File not found: 'missing.txt'
```

Example 2 — Variation

else catching an unexpected exception that should not be swallowed: the TypeError from processing propagates even though a FileNotFoundError handler is present.

```
def first_score(filepath):
    """
    If the score-parsing logic were inside try, a bug there could be
    masked by the FileNotFoundError handler. In else it propagates cleanly.
    """
    try:
        f = open(filepath, "r", encoding="utf-8")
    except FileNotFoundError:
        print("  File not found")
        return None
    else:
        with f:
            line = f.readline().strip()
```

```
        # Deliberate bug: int() of a list (TypeError)
        # This propagates — NOT swallowed by FileNotFoundError handler
        score = int([line])    # TypeError!
        return score

try:
    first_score("grades.csv")
except TypeError as e:
    print(f"  TypeError propagated from else clause: {e}")
```

Output:

```
  TypeError propagated from else clause: int() argument must be a string, a
bytes-like object or a real number, not 'list'
```

Example 3 — Real-world application

A JSON config loader where else handles all the post-load processing: validation, merging defaults, and reporting — none of which should be swallowed by the JSON parse-error handler.

```
# config_with_else.py — clear separation of load vs process
import json

DEFAULTS = {"theme": "light", "debug": False, "max_rows": 100}

def load_config(filepath):
    try:
        with open(filepath, "r", encoding="utf-8") as f:
            raw = json.load(f)
    except FileNotFoundError:
        print(f"  Config {filepath!r} not found — using defaults")
        return DEFAULTS.copy()
    except json.JSONDecodeError as e:
        print(f"  Config parse error: {e} — using defaults")
        return DEFAULTS.copy()
    else:
        # Post-load work: only runs when json.load() succeeded
        # Any bug here (KeyError, TypeError) propagates — correct
        merged = {**DEFAULTS, **raw}
        unknown = set(raw) - set(DEFAULTS)
        if unknown:
            print(f"  Warning: unknown config key(s): {unknown}")
        print(f"  Config loaded from {filepath!r}")
        return merged

cfg = load_config("settings.json")
print("  theme:", cfg["theme"])
print("  debug:", cfg["debug"])
```

Output:

```
  Config loaded from 'settings.json'
  theme: dark
  debug: True
```

The else clause is most valuable in exactly this pattern: a narrow try containing only the I/O operation, and an else containing all the logic that depends on that operation having succeeded. It makes the error-handling scope explicit and prevents success-path bugs from being silently masked.

7.5 The finally Clause: Code That Always Runs

The finally clause guarantees execution regardless of how the try block exits: normal completion, exception caught by an except clause, exception not caught and propagating to the caller, or exit via return, break, or continue. This makes it the correct and only place for cleanup that must happen unconditionally: closing files, releasing locks, deleting temporary files, restoring global state.

In everyday file-handling code, the with statement (Chapter 4) performs the role of finally automatically. The cases where explicit finally remains valuable are those where the context manager protocol is unavailable or insufficient: a resource that does not implement __exit__, cleanup logic that spans multiple resources opened at different points, or teardown code in a test or benchmark function that must run even if an assertion fails.

finally and return

A return statement in a try block does not skip the finally clause — finally runs before the function returns. More subtly, a return statement inside finally overrides any return value from the try or except block: if try returns 42 and finally returns 99, the function returns 99. This is rarely intentional and produces confusing behaviour; return statements inside finally should be avoided. The finally clause should perform only cleanup, not produce a value.

> **Note:** A return (or raise) inside finally silently swallows any exception that was propagating at the time. If try raises ValueError and finally contains return, the ValueError disappears and the caller receives the return value instead. This is almost never correct. Keep finally clauses free of return and raise unless you explicitly intend to suppress the in-flight exception.

Example 1 — Introduction

finally running after an exception, after a clean return, and after a return from except — all three cases.

```
def demo_finally(mode):
    print(f"[{mode}]")
    try:
        if mode == "exception":
            raise ValueError("deliberate")
        elif mode == "return":
            return "from try"
        else:
            x = 1 / 0   # ZeroDivisionError (not caught)
    except ValueError:
        print("  except: ValueError caught")
        return "from except"
    finally:
        print("  finally: always runs")

print(demo_finally("exception"))
print()
print(demo_finally("return"))
print()
try:
    demo_finally("uncaught")
except ZeroDivisionError:
    print("  outer: ZeroDivisionError caught after finally")
```

Output:

```
[exception]
  except: ValueError caught
  finally: always runs
from except

[return]
  finally: always runs
from try

[uncaught]
  finally: always runs
  outer: ZeroDivisionError caught after finally
```

Example 2 — Variation

Using finally to clean up a temporary file regardless of whether the processing step succeeded or failed.

```
import os, tempfile

def process_with_tempfile(data, fail=False):
    """Write data to a temp file; process it; always delete the temp file."""
    fd, tmp_path = tempfile.mkstemp(suffix=".txt")
    print(f"  Temp file created: {tmp_path}")
    try:
        with os.fdopen(fd, "w", encoding="utf-8") as f:
            f.write(data)
        if fail:
            raise RuntimeError("simulated processing failure")
        # Simulate processing
        lines = open(tmp_path, encoding="utf-8").readlines()
        print(f"  Processed {len(lines)} line(s)")
    except RuntimeError as e:
        print(f"  except: {e}")
    finally:
        if os.path.exists(tmp_path):
            os.remove(tmp_path)
            print(f"  finally: temp file deleted")

print("--- Success path ---")
process_with_tempfile("line1\nline2\nline3")
print()
print("--- Failure path ---")
process_with_tempfile("line1\nline2", fail=True)
```

Output:

```
--- Success path ---
  Temp file created: /tmp/tmpXXXXXX.txt
  Processed 3 line(s)
  finally: temp file deleted

--- Failure path ---
  Temp file created: /tmp/tmpYYYYYY.txt
  except: simulated processing failure
  finally: temp file deleted
```

Example 3 — Real-world application

A benchmarking function that uses finally to restore global state even if the benchmarked function raises; and to record elapsed time even on failure.

```
# benchmark.py — measure elapsed time; restore state; record result
import time

RESULTS = []

def benchmark(label, func, *args):",
    """
    Call func(*args), record elapsed time and outcome in RESULTS.
    finally guarantees timing and recording even when func raises.
    """
    start   = time.perf_counter()
    outcome = "error"
    result  = None
    try:
        result  = func(*args)
        outcome = "ok"
    except Exception as e:
        print(f"  [{label}] raised {type(e).__name__}: {e}")
    finally:
        elapsed = (time.perf_counter() - start) * 1000
        RESULTS.append({"label": label, "outcome": outcome,
                        "ms": round(elapsed, 2)})
    return result

def sum_file(filepath):
```

```
    with open(filepath, "r", encoding="utf-8") as f:
        return sum(int(line) for line in f)

benchmark("sum grades.csv",   sum_file, "grades.csv")
benchmark("sum missing.txt",  sum_file, "missing.txt")   # raises
benchmark("sum invalid.txt",  sum_file, "invalid.txt")   # raises

print("\nBenchmark results:")
for r in RESULTS:
    print(f"  {r['label']:<22} {r['outcome']} {r['ms']:.2f} ms")
```

Output:

```
  [sum missing.txt] raised FileNotFoundError: [Errno 2] No such file or
directory
  [sum invalid.txt] raised ValueError: invalid literal for int() with base 10:
'Name'

Benchmark results:
  sum grades.csv         ok     0.42 ms
  sum missing.txt        error  0.18 ms
  sum invalid.txt        error  0.31 ms
```

The benchmark function demonstrates the canonical finally use: record timing and outcome regardless of what happened in the try block. Without finally, a raised exception would skip the RESULTS.append() call and leave the timing data unrecorded.

7.6 Exception Chaining: raise ... from ...

When an exception is raised inside an except block, Python automatically records the original exception as the context of the new one. This implicit chaining produces a traceback that shows "During handling of the above exception, another exception occurred:" followed by both tracebacks. This is useful for debugging but can be confusing when the original exception is an implementation detail that the caller should not see.

The raise...from syntax gives explicit control over exception chaining. Writing "raise NewException(...) from original_exception" chains them explicitly, showing "The above exception was the direct cause of the following exception:" in the traceback. Writing "raise NewException(...) from None" suppresses the chain entirely, so the traceback shows only the new exception — useful when you want to present a clean high-level error without exposing low-level details.

When to Use Explicit Chaining

Explicit chaining — raise X from e — is the correct pattern when you want to wrap a low-level exception in a higher-level one that has more meaning for the caller. For example, a database access layer might catch OperationalError and raise a ConnectionError from it, so that callers only need to handle ConnectionError without knowing which underlying database library was used. The original exception is still accessible via __cause__ if needed for debugging.

Suppressing the Chain

raise X from None is appropriate when the original exception is a normal control flow signal that happens to look like an error: for example, catching StopIteration inside a generator to convert it to a simpler return, or catching a LookupError during a conditional conversion where the miss is expected. Suppressing the chain in these cases prevents the traceback from misleadingly suggesting an error occurred.

> **Note:** The chained exception is accessible on the new exception via e.__cause__ (for explicit raise X from e) or e.__context__ (for implicit chaining). Both preserve the full original traceback. When writing exception-handling code in a library, always consider whether the original exception should be exposed to the caller or suppressed.

Example 1 — Introduction

Implicit chaining (automatic), explicit chaining with raise...from, and suppression with raise...from None.

```
def implicit_chain():
    try:
        int("not a number")
    except ValueError:
        raise RuntimeError("conversion failed")  # implicit chain

def explicit_chain():
    try:
        int("not a number")
    except ValueError as e:
        raise RuntimeError("conversion failed") from e  # explicit chain

def suppressed_chain():
    try:
        int("not a number")
    except ValueError:
        raise RuntimeError("conversion failed") from None  # suppressed

for fn in [implicit_chain, explicit_chain, suppressed_chain]:
    try:
        fn()
    except RuntimeError as e:
        print(f"{fn.__name__}:")
        print(f"  __cause__:   {e.__cause__}")
        print(f"  __context__: {e.__context__}")
        print()
```

Output:

```
implicit_chain:
  __cause__:   None
  __context__: invalid literal for int() with base 10: 'not a number'

explicit_chain:
  __cause__:   invalid literal for int() with base 10: 'not a number'
  __context__: invalid literal for int() with base 10: 'not a number'

suppressed_chain:
  __cause__:   None
  __context__: None
```

Example 2 — Variation

A library function that wraps a low-level OSError in a high-level DataAccessError using explicit chaining.

```
class DataAccessError(Exception):
    """High-level error for the data access layer."""
    pass

def load_records(filepath):
    """
    Wraps OS-level errors in a DataAccessError so callers only
    need to handle one exception type from this module.
    The original OSError is preserved as __cause__ for debugging.
    """
    try:
        with open(filepath, "r", encoding="utf-8") as f:
            return f.read()
    except OSError as e:
        raise DataAccessError(
            f"Cannot load records from {filepath!r}"
        ) from e    # explicit chain: original OSError accessible via __cause__

try:
    load_records("missing.json")
except DataAccessError as e:
```

```
    print(f"Caught: {e}")
    print(f"Cause:  {e.__cause__}")
    print(f"Cause type: {type(e.__cause__).__name__}")
```

Output:

```
Caught: Cannot load records from 'missing.json'
Cause:  [Errno 2] No such file or directory: 'missing.json'
Cause type: FileNotFoundError
```

Example 3 — Real-world application

A data pipeline that re-raises from None at each stage boundary, so the caller sees a clean pipeline error rather than deep internal tracebacks.

```
# pipeline.py — stage-level exception wrapping with from None

class PipelineError(Exception):
    def __init__(self, stage, message):
        self.stage = stage
        super().__init__(f"[{stage}] {message}")

def stage_load(filepath):
    try:
        with open(filepath, "r", encoding="utf-8") as f:
            return f.read()
    except OSError as e:
        raise PipelineError("LOAD", f"Cannot read {filepath!r}") from None

def stage_parse(raw):
    import json
    try:
        return json.loads(raw)
    except json.JSONDecodeError as e:
        raise PipelineError("PARSE", f"Invalid JSON at line {e.lineno}") from
None

def stage_validate(data):
    if not isinstance(data, list):
        raise PipelineError("VALIDATE", "Expected a JSON array") from None
    return data

def run_pipeline(filepath):
    raw  = stage_load(filepath)
    data = stage_parse(raw)
    return stage_validate(data)

for path in ["valid_data.json", "missing.json", "bad_json.json"]:",
    try:
        records = run_pipeline(path)
        print(f"  OK: {len(records)} record(s) from {path!r}")
    except PipelineError as e:
        print(f"  Error at stage {e.stage}: {e}")
```

Output:

```
  OK: 3 record(s) from 'valid_data.json'
  Error at stage LOAD: [LOAD] Cannot read 'missing.json'
  Error at stage PARSE: [PARSE] Invalid JSON at line 2
```

The pipeline pattern with from None presents the caller with clean, stage-labelled errors while hiding the implementation detail of which JSON library, OS, or internal function was involved. The trade-off is that debugging is slightly harder when the original exception is suppressed; in development, temporarily changing from None to from e reveals the underlying cause.

7.7 Best Practices: What to Catch and What to Propagate

Exception handling is easy to write badly. The two most common mistakes are catching too broadly (masking bugs) and catching too narrowly (letting recoverable errors crash the program). The guiding principle is: catch exceptions at the level of abstraction where you can do something useful with them. If you can recover, report clearly, or provide a fallback, catch there. If you cannot, let the exception propagate to a caller who can.

What Not to Catch

Never write "except:" or "except Exception:" as a blanket catch unless you are writing a top-level error handler for a long-running process (a server, a daemon, a GUI event loop). These forms swallow programming errors — NameError, AttributeError, TypeError from your own bugs — and make incorrect programs appear to work. They also swallow KeyboardInterrupt (for bare except:), making programs impossible to stop. If you genuinely need a broad catch, log the exception before swallowing it, and always re-raise SystemExit and KeyboardInterrupt.

Catch, Log, Re-raise

A useful pattern for long-running or server code is to catch broadly enough to prevent crashes, log the exception with full traceback, and then either re-raise or continue depending on the severity. The logging module's logging.exception(msg) method records the current exception with its full traceback at ERROR level. This pattern preserves the benefit of broad catching (no crash) while retaining the debugging information that a bare except would destroy.

Prefer EAFP for Resources, LBYL for Validation

Recall the LBYL vs EAFP discussion from Chapter 1. EAFP (try/except) is preferred for resource access because it avoids race conditions and is more idiomatic Python. LBYL (if checks) is preferred for validating data already in memory, because it is cleaner and produces better messages. The two are not mutually exclusive: use try/except around file opens, network calls, and database queries; use if/isinstance/hasattr for validating inputs before operating on them.

> **Note:** When logging exception details, use logging.exception() or logging.error(..., exc_info=True). Both record the full traceback. Printing str(e) only records the exception message without the traceback, which is often insufficient for debugging. In scripts without the logging module, use traceback.format_exc() to get the full traceback as a string.

Example 1 — Introduction

Contrasting a naive broad catch (masks bugs) with a narrow specific catch (correct) and a logged broad catch with re-raise (acceptable for servers).

```
import traceback

records = [
    {"name": "Anika Patel",  "score": "88"},
    {"name": "Liam Torres",  "score": "N/A"},
    {"name": None,           "score": "72"},   # None name — a bug
]

# —— BAD: bare except swallows the AttributeError bug ————————————
print("Bad (bare except):")
for r in records:
    try:
        upper_name = r["name"].upper()   # AttributeError if name is None
        score      = int(r["score"])
        print(f"  {upper_name}: {score}")
    except:
        pass   # silently swallows EVERYTHING including the bug
```

```
# ── GOOD: specific catch; bug propagates ──────────────────────
print("\nGood (specific catch):")
for r in records:
    try:
        score = int(r["score"])
        print(f"  {r['name']}: {score}")
    except ValueError:
        print(f"  Skipped: bad score {r['score']!r}")
    # AttributeError from None name will propagate — correctly
```

Output:

```
Bad (bare except):
  ANIKA PATEL: 88

Good (specific catch):
  Anika Patel: 88
  Skipped: bad score 'N/A'
```

Example 2 — Variation

A server-style top-level handler: catch broadly, log with full traceback, re-raise critical signals, continue for application errors.

```
import traceback

ERROR_LOG = []  # stand-in for a proper logging system

def safe_execute(task_name, func, *args):
    """
    Top-level task runner for long-running processes.
    - Re-raises SystemExit and KeyboardInterrupt immediately.
    - Logs and continues for all other exceptions.
    """
    try:
        return func(*args)
    except (SystemExit, KeyboardInterrupt):
        raise   # always propagate system signals
    except Exception as e:
        tb = traceback.format_exc()
        ERROR_LOG.append({"task": task_name, "error": str(e), "tb": tb})
        print(f"  [{task_name}] ERROR: {type(e).__name__}: {e}")
        return None

def good_task(x):  return x * 2
def bad_task(x):   return x / 0       # ZeroDivisionError
def buggy_task(x): return x.upper()   # AttributeError (x is int)

results = []
for name, fn, arg in [("good",  good_task,  5),
                      ("bad",   bad_task,   5),
                      ("buggy", buggy_task, 5)]:
    r = safe_execute(name, fn, arg)
    if r is not None:
        results.append(r)

print(f"Results: {results}")
print(f"Errors logged: {len(ERROR_LOG)}")
for e in ERROR_LOG:
    print(f"  Task {e['task']!r}: {e['error']}")
```

Output:

```
  [bad] ERROR: ZeroDivisionError: division by zero
  [buggy] ERROR: AttributeError: 'int' object has no attribute 'upper'
Results: [10]
Errors logged: 2
  Task 'bad': division by zero
  Task 'buggy': 'int' object has no attribute 'upper'
```

Example 3 — Real-world application

A production-quality file processing loop combining all best practices: narrow catches, logged errors, re-raised signals, and a final summary.

```
# robust_processor.py — production-quality file batch with all best practices
import json, traceback

FILES = ["records_a.json", "records_b.json", "records_c.json",
         "missing.json",   "corrupt.json"]

SUMMARY = {"processed": 0, "skipped": 0, "errors": []}

def process_file(filepath):
    """Load and validate a JSON records file."""
    with open(filepath, "r", encoding="utf-8") as f:   # OSError propagates
        data = json.load(f)                             # JSONDecodeError
propagates
    if not isinstance(data, list):
        raise ValueError(f"Expected a list, got {type(data).__name__}")
    return [r for r in data if isinstance(r, dict)]

for path in FILES:
    try:
        records = process_file(path)
        SUMMARY["processed"] += len(records)
        print(f"  OK   {path}: {len(records)} record(s)")
    except (SystemExit, KeyboardInterrupt):
        raise                           # never suppress these
    except FileNotFoundError:
        SUMMARY["skipped"] += 1
        print(f"  SKIP {path}: not found")
    except json.JSONDecodeError as e:
        SUMMARY["errors"].append({"file": path, "error": str(e)})
        print(f"  ERR  {path}: JSON error at line {e.lineno}")
    except Exception as e:
        SUMMARY["errors"].append({"file": path, "error": str(e),
                                  "tb": traceback.format_exc()})
        print(f"  ERR  {path}: {type(e).__name__}: {e}")

print(f"\nSummary: {SUMMARY['processed']} records, "
      f"{SUMMARY['skipped']} skipped, {len(SUMMARY['errors'])} error(s)")
```

Output:

```
  OK   records_a.json: 4 record(s)
  OK   records_b.json: 3 record(s)
  OK   records_c.json: 5 record(s)
  SKIP missing.json: not found
  ERR  corrupt.json: JSON error at line 3

Summary: 12 records, 1 skipped, 1 error(s)
```

The robust_processor pattern — narrow catches ordered specific to general, explicit re-raise for system signals, separate handling for expected vs unexpected failures, full traceback stored for unexpected errors — represents the mature form of exception handling that production code requires. Chapters 8 and 11 extend this further with custom exception hierarchies and logging infrastructure.

Chapter 7 Summary

- The four clauses have distinct semantics: try contains the risky code; except handles named failure modes; else runs only when try completed without exception (not swallowed by any except clause); finally always runs — after normal completion, after a caught exception, after an uncaught exception, and even after a return or break.

- The else clause should contain success-path logic that must only run on clean completion. Placing it in else rather than at the end of try ensures that unexpected exceptions in that code propagate rather than being silently caught by the except clauses above.
- finally is for unconditional cleanup: closing connections, deleting temp files, restoring global state, recording timing. A return inside finally overrides any return from try or except and silently swallows in-flight exceptions — keep finally free of return and raise.
- Always catch the most specific applicable type. Put more-specific except clauses before less-specific; a parent type listed first makes all its child handlers unreachable. Use a tuple to group types that deserve identical handling: "except (TypeError, ValueError) as e:".
- raise X from e chains exceptions explicitly, preserving the original as __cause__. raise X from None suppresses the chain, presenting a clean high-level error. Implicit chaining (raising inside an except block) sets __context__ automatically.
- Never use bare "except:" or "except Exception:" for application logic — it masks programming errors and makes broken programs appear to work. For server-style top-level handlers, always re-raise SystemExit and KeyboardInterrupt, log the full traceback, and continue.
- Two-level exception handling — outer file-level catch, inner row-level catch — is the correct structure for batch processing that must distinguish fatal file-access failures from recoverable per-record data errors.
- EAFP (try/except) is preferred for resource access (files, networks, databases) where conditions can change between a check and an action. LBYL (if/isinstance) is preferred for validating data already in memory. Use logging.exception() or traceback.format_exc() to preserve full stack trace information when logging errors.

Guided Exercises

1. Write a function safe_divide(a, b) using all four clauses: try to perform the division, except ZeroDivisionError to return None with a message, else to return the result and print a success message, and finally to print "operation complete" regardless of outcome. Test with valid inputs, b=0, and non-numeric inputs (which should propagate).

> ***Hint:*** *Only the division a / b should be in try. The return statement and success print go in else. finally prints unconditionally. Do not catch TypeError — let it propagate to show it is a bug.*

2. Write a function load_json_safe(filepath) that uses try/except/else/finally. The try block should only contain the file open and json.load(). The else block should validate that the result is a dict or list and return it. Finally should print whether the file was opened successfully. Handle FileNotFoundError and json.JSONDecodeError separately with different messages.

> ***Hint:*** *Open the file and load with json.load() in try. In else, check isinstance(data, (dict, list)) and raise ValueError if not. In finally, use a flag variable set before try to print the open result.*

3. Rewrite a CSV loader from Chapter 5 to use proper two-level exception handling: an outer try/except for OSError (file-level), and an inner try/except for (ValueError, IndexError) inside the row loop (row-level). Return (records, errors) where errors is a list of strings describing each row problem.

> ***Hint:*** *Outer try wraps the open() and DictReader setup. Inner try wraps the per-row type conversion. Each level catches only what is appropriate for that level. Return (None, error_list) for file-level failures and (records, error_list) for row-level failures.*

4. Demonstrate exception chaining: write a function parse_config(text) that calls json.loads(). If it raises json.JSONDecodeError, raise a ConfigError (a custom Exception subclass) from the original using raise X from e. Show that e.__cause__ on the caught ConfigError contains the original JSONDecodeError.

> ***Hint:*** *Define ConfigError as a simple subclass of Exception. In the except block, raise ConfigError("bad config") from e. Catch ConfigError in the caller and print both str(e) and str(e.__cause__).*

5. Write a top-level task runner run_tasks(task_list) where each task is a callable. Use a broad except Exception after a specific except (SystemExit, KeyboardInterrupt) re-raise. For each Exception caught, store the task name, exception type, and message in a list and continue to the next task. Print a summary at the end.

Hint: *Loop over tasks, call each in a try. First except clause: (SystemExit, KeyboardInterrupt): raise. Second except Exception as e: append {"task": name, "type": type(e).__name__, "msg": str(e)}. Print the list after the loop.*

Challenge Tasks

1. Build a RetryHandler context manager (using @contextmanager) that retries the body of a with block up to N times on a specified exception type. Each retry should wait an increasing delay (1s, 2s, 3s ...). If all retries are exhausted, re-raise the last exception. If the body succeeds, record how many attempts were needed. Demonstrate with a function that fails the first two times and succeeds on the third.

2. Write a function audit_exceptions(func, test_cases) that calls func with each set of arguments in test_cases, catches all exceptions, and produces a structured report mapping each test case to either its return value or the exception type and message that was raised. The report should be returned as a list of dicts and also saved to a JSON file. Use raise...from None when wrapping any exceptions raised during the audit itself.

3. Build a multi-stage data pipeline processor where each stage is a function in a list. Each stage receives the output of the previous. Use a PipelineStageError(Exception) with a stage_name attribute. If a stage raises any exception, wrap it in a PipelineStageError using raise X from e, record the failed stage, and either abort the pipeline or continue with a fallback value depending on a configurable strict mode. At the end, print a detailed report of which stages succeeded, which failed, and what fallback values were used.

CHAPTER 8 Raising and Creating Custom Exceptions

Book 02: File Handling & Exception Management

> *Chapter 7 covered the full try/except/else/finally structure and the principles that govern when to catch and when to propagate. This chapter turns to the other side of exception handling: raising exceptions deliberately, wrapping low-level exceptions in higher-level ones, and defining your own exception classes. Custom exceptions are not a cosmetic feature — they are the mechanism by which a module communicates its failure modes precisely to its callers. By the end of this chapter you will know how to raise with context, design exception hierarchies that callers can catch at the right level of specificity, add attributes that carry diagnostic information, and write validation functions that raise rather than return error codes.*

8.1 raise and Re-raise

The raise statement signals that something has gone wrong. In its simplest form, raise takes an exception instance or class: raise ValueError("score must be 0–100"). If a class is passed without parentheses, Python instantiates it with no arguments. raise on its own — with no argument — re-raises the currently active exception; this is the correct idiom for catching an exception to perform some action (logging, cleanup, audit) and then letting it continue to propagate to the caller.

Re-raising with bare raise preserves the original traceback intact. This is important: if you catch an exception and then raise a new instance of the same type (raise ValueError("same message")), the traceback will point to the re-raise line rather than the original location where the error occurred, making debugging much harder. Bare raise avoids this by keeping the original call stack.

Raising in Validation

Raising exceptions is not only for error recovery — it is the primary mechanism for enforcing preconditions. A function that receives a student score should validate it immediately and raise ValueError if it is out of range, rather than allowing an invalid value to propagate silently into downstream calculations. Raising early with a clear message is the fail-fast principle from Chapter 1 applied at the function level.

> **Note:** raise ValueError vs raise ValueError(): both work, but the form with parentheses is always preferable because it makes the intent explicit and allows a message to be passed. raise ValueError raises the class and lets Python instantiate it with no message; raise ValueError("out of range") raises an instance with a descriptive message that appears in the traceback and in str(e).

Example 1 — Introduction

raise with a message, bare re-raise preserving the traceback, and raise on its own to re-raise after logging.

```
def set_score(score):
    """Raise ValueError immediately if score is out of range."""
    if not isinstance(score, int):
        raise TypeError(f"score must be int, got {type(score).__name__}")
    if not 0 <= score <= 100:
        raise ValueError(f"score {score} is out of range 0-100")
    return score

# —— Basic raise ——————————————————————————————————————————————
for val in [88, 150, "A"]:",
    try:
        result = set_score(val)
        print(f"  OK: {result}")
```

```
    except (ValueError, TypeError) as e:
        print(f"  {type(e).__name__}: {e}")

# — Bare re-raise: preserves original traceback ————————————————
def process_score(score):
    try:
        return set_score(score)
    except ValueError:
        print("  Logging the error before re-raising...")
        raise   # re-raises the original ValueError unchanged


try:
    process_score(-5)
except ValueError as e:
    print(f"  Caught after re-raise: {e}")
```

Output:

```
  OK: 88
  ValueError: score 150 is out of range 0–100
  TypeError: score must be int, got str
  Logging the error before re-raising...
  Caught after re-raise: score -5 is out of range 0–100
```

Example 2 — Variation

Demonstrating that bare raise preserves the original traceback line, while raise ValueError(...) creates a new one pointing to the re-raise site.

```
import traceback

def original_error():
    raise ValueError("original error on this line")  # line A

def bare_reraise():
    try:
        original_error()
    except ValueError:
        raise   # traceback still points to line A

def new_raise():
    try:
        original_error()
    except ValueError:
        raise ValueError("re-raised")   # traceback points HERE, not line A

# Show last line of each traceback
for fn in [bare_reraise, new_raise]:
    try:
        fn()
    except ValueError:
        tb_lines = traceback.format_exc().strip().splitlines()
        print(f"{fn.__name__}:")
        print(f"  {tb_lines[-3].strip()}")   # the offending source line
        print(f"  {tb_lines[-1]}")            # the exception message
        print()
```

Output:

```
bare_reraise:
  raise ValueError("original error on this line")  # line A
  ValueError: original error on this line

new_raise:
  raise ValueError("re-raised")   # traceback points HERE, not line A
  ValueError: re-raised
```

Example 3 — Real-world application

A student enrolment validator that raises specific exceptions at each validation step, providing actionable messages.

```
# enrolment_validator.py — fail-fast validation with specific raises
from datetime import date

VALID_YEAR_LEVELS = {7, 8, 9, 10, 11, 12}
VALID_SUBJECTS    = {"Mathematics", "English", "Science",
                     "History", "Physics", "Digital Technologies"}

def validate_enrolment(student_id, name, year_level, subject, enrol_date):
    """Validate all enrolment fields; raise ValueError for any violation."""
    if not isinstance(student_id, str) or not student_id.strip():
        raise ValueError("student_id must be a non-empty string")
    if not isinstance(name, str) or len(name.strip()) < 2:
        raise ValueError(f"name {name!r} is too short or not a string")
    if year_level not in VALID_YEAR_LEVELS:
        raise ValueError(
            f"year_level {year_level!r} not in {sorted(VALID_YEAR_LEVELS)}"
        )
    if subject not in VALID_SUBJECTS:
        raise ValueError(f"subject {subject!r} is not offered")
    if not isinstance(enrol_date, date):
        raise TypeError(f"enrol_date must be a date object, got
{type(enrol_date).__name__}")
    if enrol_date > date.today():
        raise ValueError(f"enrol_date {enrol_date} is in the future")
    return True

test_cases = [
    ("10042", "Anika Patel",  10, "Mathematics",  date(2025, 2, 1)),   # valid
    ("",      "Liam Torres",  10, "English",       date(2025, 2, 1)),   # bad
ID
    ("10044", "Priya Nair",   13, "Science",       date(2025, 2, 1)),   # bad
year
    ("10045", "Sam Wong",     11, "Pottery",       date(2025, 2, 1)),   # bad
subject
    ("10046", "Maya Chen",    10, "Physics",       date(2030, 1, 1)),   #
future date
]

for args in test_cases:
    try:
        validate_enrolment(*args)
        print(f"  OK: {args[0]} {args[1]}")
    except (ValueError, TypeError) as e:
        print(f"  {type(e).__name__}: {e}")
```

Output:

```
  OK: 10042 Anika Patel
  ValueError: student_id must be a non-empty string
  ValueError: year_level 13 not in [7, 8, 9, 10, 11, 12]
  ValueError: subject 'Pottery' is not offered
  ValueError: enrol_date 2030-01-01 is in the future
```

The enrolment validator demonstrates the fail-fast principle at its most useful: each invalid condition is detected immediately and described precisely. A caller who catches ValueError from validate_enrolment() gets a message that identifies exactly which field failed and why, without having to inspect the data themselves.

8.2 Raising with a Message vs Raising with Context

A raise statement can convey information at two levels: the message string passed to the exception constructor, and the exception chain that links it to a lower-level cause. Both matter for diagnosing failures, and choosing between them requires understanding who will read the error.

A message string is for the immediate caller — it describes what went wrong in terms that are meaningful at the current level of abstraction. A file-processing function should say "Cannot load student records from term3.csv" rather than "errno 2". The underlying OSError that caused the failure is preserved in the chain (via raise ... from) for debugging, but the message presented to the user or to a higher-level handler should speak the language of the application, not the language of the OS.

Adding Positional and Keyword Arguments

Exception constructors accept arbitrary positional arguments, accessible via e.args. By convention most built-in exceptions take a single string message: ValueError("score out of range"). Custom exceptions (Section 8.3) can define their own __init__ with named parameters that carry structured information: ScoreError(score=150, allowed_range=(0, 100)). This makes the exception both human-readable (str(e) shows the message) and machine-readable (e.score and e.allowed_range can be inspected programmatically).

> **Note:** str(e) on an exception with a single argument returns that argument as a string. For an exception with multiple positional arguments, str(e) returns a tuple representation. Custom exceptions that override __str__ can produce any representation. Always ensure that str(e) produces a useful human-readable message — this is what appears in logs, tracebacks, and user-facing error displays.

Example 1 — Introduction

Raising with a clear application-level message; inspecting e.args; and raising with multiple positional arguments.

```
# —— Single-message raise — most common form ————————————————
try:
    raise ValueError("score 150 is out of range 0-100")
except ValueError as e:
    print(f"str(e):  {e}")
    print(f"e.args:  {e.args}")
    print(f"args[0]: {e.args[0]}")

# —— Multi-argument raise — accessible via e.args ———————————
try:
    raise ValueError("score out of range", 150, (0, 100))
except ValueError as e:
    print(f"\nstr(e):    {e}")
    print(f"e.args:    {e.args}")
    msg, value, rng = e.args
    print(f"message:   {msg}")
    print(f"value:     {value}")
    print(f"range:     {rng}")
```

Output:

```
str(e):  score 150 is out of range 0-100
e.args:  ('score 150 is out of range 0-100',)
args[0]: score 150 is out of range 0-100

str(e):    ('score out of range', 150, (0, 100))
e.args:    ('score out of range', 150, (0, 100))
message:   score out of range
value:     150
range:     (0, 100)
```

Example 2 — Variation

Raising an application-level message while preserving the low-level cause for debugging; contrasting str(e) vs the full chain.

```
class RecordLoadError(Exception):
```

```
    pass

def load_csv_record(filepath, student_id):
    """Raises RecordLoadError with application context; low-level cause
preserved."""
    import csv
    try:
        with open(filepath, "r", encoding="utf-8", newline="") as f:
            reader = csv.DictReader(f)
            for row in reader:
                if row.get("StudentID") == student_id:
                    return row
            raise KeyError(student_id)
    except FileNotFoundError as e:
        raise RecordLoadError(
            f"Record file {filepath!r} not found"
        ) from e
    except KeyError as e:
        raise RecordLoadError(
            f"Student {student_id!r} not found in {filepath!r}"
        ) from e

for sid, path in [("10042","grades.csv"), ("99999","grades.csv"),
("10042","missing.csv")]:",
    try:
        row = load_csv_record(path, sid)
        print(f"  Found: {row}")
    except RecordLoadError as e:
        print(f"  RecordLoadError: {e}")
        if e.__cause__:
            print(f"  Caused by: {type(e.__cause__).__name__}: {e.__cause__}")
```

Output:

```
  Found: {'StudentID': '10042', 'Name': 'Anika Patel', 'Score': '88'}
  RecordLoadError: Student '99999' not found in 'grades.csv'
  Caused by: KeyError: '99999'
  RecordLoadError: Record file 'missing.csv' not found
  Caused by: FileNotFoundError: [Errno 2] No such file or directory:
'missing.csv'
```

Example 3 — Real-world application

A configuration parser that produces precise, context-rich error messages identifying the file, section, key, and invalid value.

```
# config_parser.py — raise with full context at every validation step
import json

REQUIRED = {
    "school_name":   str,
    "academic_year": int,
    "max_students":  int,
}

def parse_config(filepath):
    """Load and validate a JSON config; every error carries file + key
context."""
    try:
        with open(filepath, "r", encoding="utf-8") as f:
            raw = json.load(f)
    except FileNotFoundError:
        raise ValueError(f"Config file {filepath!r} does not exist") from None
    except json.JSONDecodeError as e:
        raise ValueError(
            f"Config file {filepath!r} contains invalid JSON at line
{e.lineno}"
        ) from e
```

```
    config = {}
    for key, expected_type in REQUIRED.items():
        if key not in raw:
            raise ValueError(
                f"Config {filepath!r}: required key {key!r} is missing"
            )
        value = raw[key]
        if not isinstance(value, expected_type):
            raise ValueError(
                f"Config {filepath!r}: key {key!r} must be
{expected_type.__name__}, "
                f"got {type(value).__name__} ({value!r})"
            )
        config[key] = value
    return config

# Test with a valid config, then inject errors
import io, unittest.mock

good = '{"school_name":"Brisbane
SHS","academic_year":2025,"max_students":1800}'
bad_type = '{"school_name":"Brisbane
SHS","academic_year":"2025","max_students":1800}'

for label, content in [("valid", good), ("bad type", bad_type)]:",
    with unittest.mock.patch("builtins.open",
                             return_value=io.StringIO(content)):",
        try:
            cfg = parse_config("school.conf")
            print(f"  [{label}] OK: {cfg}")
        except ValueError as e:
            print(f"  [{label}] Error: {e}")
```

Output:

```
  [valid] OK: {'school_name': 'Brisbane SHS', 'academic_year': 2025,
'max_students': 1800}
  [bad type] Error: Config 'school.conf': key 'academic_year' must be int, got
str ('2025')
```

The config parser is a model of context-rich error messages. Every raise identifies the file, the key, the expected type, and the actual value received. A user who sees one of these messages can fix the problem without opening any other documentation.

8.3 Defining Custom Exception Classes

Custom exception classes let a module communicate its failure modes precisely. Instead of raising a generic ValueError and relying on the message string to convey meaning, a module can define SchoolError, EnrolmentError, or ScoreRangeError. Callers can then catch SchoolError as a group, or EnrolmentError specifically, without parsing message strings. The exception class itself is the interface.

Defining a custom exception is minimal: subclass Exception (or a more specific built-in if appropriate) and add a docstring. The simplest custom exception is an empty class body with pass; its name alone adds specificity. A more useful exception adds an __init__ that stores structured data and a __str__ that produces a clear message. All of Python's exception infrastructure — chaining, traceback formatting, isinstance checks — works automatically for subclasses of Exception.

Naming Conventions

Custom exception names end with Error by convention: ValidationError, ParseError, ConnectionError, ScoreRangeError. This matches the naming of built-in exceptions and signals to readers that the class is an exception type. Module-level exceptions are defined at the top of the module, before any function definitions, so they are visible to both the module's own code and its importers.

Note: Always subclass Exception, not BaseException, for custom application exceptions. Subclassing BaseException would make your exception bypass "except Exception:" handlers in callers, which violates the principle of least surprise. The only classes that should inherit directly from BaseException are system-level signals like SystemExit and KeyboardInterrupt.

Example 1 — Introduction

Three custom exception classes: a base class, a minimal subclass, and a subclass with a custom __init__ and __str__.

```
# ── Minimal custom exceptions – name alone adds value ──────────────
class SchoolError(Exception):
    """Base class for all school-application errors."""
    pass

class EnrolmentError(SchoolError):
    """Raised when an enrolment operation fails."""
    pass

# ── Custom exception with structured data ──────────────────────────
class ScoreRangeError(SchoolError):
    """Raised when a score is outside the allowed range."""

    def __init__(self, score, low=0, high=100):
        self.score = score
        self.low   = low
        self.high  = high
        super().__init__(f"Score {score} is outside allowed range {low}-
{high}")

# ── Using them ─────────────────────────────────────────────────────
def enrol(student_id, score):
    if not student_id:
        raise EnrolmentError(f"Student ID cannot be empty")
    if not 0 <= score <= 100:
        raise ScoreRangeError(score)
    return True

for sid, sc in [("10042", 88), ("", 72), ("10044", 150)]:",
    try:
        enrol(sid, sc)
        print(f"  Enrolled: {sid} score={sc}")
    except ScoreRangeError as e:
        print(f"  ScoreRangeError: {e}  (score attr={e.score})")
    except EnrolmentError as e:
        print(f"  EnrolmentError: {e}")

# ── Hierarchy check ────────────────────────────────────────────────
print(issubclass(ScoreRangeError, SchoolError))
print(issubclass(EnrolmentError,  SchoolError))
print(issubclass(SchoolError,     Exception))
```

Output:

```
  Enrolled: 10042 score=88
  EnrolmentError: Student ID cannot be empty
  ScoreRangeError: Score 150 is outside allowed range 0-100  (score attr=150)
True
True
True
```

Example 2 — Variation

Catching at different levels of the hierarchy: SchoolError catches all school-app errors; a specific subclass catches only one.

```
# Using the hierarchy from Example 8.3.1
```

```
def process_batch(records):
    """Process records; collect all school errors; let others propagate."""
    results, school_errors = [], []
    for rec in records:
        try:
            enrol(rec["id"], rec["score"])
            results.append(rec)
        except SchoolError as e:
            # Catches BOTH EnrolmentError and ScoreRangeError
            school_errors.append({"record": rec, "error": str(e),
                                  "type": type(e).__name__})
    return results, school_errors

batch = [
    {"id": "10042", "score": 88},
    {"id": "",      "score": 72},
    {"id": "10044", "score": 95},
    {"id": "10045", "score": 120},
]

ok, errors = process_batch(batch)
print(f"Processed: {len(ok)}, Errors: {len(errors)}")
for e in errors:
    print(f"  [{e['type']}] {e['error']}  (record={e['record']})")
```

Output:

```
Processed: 2, Errors: 2
  [EnrolmentError] Student ID cannot be empty  (record={'id': '', 'score': 72})
  [ScoreRangeError] Score 120 is outside allowed range 0-100  (record={'id':
'10045', 'score': 120})
```

Example 3 — Real-world application

A complete custom exception module for a school records system, with a base error, functional sub-errors, and a catch-all handler that generates a structured error report.

```
# school_exceptions.py — exception hierarchy for a school records system

class SchoolError(Exception):
    """Base for all school-application errors."""

class DataError(SchoolError):
    """Raised when input data is invalid or inconsistent."""
    def __init__(self, field, value, reason):
        self.field  = field
        self.value  = value
        self.reason = reason
        super().__init__(f"Field {field!r}={value!r}: {reason}")

class PersistenceError(SchoolError):
    """Raised when a load or save operation fails."""
    def __init__(self, operation, path, cause=None):
        self.operation = operation
        self.path      = path
        msg = f"Cannot {operation} {path!r}"
        super().__init__(msg)

class DuplicateError(DataError):
    """Raised when a record with the same key already exists."""
    def __init__(self, field, value):
        super().__init__(field, value, "already exists")


def add_student(db, sid, name, score):",
    if sid in db:
        raise DuplicateError("student_id", sid)
```

```
    if not 0 <= score <= 100:
        raise DataError("score", score, "must be 0-100")
    if len(name) < 2:
        raise DataError("name", name, "too short")
    db[sid] = {"name": name, "score": score}

database = {"10042": {"name": "Anika Patel", "score": 88}}

operations = [
    ("10043", "Liam Torres",  72),   # valid
    ("10042", "Anika Patel",  88),   # duplicate
    ("10044", "",             95),   # bad name
    ("10045", "Sam Wong",    110),   # bad score
]

for sid, name, score in operations:
    try:
        add_student(database, sid, name, score)
        print(f"  Added:   {sid} {name}")
    except DuplicateError as e:
        print(f"  Dup:     {e}")
    except DataError as e:
        print(f"  Data:    {e}  (field={e.field!r})")
```

Output:

```
  Added:   10043 Liam Torres
  Dup:     Field 'student_id'='10042': already exists
  Data:    Field 'name'='': too short  (field='name')
  Data:    Field 'score'=110: must be 0-100  (field='score')
```

The school_exceptions module illustrates the value of structured exception hierarchies. A caller can catch SchoolError broadly to handle all school-application errors in one place, or catch DuplicateError specifically to handle the unique-ID conflict with a user-facing message. The structured attributes (field, value, reason) make the errors programmatically inspectable without parsing message strings.

8.4 Exception Hierarchies: Subclassing for Specificity

A well-designed exception hierarchy mirrors the logical structure of the module's failure modes. The hierarchy should be deep enough to allow callers to catch at the right level of specificity, but not so deep that it becomes a burden to maintain. A module with three or four distinct failure categories typically needs one base class and three or four leaf classes; deeper nesting is rarely justified unless different callers genuinely need different levels of specificity.

The key design question is: which callers will catch which exceptions? A high-level application loop that must not crash can catch the base SchoolError and log everything. A specific UI component that handles duplicate student IDs with a user-facing message needs to catch DuplicateError. A data import wizard that handles file access failures differently from data validation failures needs both PersistenceError and DataError. Design the hierarchy around the catching patterns of your callers, not the internal implementation details of your code.

Mixin Exceptions

Occasionally a class needs to be catchable both as part of your hierarchy and as a built-in type. For example, a ValidationError that should be catchable as both SchoolError and ValueError can inherit from both: class ValidationError(SchoolError, ValueError). This allows existing code that catches ValueError to continue working while new code can catch ValidationError or SchoolError specifically. Multiple inheritance for exceptions is legitimate and common in Python's standard library (StopAsyncIteration inherits from both Exception and BaseException-derived types).

Note: When subclassing built-in exceptions, always call super().__init__() with the message string. If you define __init__ without calling super(), str(e) will return an empty string rather than your message. The pattern is: def __init__(self, msg, *extra): super().__init__(msg); self.extra = extra.

Example 1 — Introduction

A three-level exception hierarchy: base, functional categories, and specific leaf exceptions.

```
# ── Three-level hierarchy ──────────────────────────────────────

class AppError(Exception):
    """Root of all application errors."""

# ── Level 2: functional categories ─────────────────────────────
class IOError_(AppError):
    """File, network, or storage access failures."""

class ValidationError(AppError):
    """Input data fails a business rule."""

class AuthError(AppError):
    """Authentication or authorisation failure."""

# ── Level 3: specific leaf exceptions ──────────────────────────
class FileReadError(IOError_):
    def __init__(self, path):
        super().__init__(f"Cannot read {path!r}")
        self.path = path

class SchemaError(ValidationError):
    def __init__(self, key, expected, got):
        super().__init__(f"{key!r}: expected {expected}, got {got!r}")
        self.key = key

class PermissionDeniedError(AuthError):
    def __init__(self, user, resource):
        super().__init__(f"User {user!r} cannot access {resource!r}")
        self.user     = user
        self.resource = resource

# Show the hierarchy in action
errors = [
    FileReadError("data/grades.csv"),
    SchemaError("year_level", "int", "ten"),
    PermissionDeniedError("guest", "admin_panel"),
]

print("Catching at root level (AppError):")
for e in errors:
    try:
        raise e
    except AppError as caught:
        print(f"  {type(caught).__name__}: {caught}")
```

Output:

```
Catching at root level (AppError):
  FileReadError: Cannot read 'data/grades.csv'
  SchemaError: 'year_level': expected int, got 'ten'
  PermissionDeniedError: User 'guest' cannot access 'admin_panel'
```

Example 2 — Variation

Demonstrating how callers catch at different levels: a high-level handler catches AppError; specific handlers catch only what they can manage.

```
# Continued from Example 8.4.1
```

```
def handle_at_right_level(error):",
    """Simulate a caller catching at different levels of specificity."""
    try:
        raise error
    except FileReadError as e:
        print(f"  UI handler: show file-missing dialog for {e.path!r}")
    except ValidationError as e:
        print(f"  Form handler: highlight field {getattr(e, 'key', 'unknown')!
r}")
    except AuthError:
        print("  Auth handler: redirect to login page")
    except AppError as e:
        print(f"  Catch-all: log and show generic error: {e}")

for err in errors:
    handle_at_right_level(err)
```

Output:

```
  UI handler: show file-missing dialog for 'data/grades.csv'
  Form handler: highlight field 'year_level'
  Auth handler: redirect to login page
```

Example 3 — Real-world application

A complete exception module for a school data pipeline, with hierarchy, attributes, and a structured error report builder.

```
# pipeline_exceptions.py — production exception hierarchy + error reporter

class PipelineError(Exception):
    """Base for all data pipeline errors."""
    def __init__(self, message, stage=None):
        self.stage = stage
        super().__init__(f"[{stage}] {message}" if stage else message)

class LoadError(PipelineError):
    def __init__(self, path, stage="LOAD"):
        self.path = path
        super().__init__(f"Cannot load {path!r}", stage)

class ParseError(PipelineError):
    def __init__(self, line, reason, stage="PARSE"):
        self.line   = line
        self.reason = reason
        super().__init__(f"Line {line}: {reason}", stage)

class TransformError(PipelineError):
    def __init__(self, field, value, reason, stage="TRANSFORM"):
        self.field  = field
        self.value  = value
        super().__init__(f"Field {field!r}={value!r}: {reason}", stage)


def build_error_report(errors):
    """Summarise a list of PipelineErrors into a structured dict."""
    from collections import Counter
    by_stage = Counter(e.stage for e in errors)
    return {
        "total":    len(errors),
        "by_stage": dict(by_stage),
        "details":  [{"stage": e.stage, "type": type(e).__name__,
                      "message": str(e)} for e in errors],
    }

pipeline_errors = [
    LoadError("missing.csv"),
```

```
    ParseError(3, "not enough columns"),
    ParseError(7, "non-numeric score"),
    TransformError("year_level", "Year Ten", "must be integer"),
]

import json
report = build_error_report(pipeline_errors)
print(json.dumps(report, indent=2))
```

Output:

```
{
  "total": 4,
  "by_stage": {
    "LOAD": 1,
    "PARSE": 2,
    "TRANSFORM": 1
  },
  "details": [
    {"stage": "LOAD", "type": "LoadError", "message": "[LOAD] Cannot load
'missing.csv'"},
    {"stage": "PARSE", "type": "ParseError", "message": "[PARSE] Line 3: not
enough columns"},
    {"stage": "PARSE", "type": "ParseError", "message": "[PARSE] Line 7: non-
numeric score"},
    {"stage": "TRANSFORM", "type": "TransformError", "message": "[TRANSFORM]
Field 'year_level'='Year Ten': must be integer"}
  ]
}
```

The structured error report in Example 8.4.3 makes the pipeline's failure modes machine-readable. Any monitoring system, dashboard, or reporting tool can consume the JSON output without parsing message strings. This is the practical value of well-designed custom exceptions: the structure in the exception class becomes the structure in the error report.

8.5 Adding Attributes to Custom Exceptions

The most useful custom exceptions carry structured data as attributes, not just a formatted string. An exception with attributes can be caught and interrogated: the handler can read e.field, e.value, or e.line_number and make context-specific decisions without parsing the message string. This is the difference between an exception that reports "Invalid score 150 on line 7" and an exception that knows e.score == 150 and e.line == 7.

The pattern for adding attributes is consistent: define __init__ with the relevant parameters, store them as instance attributes, and call super().__init__(formatted_message). The formatted message should be human-readable and include all the attribute values, so that str(e) and repr(e) produce useful output in logs and tracebacks even when the caller does not inspect the attributes individually.

Serialising Exception Attributes

For applications that need to log or transmit exception data, a to_dict() method on custom exceptions is a useful convention. It returns a dict containing the exception type, message, and all structured attributes. This makes the exception data JSON-serialisable and queryable in log aggregation tools without any string parsing. The method is not part of the Python protocol but is a widely-adopted convention in production exception hierarchies.

> **Note:** Exception attributes are only accessible on the exception instance, which is only available inside the except clause and while the exception is assigned to the as variable. After the except block, Python deletes the binding to break reference cycles. Store any attributes you need after the except block: save_me = e.score inside the except, then use save_me outside.

Example 1 — Introduction

An exception with multiple structured attributes and a formatted __str__; demonstrating attribute access in the handler.

```
class RecordValidationError(Exception):
    """Validation failure for a single data record."""

    def __init__(self, record_id, field, value, constraint):",
        self.record_id  = record_id
        self.field      = field
        self.value      = value
        self.constraint = constraint
        super().__init__(
            f"Record {record_id!r}: field {field!r}={value!r} violates
{constraint!r}"
        )

def validate_record(record):
    if not 0 <= record["score"] <= 100:
        raise RecordValidationError(
            record["id"], "score", record["score"], "0 ≤ score ≤ 100"
        )
    if record["year_level"] not in range(7, 13):
        raise RecordValidationError(
            record["id"], "year_level", record["year_level"], "7 ≤ year ≤ 12"
        )

records = [
    {"id": "10042", "score": 88,  "year_level": 10},
    {"id": "10043", "score": 150, "year_level": 10},
    {"id": "10044", "score": 75,  "year_level": 15},
]

for rec in records:
    try:
        validate_record(rec)
        print(f"  OK: {rec['id']}")
    except RecordValidationError as e:
        print(f"  Error: {e}")
        print(f"    record_id={e.record_id!r}, field={e.field!r},
value={e.value!r}")
```

Output:

```
  OK: 10042
  Error: Record '10043': field 'score'=150 violates '0 ≤ score ≤ 100'
    record_id='10043', field='score', value=150
  Error: Record '10044': field 'year_level'=15 violates '7 ≤ year ≤ 12'
    record_id='10044', field='year_level', value=15
```

Example 2 — Variation

A to_dict() method on a custom exception; serialising exception data to JSON for structured logging.

```
import json
from datetime import datetime

class AuditableError(Exception):
    """Custom exception with to_dict() for structured logging."""

    def __init__(self, code, message, **context):
        self.code      = code
        self.context   = context
        self.timestamp = datetime.now().isoformat()
        super().__init__(f"[{code}] {message}")

    def to_dict(self):
        return {
            "type":      type(self).__name__,
```

```
            "code":      self.code,
            "message":   str(self),
            "timestamp": self.timestamp,
            **self.context,
        }

class FileAuditError(AuditableError):
    pass

class DataAuditError(AuditableError):
    pass

errors_log = []

raised = [
    FileAuditError("FILE_001", "Cannot open config", path="school.conf"),
    DataAuditError("DATA_042", "Score out of range", student="10043",
score=150),
]

for e in raised:
    errors_log.append(e.to_dict())

print(json.dumps(errors_log, indent=2))
```

Output:

```
[
  {
    "type": "FileAuditError",
    "code": "FILE_001",
    "message": "[FILE_001] Cannot open config",
    "timestamp": "2025-08-14T10:22:04",
    "path": "school.conf"
  },
  {
    "type": "DataAuditError",
    "code": "DATA_042",
    "message": "[DATA_042] Score out of range",
    "timestamp": "2025-08-14T10:22:04",
    "student": "10043",
    "score": 150
  }
]
```

Example 3 — Real-world application

A batch validator that collects RecordValidationErrors with all their attributes and writes a structured validation report to JSON.

```
# batch_validator.py — collect rich exception data; write validation report
import json
from datetime import date

class FieldError(Exception):
    def __init__(self, record_id, line, field, value, rule):
        self.record_id = record_id
        self.line      = line
        self.field     = field
        self.value     = value
        self.rule      = rule
        super().__init__(
            f"Line {line}, {record_id!r}: {field!r}={value!r} — {rule}"
        )
    def to_dict(self):
        return {"record_id": self.record_id, "line": self.line,
                "field": self.field, "value": self.value, "rule": self.rule}
```

```
RECORDS = [
    {"id": "10042", "name": "Anika Patel",  "score": 88,  "year": 10},
    {"id": "10043", "name": "Liam Torres",  "score": 150, "year": 10},
    {"id": "10044", "name": "",             "score": 95,  "year": 10},
    {"id": "10045", "name": "Sam Wong",     "score": 81,  "year": 15},
]

def validate_batch(records):
    valid, errors = [], []
    for lineno, rec in enumerate(records, 1):
        try:
            if not 0 <= rec["score"] <= 100:
                raise FieldError(rec["id"], lineno, "score",
                                 rec["score"], "0-100 required")
            if len(rec["name"].strip()) < 2:
                raise FieldError(rec["id"], lineno, "name",
                                 rec["name"], "minimum 2 characters")
            if rec["year"] not in range(7, 13):
                raise FieldError(rec["id"], lineno, "year",
                                 rec["year"], "must be 7-12")
            valid.append(rec)
        except FieldError as e:
            errors.append(e.to_dict())
    return valid, errors

valid, errors = validate_batch(RECORDS)
report = {
    "date":    date.today().isoformat(),
    "total":   len(RECORDS),
    "valid":   len(valid),
    "invalid": len(errors),
    "errors":  errors,
}
print(json.dumps(report, indent=2))
```

Output:

```
{
  "date": "2025-08-14",
  "total": 4,
  "valid": 1,
  "invalid": 3,
  "errors": [
    {"record_id": "10043", "line": 2, "field": "score", "value": 150, "rule":
"0-100 required"},
    {"record_id": "10044", "line": 3, "field": "name", "value": "", "rule":
"minimum 2 characters"},
    {"record_id": "10045", "line": 4, "field": "year", "value": 15, "rule":
"must be 7-12"}
  ]
}
```

The to_dict() convention transforms a list of caught exceptions into a structured validation report that can be saved as a JSON file, displayed in a UI, or sent to a monitoring service. None of this requires parsing message strings — the structure is in the exception attributes.

8.6 When to Use Custom Exceptions vs Built-ins

Custom exceptions add value when two conditions are met: the failure mode is specific to your module (not already described precisely by a built-in exception), and callers need to handle that specific failure mode differently from other errors. When either condition is absent, a built-in exception is the right choice.

Use built-in exceptions for failures that are genuinely described by the built-in semantics: ValueError for an invalid value, TypeError for a wrong type, KeyError for a missing dict key, FileNotFoundError for a missing file. Raising ValueError("score must be 0–100") from your validation code is correct and idiomatic. Callers already know how to handle ValueError; adding a custom ScoreError only creates work without adding precision — unless callers specifically need to distinguish ScoreError from other ValueErrors in their code.

When Custom Exceptions Are Necessary

Custom exceptions are necessary when: the caller needs to catch exactly one failure mode from your module without catching unrelated failures of the same built-in type; the exception needs to carry structured data as attributes; the failure mode has a name that communicates more than the generic built-in type; or you are building a library where the public API should be stable even if the implementation changes. A library that raises FileNotFoundError couples its public API to the fact that it uses files internally. If it later switches to a database, the exception type changes. A library that raises DataNotFoundError can change its storage layer without breaking callers.

> **Note:** Raising ValueError is almost always correct for input validation. Raising a custom ValidationError adds value only if callers need to catch ValidationError specifically — for example, to display a form validation UI — while also catching (or not catching) other ValueErrors from unrelated code. If callers will always handle both the same way, the custom exception adds nothing.

Example 1 — Introduction

Side-by-side comparison: when a built-in exception is more appropriate vs when a custom exception adds genuine value.

```
# ── Built-in is correct here ──────────────────────────────────────────
# Callers handle ValueError from many places; no new distinction needed
def set_year_level(year):
    if year not in range(7, 13):
        raise ValueError(f"year_level must be 7-12, got {year}")
    return year

# ── Custom exception adds value here ─────────────────────────────────
# Callers need to distinguish "enrolment conflict" from other ValueErrors
class EnrolmentConflictError(Exception):
    """A student is already enrolled in this subject for this term."""
    def __init__(self, student_id, subject, term):
        self.student_id = student_id
        self.subject    = subject
        self.term       = term
        super().__init__(
            f"{student_id!r} is already enrolled in {subject!r} for {term!r}"
        )

ENROLMENTS = {("10042", "Mathematics", "2025-T1")}

def enrol(student_id, subject, term):
    key = (student_id, subject, term)
    if key in ENROLMENTS:
        raise EnrolmentConflictError(student_id, subject, term)
    ENROLMENTS.add(key)

# Caller can catch the conflict specifically:
try:
    enrol("10042", "Mathematics", "2025-T1")
except EnrolmentConflictError as e:
    print(f"Conflict: {e}")
    print(f"  student={e.student_id!r}, subject={e.subject!r}")
```

Output:

```
Conflict: '10042' is already enrolled in 'Mathematics' for '2025-T1'
  student='10042', subject='Mathematics'
```

Example 2 — Variation

A library function that catches built-in OSError and re-raises as a custom StorageError, decoupling the public API from the storage implementation.

```
# storage.py — public API raises StorageError regardless of storage backend

class StorageError(Exception):
    """Public exception for all storage-layer failures."""
    def __init__(self, operation, key, message):
        self.operation = operation
        self.key       = key
        super().__init__(f"{operation} failed for {key!r}: {message}")

class FileStorage:
    """Storage backend using the local filesystem."""
    def __init__(self, base_dir):
        import os; os.makedirs(base_dir, exist_ok=True)
        self.base_dir = base_dir

    def load(self, key):
        import json, os
        path = os.path.join(self.base_dir, key + ".json")
        try:
            with open(path, "r", encoding="utf-8") as f:
                return json.load(f)
        except FileNotFoundError:
            raise StorageError("load", key, "record not found") from None
        except (OSError, json.JSONDecodeError) as e:
            raise StorageError("load", key, str(e)) from e

    def save(self, key, data):
        import json, os
        path = os.path.join(self.base_dir, key + ".json")
        try:
            with open(path, "w", encoding="utf-8") as f:
                json.dump(data, f)
        except OSError as e:
            raise StorageError("save", key, str(e)) from e

store = FileStorage("db")
store.save("student_10042", {"name": "Anika Patel", "score": 88})

for key in ["student_10042", "student_99999"]:",
    try:
        record = store.load(key)
        print(f"  Loaded {key}: {record}")
    except StorageError as e:
        print(f"  StorageError [{e.operation}] key={e.key!r}: {e}")
```

Output:

```
  Loaded student_10042: {'name': 'Anika Patel', 'score': 88}
  StorageError [load] key='student_99999': load failed for 'student_99999':
record not found
```

Example 3 — Real-world application

A decision table for choosing between built-in and custom exceptions, implemented as a set of functions demonstrating each case.

```
# —— Decision: use built-in — type error describes the problem precisely ——
def multiply_score(score, factor):",
    if not isinstance(factor, (int, float)):
        raise TypeError(f"factor must be numeric, got {type(factor).__name__}")
    return score * factor

# —— Decision: use built-in — value error is idiomatic for invalid input ——
def parse_grade_letter(letter):
    grades = {"A+": 98, "A": 92, "B+": 82, "B": 75, "C": 65, "F": 40}
    if letter not in grades:
        raise ValueError(f"Unknown grade letter {letter!r}")
    return grades[letter]
```

```
# ── Decision: custom — callers need to handle this specific failure ────
class GradeLockedError(Exception):
    """A grade that has been finalised cannot be modified."""
    def __init__(self, student_id, subject):
        super().__init__(f"Grade for {student_id!r}/{subject!r} is locked")
        self.student_id = student_id
        self.subject    = subject

LOCKED = {("10042", "Mathematics")}

def update_grade(student_id, subject, new_score):
    if (student_id, subject) in LOCKED:
        raise GradeLockedError(student_id, subject)
    return new_score

# Demonstrate each
for fn, args in [
    (multiply_score,   (88, "x")),
    (parse_grade_letter, ("Z",)),
    (update_grade,     ("10042", "Mathematics", 95)),
]:
    try:
        fn(*args)
    except GradeLockedError as e:
        print(f"  GradeLockedError: {e}")
    except (TypeError, ValueError) as e:
        print(f"  {type(e).__name__}: {e}")
```

Output:

```
  TypeError: factor must be numeric, got str
  ValueError: Unknown grade letter 'Z'
  GradeLockedError: Grade for '10042'/'Mathematics' is locked
```

The decision pattern is clear in Example 8.6.3: TypeError and ValueError need no custom subclass because they are precisely descriptive. GradeLockedError earns its existence because callers need to specifically distinguish this failure — a grade lock — from a generic value or type error, and respond differently (show a lock warning, not a generic error dialog).

8.7 Defensive Coding: Validation Functions That Raise

Defensive programming means assuming inputs may be wrong and checking them before use. Validation functions that raise exceptions on invalid data are the primary tool. The pattern is simple: accept the candidate value, apply every applicable rule, and raise a specific exception immediately on the first violation. The caller either catches the exception and handles it, or lets it propagate to a higher-level handler.

Validation functions belong at the boundary between untrusted data and trusted code. When reading from a file, a network, a database, or user input, the data must be validated before it is used. After validation, the rest of the code can proceed under the assumption that the data is correct. This separation — validate at the boundary, trust inside — keeps internal logic free of defensive checks and makes the validation rules easy to find, test, and update.

Composing Validators

Individual validators for single fields compose into a record validator: call each field validator in sequence, collect all errors (rather than stopping at the first), and raise a single exception listing all problems. This pattern — sometimes called accumulating validation — produces more useful error messages than stopping at the first failure, because the caller can see and fix all problems at once rather than discovering them one at a time.

Note: Validation functions should raise, not return error codes or status flags. Returning False or None on failure requires every caller to check the return value; raising guarantees that the error is handled (or at least not silently ignored). Callers who want to continue on validation failure use try/except; callers who want to propagate the error do nothing.

Example 1 — Introduction

A suite of single-field validators that each raise on the first violation they detect.

```
from datetime import date

def validate_student_id(value):
    if not isinstance(value, str):
        raise TypeError(f"student_id must be str, got {type(value).__name__}")
    if not value.strip():
        raise ValueError("student_id cannot be empty")
    if not value.strip().isdigit():
        raise ValueError(f"student_id must be numeric, got {value!r}")

def validate_name(value):
    if not isinstance(value, str):
        raise TypeError(f"name must be str, got {type(value).__name__}")
    if len(value.strip()) < 2:
        raise ValueError(f"name {value!r} is too short (min 2 chars)")

def validate_score(value):
    if not isinstance(value, int):
        raise TypeError(f"score must be int, got {type(value).__name__}")
    if not 0 <= value <= 100:
        raise ValueError(f"score {value} must be 0-100")

def validate_year_level(value):
    if value not in range(7, 13):
        raise ValueError(f"year_level {value} must be 7-12")

test_values = [
    ("student_id", validate_student_id, ["10042", "abc", "", 42]),
    ("name",       validate_name,       ["Anika Patel", "A", None]),
    ("score",      validate_score,      [88, 150, 3.5]),
]

for field, fn, vals in test_values:
    for v in vals:
        try:
            fn(v)
            print(f"  {field}={v!r}  OK")
        except (ValueError, TypeError) as e:
            print(f"  {field}={v!r}  {type(e).__name__}: {e}")
```

Output:

```
  student_id='10042'  OK
  student_id='abc'  ValueError: student_id must be numeric, got 'abc'
  student_id=''  ValueError: student_id cannot be empty
  student_id=42  TypeError: student_id must be str, got int
  name='Anika Patel'  OK
  name='A'  ValueError: name 'A' is too short (min 2 chars)
  name=None  TypeError: name must be str, got NoneType
  score=88  OK
  score=150  ValueError: score 150 must be 0-100
  score=3.5  TypeError: score must be int, got float
```

Example 2 — Variation

An accumulating validator that collects all errors rather than stopping at the first, and raises a single exception listing everything wrong.

```
class MultiFieldError(Exception):
```

```
    """Raised when multiple field validations fail; carries all errors."""
    def __init__(self, errors):
        self.errors = errors
        lines = "\n".join(f"  - {e}" for e in errors)
        super().__init__(f"{len(errors)} validation error(s):\n{lines}")

def validate_record_all(record):
    """Collect all validation errors; raise MultiFieldError if any."""
    errors = []

    def try_validate(fn, value):
        try: fn(value)
        except (ValueError, TypeError) as e: errors.append(str(e))

    try_validate(validate_student_id, record.get("id", ""))
    try_validate(validate_name,       record.get("name", ""))
    try_validate(validate_score,      record.get("score", 0))
    try_validate(validate_year_level, record.get("year", 0))

    if errors:
        raise MultiFieldError(errors)

# A record with three errors
bad_record = {"id": "abc", "name": "A", "score": 150, "year": 10}
try:
    validate_record_all(bad_record)
except MultiFieldError as e:
    print(e)
    print(f"\nError count accessible: {len(e.errors)}")
```

Output:

```
3 validation error(s):
  - student_id must be numeric, got 'abc'
  - name 'A' is too short (min 2 chars)
  - score 150 must be 0-100

Error count accessible: 3
```

Example 3 — Real-world application

A production-grade student record importer that validates, collects errors, saves valid records, and writes a structured import report.

```
# importer.py — validate-then-import with full error reporting
import json
from datetime import date

class ImportError_(Exception):
    def __init__(self, line, field, value, reason):
        self.line   = line
        self.field  = field
        self.value  = value
        self.reason = reason
        super().__init__(f"Line {line}: {field}={value!r}: {reason}")
    def to_dict(self):
        return vars(self) | {"message": str(self)}

INCOMING = [
    {"id": "10046", "name": "Zara Hill",   "score": 78, "year": 10},
    {"id": "abc",   "name": "Bad ID",      "score": 75, "year": 10},
    {"id": "10048", "name": "Ben Chu",     "score": 84, "year": 11},
    {"id": "10049", "name": "A",           "score": 88, "year": 12},
    {"id": "10050", "name": "Sara Kim",    "score": 92, "year": 99},
]

valid_records, import_errors = [], []
```

```
for lineno, rec in enumerate(INCOMING, 1):
    try:
        validate_student_id(rec.get("id", ""))
        validate_name(rec.get("name", ""))
        validate_score(rec.get("score", 0))
        validate_year_level(rec.get("year", 0))
        valid_records.append(rec)
    except (ValueError, TypeError) as e:
        # Determine which field caused the error from the message
        for field in ("student_id", "name", "score", "year_level"):
            if field in str(e):
                import_errors.append(
                    ImportError_(lineno, field, rec.get(field[:2]),
str(e)).to_dict()
                )
                break
        else:
            import_errors.append({"line": lineno, "message": str(e)})

report = {
    "date":      date.today().isoformat(),
    "total":     len(INCOMING),
    "imported":  len(valid_records),
    "rejected":  len(import_errors),
    "errors":    import_errors,
}
print(json.dumps(report, indent=2))
```

Output:

```
{
  "date": "2025-08-14",
  "total": 5,
  "imported": 2,
  "rejected": 3,
  "errors": [
    {"line": 2, "message": "student_id must be numeric, got 'abc'"},
    {"line": 4, "message": "name 'A' is too short (min 2 chars)"},
    {"line": 5, "message": "year_level 99 must be 7-12"}
  ]
}
```

The importer combines every technique from this chapter: specific raises with messages, custom exception classes with to_dict(), accumulating error collection, and a structured JSON report. This is the complete form of defensive coding: validate at the boundary, collect all failures, report with enough structure to act on each one individually.

Chapter 8 Summary

- raise ValueError("message") is the correct form for explicit raises: it provides a descriptive message, makes intent clear, and appears in tracebacks. Bare raise (no argument) re-raises the current exception with the original traceback intact — preferred over raise ValueError(same_message) which shifts the traceback to the re-raise site.
- raise X from e chains explicitly: the original exception is stored in e.__cause__ and shown in the traceback as "the direct cause". raise X from None suppresses the chain for clean public API errors. Bare raise in an except block preserves the original as __context__ (implicit chaining).
- Custom exception classes are defined by subclassing Exception. The simplest form is an empty body with pass; the most useful form adds a custom __init__ storing structured attributes, calls super().__init__(message), and defines to_dict() for serialisation.
- Exception hierarchies mirror the failure-mode structure of a module. Design them around the catching patterns of callers: a base class for broad catches, specific leaf classes for precise handling. Deeper than three levels is rarely justified.

- Adding attributes to custom exceptions (e.field, e.score, e.line) makes exceptions machine-readable: handlers can inspect attributes programmatically rather than parsing message strings. A to_dict() method enables structured logging and JSON serialisation.
- Use built-in exceptions (ValueError, TypeError, KeyError) when they precisely describe the failure. Use custom exceptions when callers need to distinguish your specific failure mode from other instances of the same built-in type, or when the exception needs to carry structured attributes.
- Validation functions raise at the boundary between untrusted and trusted data. Single-field validators raise on the first violation. Accumulating validators collect all violations and raise a MultiFieldError listing everything wrong — preferable for forms and import pipelines where the user needs to see and fix all problems at once.
- The complete defensive coding pattern: validate at the boundary, collect errors into structured exception objects, raise with full context, catch at the right level of specificity, and produce a JSON error report with enough detail to act on each failure individually.

Guided Exercises

1. Write a validate_email(email) function that raises ValueError with a descriptive message if the email does not contain exactly one "@" and at least one "." after the "@". Test it with valid and invalid email addresses.

> ***Hint:*** *Use email.count("@") == 1 and email.partition("@")[2].count(".") >= 1. Raise separate ValueError messages for each violation so the caller knows exactly which rule failed.*

2. Define a custom exception hierarchy: AppError as base, then FileError(AppError) and DataError(AppError) as functional categories, then CorruptFileError(FileError) and MissingFieldError(DataError) as specific leaves. Write a function that raises each type and show that catching AppError catches all of them.

> ***Hint:*** *Each leaf should have a custom __init__ that stores relevant attributes and calls super().__init__(message). Demonstrate with a loop that raises each, catches AppError, and prints type(e).__name__ and str(e).*

3. Write a custom exception SchemaError that stores field, expected_type, and actual_value as attributes. Define __init__, __str__, and to_dict(). Raise it from a function that validates a dict against a schema {field: type}. Test with a dict that has three fields, two of which fail.

> ***Hint:*** *In __init__, store the three attributes and call super().__init__(formatted message). In to_dict(), return a dict with "field", "expected", "actual", and "message" keys. Loop over the schema dict and raise on the first type mismatch found.*

4. Write an accumulating validator validate_all(record, rules) where rules is a list of (field_name, validator_function) pairs. Collect all validation errors into a list and raise a MultiValidationError(errors_list) if any errors occurred. Test with a record that has three fields and two violations.

> ***Hint:*** *Loop over rules, call each validator in a try/except, and append str(e) to an errors list. After the loop, if errors: raise MultiValidationError(errors). The MultiValidationError should store the list and format all errors in its __str__.*

5. Write a function safe_load(filepath) that wraps both OSError and json.JSONDecodeError in a custom LoadError(path, message). Use raise LoadError(...) from e so the original cause is preserved. Verify that e.__cause__ on a caught LoadError gives the original exception.

> ***Hint:*** *Define LoadError(Exception) with __init__(path, message). Wrap the file open and json.load in a try. In each except clause, raise LoadError(filepath, str(e)) from e. Catch LoadError in the caller and print e.__cause__ and type(e.__cause__).*

Challenge Tasks

1. Build a complete validation library for student records. Define a base SchoolValidationError and at least five specific exceptions: MissingFieldError, TypeMismatchError, RangeError, FormatError, and DuplicateKeyError. Each should carry structured attributes and a to_dict() method. Write a validate_student_record(record, existing_ids) function that runs all validations and raises a BatchValidationError(list_of_errors) collecting all failures. Demonstrate with a batch of five records containing at least one of each error type.
2. Implement a retry decorator @retry(exceptions, max_attempts, delay) that retries the decorated function up to max_attempts times when it raises one of the specified exceptions. On the final failed attempt, re-raise the last exception with a RetryExhaustedError chained from it using raise X from e. The RetryExhaustedError should store the number of attempts and the last exception as attributes. Demonstrate with a function that fails three times then succeeds on attempt four.
3. Design and implement a pipeline exception system for a multi-stage data processing pipeline. Each stage (load, parse, transform, validate, export) should have its own exception class inheriting from a PipelineError base. Write a run_pipeline(stages, data) function that runs each stage, catches stage-specific exceptions, stores them with stage name and elapsed time, and produces a final PipelineReport that can be serialised to JSON. Include both strict mode (abort on first failure) and lenient mode (continue with fallback on failure, record all errors). Demonstrate with a pipeline where the parse stage fails on some records but the pipeline continues.

CHAPTER 9 File System Navigation with os and pathlib

Book 02: File Handling & Exception Management

> *The previous eight chapters have opened, read, written, and managed individual files. This chapter zooms out to the file system itself: navigating directory trees, listing and filtering files by name and type, creating and deleting directories safely, walking entire subdirectory hierarchies, and working with temporary files. Python provides two overlapping APIs for this work — the traditional os.path module and the modern pathlib package — and this chapter covers both so you can read existing code that uses either and write new code that uses the right tool for each job. The chapter closes with three complete real-world tools that combine everything: a file organiser, a batch renamer, and a disk-usage reporter.*

9.1 os.path vs pathlib — Two APIs for the Same Job

Python has two distinct APIs for working with file paths and the file system. The os.path module has been part of the standard library since Python 2 and represents paths as plain strings. Every operation is a function call that accepts a string and returns a string: os.path.join("data", "grades.csv") returns the string "data/grades.csv" on Unix. The module is functional, reliable, and widely used in existing codebases.

pathlib was introduced in Python 3.4 and takes an object-oriented approach. A Path object represents a filesystem path and carries methods for navigation, inspection, reading, writing, and manipulation. Instead of calling os.path.join("data", "grades.csv"), you write Path("data") / "grades.csv". The result is a Path object rather than a string, and that object knows how to inspect itself, open itself, and navigate to its children and parent without importing anything beyond Path. pathlib is the preferred style in modern Python code.

Choosing Between Them

For new code, use pathlib. It is more readable, eliminates the need to import multiple functions, and integrates cleanly with open() (which accepts Path objects directly since Python 3.6). For reading and maintaining existing code, knowing os.path is essential — it appears in virtually every Python project written before 2018. Both APIs are cross-platform: they select the correct path separator (/ on Unix, \ on Windows) automatically. Never hard-code separators in path strings.

A practical bridge between the two APIs is the Path() constructor, which accepts both string paths and existing Path objects. Wrapping any path argument with Path(p) at the entry point of a function makes the function work correctly regardless of whether the caller passes a string or a Path. The reverse — calling str(path) to convert a Path to a string for legacy code — is equally simple.

> **Note:** os.path.join() is the correct string-based path builder. Never concatenate path components with + or hard-code "/" or "\\". os.path.join("data", "grades.csv") produces "data/grades.csv" on Unix and "data\\grades.csv" on Windows automatically. The pathlib / operator provides the same guarantee.

Example 1 — Introduction

Five common file-system operations written first with os.path, then with pathlib — identical results, different style.

```
import os
from pathlib import Path

base = "school/data"
file = "grades.csv"
```

```
# — os.path ────────────────────────────────────────────────────
full_path  = os.path.join(base, file)
exists     = os.path.exists(full_path)
is_file    = os.path.isfile(full_path)
size       = os.path.getsize(full_path) if exists else 0
parent_dir = os.path.dirname(full_path)
stem       = os.path.splitext(file)[0]

print("os.path:")
print(f"  full:   {full_path}")
print(f"  exists: {exists}  is_file: {is_file}  size: {size}")
print(f"  parent: {parent_dir}  stem: {stem}")

# — pathlib ────────────────────────────────────────────────────
p = Path(base) / file

print("\npathlib:")
print(f"  full:   {p}")
print(f"  exists: {p.exists()}  is_file: {p.is_file()}",
      f"  size: {p.stat().st_size if p.exists() else 0}")
print(f"  parent: {p.parent}  stem: {p.stem}")
```

Output:

```
os.path:
  full:   school/data/grades.csv
  exists: True  is_file: True  size: 312
  parent: school/data  stem: grades

pathlib:
  full:   school/data/grades.csv
  exists: True  is_file: True  size: 312
  parent: school/data  stem: grades
```

Example 2 — Variation

A path-normalising helper that accepts either a str or a Path and always returns a Path; demonstrating both APIs on mtime.

```
import os
from pathlib import Path
from datetime import datetime

def as_path(p):
    """Accept str or Path; always return a Path."""
    return Path(p)

def file_info(p):
    """Return a dict of file metadata, accepting str or Path."""
    path = as_path(p)
    if not path.exists():
        return None
    st = path.stat()
    return {
        "name":     path.name,
        "size":     st.st_size,
        "modified": datetime.fromtimestamp(st.st_mtime).strftime("%Y-%m-%d %H:
%M"),
        "is_file":  path.is_file(),
    }

# Works with both str and Path inputs
for p in ["school/data/grades.csv", Path("school/data/enrolments.csv")]:",
    info = file_info(p)
    if info:
        print(f"  {info['name']:<25} {info['size']:>6} bytes
{info['modified']}")
```

```
    else:
        print(f"  {str(p)!r}: not found")
```

Output:

```
  grades.csv                    312 bytes  2025-08-14 10:22
  enrolments.csv                188 bytes  2025-08-14 10:22
```

Example 3 — Real-world application

A project health checker that validates the expected directory and file layout of a school application, using os.path for the legacy checks and pathlib for the new ones.

```
# project_health.py — validate that all expected paths exist
import os
from pathlib import Path

PROJECT_ROOT = Path("school_app")

# Expected structure
REQUIRED_DIRS  = ["data", "reports", "logs", "config"]
REQUIRED_FILES = [
    "config/school.conf",
    "data/students.csv",
    "data/courses.json",
]

def check_health(root):
    root = Path(root)
    ok, missing = [], []

    # Check directories with pathlib
    for d in REQUIRED_DIRS:
        target = root / d
        if target.is_dir():
            ok.append(f"  DIR  {target}")
        else:
            missing.append(f"  DIR  {target}")

    # Check files using os.path (illustrating interoperability)
    for f in REQUIRED_FILES:
        target = os.path.join(str(root), f)
        if os.path.isfile(target):
            size = os.path.getsize(target)
            ok.append(f"  FILE {target}  ({size} bytes)")
        else:
            missing.append(f"  FILE {target}")

    print(f"Health check for {root!r}:")
    print(f"  {len(ok)} item(s) present, {len(missing)} missing")
    if missing:
        print("  Missing:")
        for m in missing:
            print(f"    ✗ {m}")
    else:
        print("  All required paths present. ✓")

check_health(PROJECT_ROOT)
```

Output:

```
Health check for 'school_app':
  5 item(s) present, 2 missing
  Missing:
    ✗   DIR  school_app/logs
    ✗   FILE school_app/data/courses.json
```

The project health checker demonstrates the practical interoperability of the two APIs: new code uses pathlib; legacy-compatible checks use os.path; Path(str) and str(path) bridge between them. From this point on, examples in this chapter use pathlib as the primary API, with os.path shown where it adds a meaningful contrast.

9.2 pathlib.Path: Construction, Navigation, and Properties

A Path object is constructed from a string, another Path, or a sequence of parts joined automatically: Path("school/data/grades.csv"), Path("school", "data", "grades.csv"), and Path("school") / "data" / "grades.csv" all produce the same path. The / operator is the idiomatic choice for building paths from a base: it is readable, avoids the awkward os.path.join() call, and immediately signals that path construction is happening.

Once constructed, a Path exposes the components of its path as properties. name returns the final component (the filename including extension). stem returns the filename without its final suffix. suffix returns the final extension including the dot. suffixes returns a list of all extensions for multiply-suffixed files. parent returns the containing directory as a new Path. parts returns a tuple of all path components from root to filename. These properties are read-only; they do not make filesystem calls and never raise an exception.

Filesystem Methods

The methods that actually interact with the filesystem are clearly distinguished from the properties by their verb names. exists() returns True if the path exists. is_file() and is_dir() distinguish files from directories. stat() returns an os.stat_result with the file's size (st_size), last-modification time (st_mtime as a Unix timestamp), and creation time (st_ctime). resolve() converts the path to an absolute canonical path, resolving any symlinks. read_text() and write_text() read and write the file's entire contents as a string in a single call, handling the open/close lifecycle automatically.

> **Note:** Path properties (name, stem, suffix, parent, parts) are pure string operations — they never touch the filesystem and cannot raise exceptions even if the path does not exist. Filesystem methods (exists, is_file, stat, read_text) do touch the filesystem and can raise OSError. Keep this distinction in mind when building paths programmatically.

Example 1 — Introduction

Path properties: name, stem, suffix, parent, parts, and resolve() on the same path object.

```
from pathlib import Path

p = Path("school/data/term3_grades.csv")

print(f"str:      {p}")
print(f"name:     {p.name}")
print(f"stem:     {p.stem}")
print(f"suffix:   {p.suffix}")
print(f"parent:   {p.parent}")
print(f"parts:    {p.parts}")
print(f"resolve: {p.resolve()}")

# Chaining parent to navigate up the tree
print(f"grandparent: {p.parent.parent}")

# Building sibling paths
sibling = p.parent / "term3_report.txt"
print(f"sibling: {sibling}")

# Path.home() and Path.cwd()
print(f"home:     {Path.home()}")
print(f"cwd:      {Path.cwd().name}  (last part only)")
```

Output:
```
str:     school/data/term3_grades.csv
name:    term3_grades.csv
stem:    term3_grades
suffix:  .csv
parent:  school/data
parts:   ('school', 'data', 'term3_grades.csv')
resolve: /home/anika/school/data/term3_grades.csv
grandparent: school
sibling: school/data/term3_report.txt
home:    /home/anika
cwd:     school  (last part only)
```

Example 2 — Variation

stat() for size and modification time; read_text() and write_text() for whole-file I/O in one call.

```
from pathlib import Path
from datetime import datetime

p = Path("school/data/grades.csv")

# ── stat(): size and timestamps ──────────────────────────────
st = p.stat()
mtime = datetime.fromtimestamp(st.st_mtime)
print(f"size:     {st.st_size} bytes")
print(f"modified: {mtime.strftime('%Y-%m-%d %H:%M:%S')}")

# ── read_text(): entire file in one call ──────────────────────
content = p.read_text(encoding="utf-8")
lines   = content.splitlines()
print(f"lines:    {len(lines)}")
print(f"header:   {lines[0]!r}")

# ── write_text(): entire file in one call ─────────────────────
out_path = Path("school/data/grades_upper.csv")
out_path.write_text(content.upper(), encoding="utf-8")
print(f"written:  {out_path.name}  ({out_path.stat().st_size} bytes)")
```

Output:
```
size:     312 bytes
modified: 2025-08-14 10:22:04
lines:    5
header:   'StudentID,Name,Subject,Score'
written:  grades_upper.csv  (312 bytes)
```

Example 3 — Real-world application

A file metadata reporter that builds a structured summary of every file in a directory using Path properties and stat().

```
# metadata_reporter.py — rich metadata for every file in a directory
from pathlib import Path
from datetime import datetime

def file_metadata(filepath):
    """Return a dict of metadata for a single file."""
    p   = Path(filepath)
    st  = p.stat()
    return {
        "name":     p.name,
        "stem":     p.stem,
        "suffix":   p.suffix,
        "size":     st.st_size,
        "modified": datetime.fromtimestamp(st.st_mtime).isoformat(),
        "parent":   str(p.parent),
    }
```

```
def report_directory(directory):
    """Print a metadata table for every file in directory."""
    root  = Path(directory)
    files = sorted(f for f in root.iterdir() if f.is_file())
    if not files:
        print(f"  No files found in {directory!r}")
        return

    total_size = sum(f.stat().st_size for f in files)
    print(f"Directory: {root.resolve()}")
    print(f"Files: {len(files)}  Total: {total_size:,} bytes")
    print(f"  {'Name':<28} {'Ext':<6} {'Size':>8}  Modified")
    print("  " + "-" * 60)
    for f in files:
        meta = file_metadata(f)
        mtime = meta["modified"][:16].replace("T", " ")
        print(f"  {meta['name']:<28} {meta['suffix']:<6}",
              f"{meta['size']:>8}  {mtime}")

report_directory("school/data")
```

Output:

```
Directory: /home/anika/school/data
Files: 4  Total: 1,024 bytes
  Name                          Ext      Size  Modified
  ------------------------------------------------------------
  courses.json                  .json     188  2025-08-14 09:14
  enrolments.csv                .csv      188  2025-08-14 10:22
  grades.csv                    .csv      312  2025-08-14 10:22
  students.csv                  .csv      336  2025-08-14 09:45
```

The metadata reporter pattern — list, sort, stat, format — is the foundation of every file-browsing or file-management tool. Section 9.3 extends this with filtering by name pattern, and Section 9.5 extends it further to walk entire directory trees.

9.3 Listing Directory Contents: iterdir() and glob()

Path.iterdir() yields every item in a directory — files and subdirectories alike — as Path objects. It does not recurse into subdirectories; it yields only the direct children. The order is filesystem-dependent and not guaranteed to be alphabetical, so always sort the results when order matters: sorted(p.iterdir()). Filtering is done with standard Python: a list comprehension with is_file(), is_dir(), or a suffix check selects the items you need.

For pattern-based filtering, Path.glob(pattern) is more expressive. It accepts shell-style glob patterns: "*.csv" matches all CSV files in the directory; "**/*.csv" matches all CSV files in the directory and all its subdirectories recursively; "term[0-9]_*.txt" matches files whose name starts with "term" followed by a single digit. The double-star ** is the recursive wildcard; glob() with ** can be slow on deep directory trees because it traverses every subdirectory.

rglob()

Path.rglob(pattern) is shorthand for glob("**/pattern") — it always searches recursively. rglob("*.csv") finds every CSV file anywhere in the directory tree. For recursive searches, rglob() is slightly more readable than the glob("**/*.csv") form and is the idiomatic choice. Both return a generator; wrap in list() if you need to iterate multiple times or check the count.

> **Note:** glob() and rglob() return generators, not lists. They are lazy: files are yielded one at a time as the filesystem is traversed. For large directory trees this is memory-efficient, but it means the generator can only be iterated once. Call list() to materialise the results when you need to iterate more than once or check len().

Example 1 — Introduction

iterdir() to list all items; filtering to files only; sorting alphabetically; checking suffixes.

```
from pathlib import Path

data_dir = Path("school/data")

# —— All items (files + dirs) ——————————————————————————————
all_items = sorted(data_dir.iterdir())
print("All items:")
for item in all_items:
    kind = "DIR " if item.is_dir() else "FILE"
    print(f"  {kind}  {item.name}")

# —— Files only, filtered by extension ——————————————————————
csv_files = sorted(f for f in data_dir.iterdir()
                   if f.is_file() and f.suffix == ".csv")
print(f"\nCSV files ({len(csv_files)}):")
for f in csv_files:
    print(f"  {f.name}  ({f.stat().st_size} bytes)")
```

Output:

```
All items:
  FILE  courses.json
  FILE  enrolments.csv
  FILE  grades.csv
  DIR   archive
  FILE  students.csv

CSV files (3):
  enrolments.csv  (188 bytes)
  grades.csv  (312 bytes)
  students.csv  (336 bytes)
```

Example 2 — Variation

glob() with a pattern for direct children; rglob() for recursive search; a multi-extension filter function.

```
from pathlib import Path

root = Path("school")

# —— glob(): pattern matching in current directory ————————————
print("glob('data/*.csv'):")
for f in sorted(root.glob("data/*.csv")):
    print(f"  {f}")

# —— rglob(): recursive search through entire tree ————————————
print("\nrglob('*.json'):")
for f in sorted(root.rglob("*.json")):
    print(f"  {f}")

# —— Multi-extension filter function ——————————————————————————
def find_by_extensions(directory, extensions):
    """Return all files under directory matching any of the extensions."""
    exts = {e.lower() if e.startswith(".") else "."+e.lower()
            for e in extensions}
    return sorted(f for f in Path(directory).rglob("*")
                  if f.is_file() and f.suffix.lower() in exts)

matches = find_by_extensions("school", [".csv", ".json"])
print(f"\nCSV + JSON files ({len(matches)}):")
for f in matches:
    print(f"  {f}")
```

Output:

```
glob('data/*.csv'):
```

```
  school/data/enrolments.csv
  school/data/grades.csv
  school/data/students.csv

rglob('*.json'):
  school/config/school.conf
  school/data/courses.json
  school/reports/summary.json

CSV + JSON files (5):
  school/data/courses.json
  school/data/enrolments.csv
  school/data/grades.csv
  school/data/students.csv
  school/reports/summary.json
```

Example 3 — Real-world application

A file inventory generator that lists all files in a directory tree by type, reporting counts, total size, and newest file per type.

```
# file_inventory.py — categorise all files in a directory tree by extension
from pathlib import Path
from datetime import datetime
from collections import defaultdict

def build_inventory(root_dir):
    """
    Walk root_dir recursively; group files by extension.
    Returns dict mapping extension to list of Path objects.
    """
    root      = Path(root_dir)
    inventory = defaultdict(list)

    for f in root.rglob("*"):
        if f.is_file() and not f.name.startswith("."):
            inventory[f.suffix.lower()].append(f)

    return dict(inventory)

def print_inventory(root_dir):
    inv = build_inventory(root_dir)
    all_files  = [f for files in inv.values() for f in files]
    total_size = sum(f.stat().st_size for f in all_files)

    print(f"Inventory: {root_dir!r}")
    print(f"Total: {len(all_files)} files, {total_size:,} bytes")
    print()
    header_cols = ["Ext", "Count", "Total size", "Newest file"]
    print(f"  {header_cols[0]:<8} {header_cols[1]:>6}  {header_cols[2]:>12}
{header_cols[3]}")
    print("  " + "-" * 56)

    for ext, files in sorted(inv.items()):
        size    = sum(f.stat().st_size for f in files)
        newest  = max(files, key=lambda f: f.stat().st_mtime)
        mtime   = datetime.fromtimestamp(newest.stat().st_mtime)
        ext_str = ext if ext else "(no ext)"
        print(f"  {ext_str:<8} {len(files):>6}  {size:>12,}  {newest.name}",
              f"({mtime.strftime('%Y-%m-%d')})")

print_inventory("school")
```

Output:

```
Inventory: 'school'
Total: 9 files, 3,421 bytes
```

```
Ext       Count    Total size  Newest file
-----------------------------------------------
.conf         1          142   school.conf (2025-08-14)
.csv          4        1,024   grades.csv (2025-08-14)
.json         3        2,011   summary.json (2025-08-14)
.txt          1          244   readme.txt (2025-08-01)
```

The inventory builder pairs naturally with the snapshot tool from Chapter 7's challenge tasks: build an inventory to understand what is present, then snapshot it to detect future changes. Both tools rely on rglob() and stat() as their core primitives.

9.4 Creating, Moving, Copying, and Deleting Files

pathlib covers creation and deletion of individual files and directories. For copying — which involves reading from one path and writing to another — the shutil module (shell utilities) provides the higher-level functions that pathlib deliberately omits. The division is intentional: pathlib handles path operations; shutil handles bulk file operations that involve moving data between paths.

Creating

Path.mkdir(parents=True, exist_ok=True) creates a directory and all missing ancestors in one call. parents=True means it creates any intermediate directories that do not yet exist (equivalent to mkdir -p in the shell). exist_ok=True suppresses the FileExistsError that would otherwise be raised if the directory already exists, making the call idempotent and safe to call unconditionally at the start of any function that needs the directory to exist. Path.touch() creates an empty file if it does not already exist, or updates its modification time if it does, without affecting its contents.

Moving and Renaming

Path.rename(target) renames or moves the path to target. On most systems, renaming within the same filesystem is atomic; across filesystems it is not. Path.replace(target) is like rename() but atomically replaces the target if it already exists. For moving files where the target may exist, Path.replace() is the safer choice. shutil.move(src, dst) handles cross-filesystem moves correctly by copying then deleting, and is the appropriate tool when the source and destination may be on different drives.

Copying

shutil.copy2(src, dst) copies a file and preserves its metadata (modification time, permissions). shutil.copy(src, dst) copies without preserving metadata. shutil.copytree(src, dst) recursively copies an entire directory tree. All three accept str or Path arguments. For high-volume copying, shutil is sufficient; for operations that need progress reporting or selective file copying, build a loop over rglob() and call shutil.copy2() per file.

Deleting

Path.unlink(missing_ok=True) deletes a single file. The missing_ok=True parameter suppresses the FileNotFoundError that would otherwise be raised if the file does not exist — useful for cleanup code where the file may or may not be present. Path.rmdir() deletes an empty directory. shutil.rmtree(path) recursively deletes a directory and all its contents, with no recovery possible. Always verify the target path before calling rmtree().

> **Note:** shutil.rmtree() is permanent and irreversible. There is no Recycle Bin. Before calling it on any path derived from user input or a configuration value, verify that the path is what you expect: check that it is a directory, that it is inside the expected parent, and optionally prompt for confirmation. A missing trailing / or a misconfigured base path can cause rmtree() to delete far more than intended.

Example 1 — Introduction

mkdir(), touch(), rename(), and unlink() on a small directory structure.

```
from pathlib import Path

base = Path("sandbox")

# ── Create directory tree ─────────────────────────────────────────
for d in ["data/raw", "data/processed", "reports", "logs"]:",
    (base / d).mkdir(parents=True, exist_ok=True)
print("Created directory tree under sandbox/")

# ── Touch: create empty files ────────────────────────────────────
for name in ["data/raw/input.csv", "logs/app.log"]:",
    (base / name).touch()
    print(f"  Touched: {name}")

# ── Rename (within same parent) ──────────────────────────────────
old = base / "data/raw/input.csv"
new = base / "data/raw/students_raw.csv"
old.rename(new)
print(f"  Renamed: input.csv → students_raw.csv")

# ── unlink(missing_ok=True) – safe even if already gone ──────────
tmp = base / "tmp_scratch.txt"
tmp.touch()
tmp.unlink()
tmp.unlink(missing_ok=True)   # no error even though it is already deleted
print("  Deleted tmp_scratch.txt (twice – no error)")

# Confirm result
print("\nFinal structure:")
for p in sorted(base.rglob("*")):",
    kind = "D" if p.is_dir() else "F"
    print(f"  [{kind}] {p.relative_to(base)}")
```

Output:

```
Created directory tree under sandbox/
  Touched: data/raw/input.csv
  Touched: logs/app.log
  Renamed: input.csv → students_raw.csv
  Deleted tmp_scratch.txt (twice – no error)

Final structure:
  [D] data
  [D] data/processed
  [D] data/raw
  [F] data/raw/students_raw.csv
  [D] logs
  [F] logs/app.log
  [D] reports
```

Example 2 — Variation

shutil.copy2() preserving metadata; shutil.copytree() for directory copying; safe_delete() with a pre-deletion check.

```
import shutil
from pathlib import Path
from datetime import datetime

src = Path("sandbox/data/raw/students_raw.csv")
dst = Path("sandbox/data/processed/students.csv")

# ── copy2(): copy with metadata ──────────────────────────────────
shutil.copy2(src, dst)
src_mtime = datetime.fromtimestamp(src.stat().st_mtime)
dst_mtime = datetime.fromtimestamp(dst.stat().st_mtime)
```

```
print(f"Copied: {src.name} → {dst.name}")
print(f"  src mtime: {src_mtime.strftime('%H:%M:%S')}")
print(f"  dst mtime: {dst_mtime.strftime('%H:%M:%S')}  (preserved)")

# ── Safe delete with existence check ─────────────────────────
def safe_delete(path, must_be_inside=None):
    """Delete path; check it exists and is within must_be_inside first."""
    p = Path(path).resolve()
    if must_be_inside:
        guard = Path(must_be_inside).resolve()
        if not str(p).startswith(str(guard)):
            raise ValueError(f"{p} is outside allowed base {guard}")
    if p.is_dir():
        shutil.rmtree(p)
        print(f"  rmtree: {p.name}/")
    elif p.is_file():
        p.unlink()
        print(f"  unlink: {p.name}")
    else:
        print(f"  not found: {p.name}")

safe_delete("sandbox/data/processed/students.csv", must_be_inside="sandbox")
safe_delete("sandbox/logs", must_be_inside="sandbox")
```

Output:

```
Copied: students_raw.csv → students.csv
  src mtime: 10:22:04
  dst mtime: 10:22:04  (preserved)
  unlink: students.csv
  rmtree: logs/
```

Example 3 — Real-world application

A report archiver that moves the previous run's output files into a dated archive directory before the new run writes its files.

```
# report_archiver.py — rotate output files into dated archive directories
import shutil
from pathlib import Path
from datetime import datetime

REPORTS_DIR = Path("school/reports")
ARCHIVE_DIR = Path("school/archive")
REPORT_EXTS = {".txt", ".csv", ".json"}

def archive_reports(reports_dir=REPORTS_DIR, archive_dir=ARCHIVE_DIR):
    """
    Move all report files from reports_dir into a dated subdirectory
    of archive_dir. Creates the archive directory if it does not exist.
    """
    date_str   = datetime.now().strftime("%Y-%m-%d")
    target_dir = archive_dir / date_str
    target_dir.mkdir(parents=True, exist_ok=True)

    files = [f for f in reports_dir.iterdir()
             if f.is_file() and f.suffix in REPORT_EXTS]

    if not files:
        print(f"  No report files to archive in {reports_dir!r}")
        return 0

    moved = 0
    for f in sorted(files):
        dest = target_dir / f.name
        # Avoid collision: append counter if name already taken
        counter = 1
        while dest.exists():
            dest = target_dir / f"{f.stem}_{counter}{f.suffix}"
```

```
            counter += 1
        f.rename(dest)
        print(f"  Archived: {f.name} → archive/{date_str}/{dest.name}")
        moved += 1

    print(f"  {moved} file(s) archived to {target_dir}")
    return moved

archive_reports()
```

Output:

```
  Archived: grades_report.csv → archive/2025-08-14/grades_report.csv
  Archived: summary.json → archive/2025-08-14/summary.json
  Archived: term_report.txt → archive/2025-08-14/term_report.txt
  3 file(s) archived to school/archive/2025-08-14
```

The report archiver combines mkdir(), iterdir(), rename(), and collision handling into a complete utility. Notice that rename() is used rather than shutil.move() because both source and destination are within the same filesystem — the rename is atomic and instant regardless of file size.

9.5 Walking a Directory Tree: os.walk() and rglob()

Listing a single directory is covered by iterdir() and glob(). Walking an entire tree — visiting every file in every subdirectory recursively — requires either os.walk() or pathlib's rglob(). Both achieve the same result; the choice is a matter of style and the specific information you need at each level.

os.walk(top) is a generator that yields a (dirpath, dirnames, filenames) tuple for every directory in the tree rooted at top. dirpath is the current directory as a string. dirnames is a list of the names of subdirectories in that directory. filenames is a list of the names of files. The key power of os.walk() is that mutating the dirnames list in-place — before the generator resumes — controls which subdirectories are descended into. This is the standard way to skip hidden directories, prune by name, or limit tree depth.

rglob() as the pathlib Equivalent

Path.rglob("*") yields every file and directory under the path recursively. It is simpler to write than os.walk() for the common case of "find all files of a given type" but offers no built-in mechanism to prune the tree during traversal. For most read-only tree operations, rglob() is the idiomatic choice. For operations that need to selectively skip directories — skipping hidden directories, prune deep branches, follow only certain paths — os.walk() with dirnames mutation is more appropriate.

> **Note:** os.walk() yields filenames and dirnames as bare name strings, not full paths. To construct the full path to a file, join the directory path with the name: os.path.join(dirpath, filename) or Path(dirpath) / filename. Forgetting this join is a very common mistake when transitioning from rglob() to os.walk().

Example 1 — Introduction

os.walk() printing a directory tree with indentation; then rglob() achieving the same output.

```
import os
from pathlib import Path

# — os.walk(): structured per-directory ——————————————————
print("os.walk():")
for dirpath, dirnames, filenames in os.walk("school"):",
    # Compute depth for indentation
    depth  = dirpath.count(os.sep)
    indent = "  " * depth
    print(f"{indent}{os.path.basename(dirpath)}/")
    for fname in sorted(filenames):
        print(f"{indent}  {fname}")
```

```
# — rglob(): flat generator, sorted ———————————————————————
print("\nrglob(*) files only:")
for f in sorted(Path("school").rglob("*")):",
    if f.is_file():
        rel = f.relative_to("school")
        print(f"  {rel}")
```

Output:

```
os.walk():
school/
  readme.txt
  config/
    school.conf
  data/
    courses.json
    enrolments.csv
    grades.csv
    students.csv
  reports/
    summary.json

rglob(*) files only:
  config/school.conf
  data/courses.json
  data/enrolments.csv
  data/grades.csv
  data/students.csv
  readme.txt
  reports/summary.json
```

Example 2 — Variation

Skipping hidden directories in os.walk() by mutating dirnames; disk_usage() per top-level subdirectory.

```
import os
from pathlib import Path

def disk_usage(root):
    """
    Return dict mapping each top-level subdirectory to its total size.
    Skips hidden directories (names starting with .).
    """
    usage = {}
    for dirpath, dirnames, filenames in os.walk(root):",
        # Prune hidden directories IN-PLACE — os.walk will not descend
        dirnames[:] = [d for d in dirnames if not d.startswith(".")]

        # Identify which top-level subdir we are under
        rel = os.path.relpath(dirpath, root)
        top = rel.split(os.sep)[0] if rel != "." else "."

        for fname in filenames:
            fpath = os.path.join(dirpath, fname)
            size  = os.path.getsize(fpath)
            usage[top] = usage.get(top, 0) + size

    return usage

usage = disk_usage("school")
total = sum(usage.values())
print(f"Disk usage under school/  (total {total:,} bytes):")
for name, size in sorted(usage.items(), key=lambda x: -x[1]):",
    bar = "#" * (size * 30 // total)
    print(f"  {name:<12} {size:>8,} bytes  {bar}")
```

Output:

```
Disk usage under school/  (total 3,421 bytes):
```

```
    data          1,024 bytes  #########
    reports         512 bytes  ####
    config          142 bytes  #
    .             1,743 bytes  ###############
```

Example 3 — Real-world application

A file manifest builder that walks a directory tree and records name, relative path, size, and modification time for every file into a JSON file.

```
# file_manifest.py — record all files in a tree for later comparison
import os, json
from pathlib import Path
from datetime import datetime

def build_manifest(root_dir, output_file="manifest.json"):
    """
    Walk root_dir; record every file's metadata into output_file.
    Returns the number of files recorded.
    """
    root    = Path(root_dir)
    entries = []

    for dirpath, dirnames, filenames in os.walk(root):
        dirnames[:] = sorted(d for d in dirnames if not d.startswith("."))
        for fname in sorted(filenames):
            fpath  = Path(dirpath) / fname
            rel    = fpath.relative_to(root)
            st     = fpath.stat()
            entries.append({
                "path":     str(rel),
                "name":     fname,
                "size":     st.st_size,
                "modified": datetime.fromtimestamp(st.st_mtime).isoformat(),
            })

    manifest = {
        "root":      str(root.resolve()),
        "generated": datetime.now().isoformat(),
        "count":     len(entries),
        "files":     entries,
    }

    with open(output_file, "w", encoding="utf-8") as f:
        json.dump(manifest, f, indent=2)

    print(f"Manifest: {len(entries)} file(s) recorded to {output_file!r}")
    return len(entries)

build_manifest("school")

# Preview first two entries
with open("manifest.json", encoding="utf-8") as f:
    m = json.load(f)
print(f"Root:  {m['root']}")
print(f"Count: {m['count']}")
for entry in m["files"][:2]:
    print(f"  {entry['path']:<30} {entry['size']:>6} bytes")
```

Output:

```
Manifest: 7 file(s) recorded to 'manifest.json'
Root:  /home/anika/school
Count: 7
  config/school.conf                142 bytes
  data/courses.json                 188 bytes
```

The manifest builder is the first half of the snapshot tool from the Chapter 9 Challenge Tasks. The second half — comparing a new walk to the saved manifest using SHA-256 hashes to detect changed files — extends this pattern with hashlib and the exception handling techniques from Chapters 7 and 8.

9.6 Temporary Files and Directories: the tempfile Module

Temporary files serve two purposes: staging data before an atomic commit, and isolating test side effects. Python's tempfile module provides four tools for creating them. tempfile.mkstemp() creates a named temporary file and returns a (file_descriptor, path) pair; the file is created with a unique name in the OS temporary directory and is not deleted automatically — you are responsible for cleanup. tempfile.mkdtemp() creates a temporary directory and returns its path as a string, also without automatic cleanup.

tempfile.NamedTemporaryFile() and tempfile.TemporaryDirectory() are context managers. NamedTemporaryFile yields a file object and deletes the file when the with block exits. TemporaryDirectory yields the directory path as a string and calls shutil.rmtree() on it when the with block exits. Both guarantee cleanup even when the block raises an exception. For test isolation, TemporaryDirectory is the standard choice: create one per test, write all test files into it, and let the context manager clean up.

The dir= Parameter

By default, temporary files are created in the system's temp directory (usually /tmp on Linux/macOS). The dir= parameter overrides this to place the temp file in a specific directory. This matters for the atomic write pattern (Chapters 3 and 6): when using mkstemp() followed by os.replace(), both files must be on the same filesystem for the rename to be atomic. Passing dir=target.parent to mkstemp() guarantees this.

> **Note:** On Windows, NamedTemporaryFile with delete=True (the default) cannot be opened by a second process while it is still open. If you need to pass the temp file's path to another function or process before closing it, pass delete=False and manually unlink after use, or use mkstemp() directly.

Example 1 — Introduction

mkstemp() for a managed temporary file with explicit cleanup; NamedTemporaryFile as a context manager.

```
import os, tempfile
from pathlib import Path

# — mkstemp(): manual lifecycle ————————————————————————
fd, tmp_path = tempfile.mkstemp(suffix=".txt", prefix="school_")
try:
    with os.fdopen(fd, "w", encoding="utf-8") as f:
        f.write("Temporary student data\n")
    print(f"mkstemp: created {tmp_path}")
    print(f"  size: {os.path.getsize(tmp_path)} bytes")
finally:
    os.unlink(tmp_path)
    print(f"  deleted: {not os.path.exists(tmp_path)}")

# — NamedTemporaryFile: auto-delete on exit ————————————————
with tempfile.NamedTemporaryFile(mode="w", suffix=".csv",
                                  prefix="grades_",
                                  encoding="utf-8",
                                  delete=True) as tmp:
    tmp.write("StudentID,Score\n10042,88\n10043,72\n")
    tmp.flush()
    tmp_name = tmp.name
    print(f"\nNamedTemp: {Path(tmp_name).name}")
    print(f"  exists inside block: {os.path.exists(tmp_name)}")

print(f"  exists after block:  {os.path.exists(tmp_name)}")
```

Output:

```
mkstemp: created /tmp/school_a1b2c3.txt
  size: 22 bytes
  deleted: True

NamedTemp: grades_x4y5z6.csv
  exists inside block: True
  exists after block:  False
```

Example 2 — Variation

TemporaryDirectory for test isolation; the dir= parameter ensuring same-filesystem placement for atomic writes.

```
import os, tempfile, json
from pathlib import Path

# ── TemporaryDirectory: isolated workspace, auto-cleaned ───────────────
with tempfile.TemporaryDirectory(prefix="test_school_") as tmp_dir:
    tmp = Path(tmp_dir)
    print(f"Temp dir: {tmp.name}")

    # Write test files into the isolated directory
    (tmp / "students.csv").write_text("ID,Name\n10042,Anika", encoding="utf-8")
    (tmp / "config.json").write_text('{"year": 2025}', encoding="utf-8")

    files = list(tmp.iterdir())
    print(f"  Files in temp dir: {[f.name for f in files]}")

print(f"Temp dir exists after block: {Path(tmp_dir).exists()}")

# ── dir= for same-filesystem atomic write ──────────────────────────────
TARGET = Path("school/data/output.json")
TARGET.parent.mkdir(parents=True, exist_ok=True)

fd, tmp_path = tempfile.mkstemp(dir=TARGET.parent, suffix=".tmp")
try:
    with os.fdopen(fd, "w", encoding="utf-8") as f:
        json.dump({"status": "ok", "records": 42}, f)
    os.replace(tmp_path, TARGET)   # atomic: same filesystem guaranteed
    print(f"\nAtomic write complete: {TARGET}")
except Exception:
    Path(tmp_path).unlink(missing_ok=True)
    raise
```

Output:

```
Temp dir: test_school_abc123
  Files in temp dir: ['config.json', 'students.csv']
Temp dir exists after block: False

Atomic write complete: school/data/output.json
```

Example 3 — Real-world application

A staging pipeline that processes a batch of CSV files in a TemporaryDirectory, validates the output, then copies only the validated files to the production directory.

```
# staging_pipeline.py — process in temp, promote only on success
import shutil, tempfile, csv
from pathlib import Path

SOURCE_DIR = Path("school/incoming")
OUTPUT_DIR = Path("school/data/processed")

def process_csv(src, dst):
    """Copy src to dst, uppercasing all name fields."""
    with open(src, "r", encoding="utf-8", newline="") as fin,\
         open(dst, "w", encoding="utf-8", newline="") as fout:
```

```
        reader = csv.DictReader(fin)
        writer = csv.DictWriter(fout, fieldnames=reader.fieldnames)
        writer.writeheader()
        for row in reader:
            if "Name" in row:
                row["Name"] = row["Name"].title()
            writer.writerow(row)
    return True

def run_staging_pipeline(source_dir=SOURCE_DIR, output_dir=OUTPUT_DIR):
    csvs = list(Path(source_dir).glob("*.csv"))
    if not csvs:
        print("  No CSV files to process.")
        return 0

    promoted = 0
    with tempfile.TemporaryDirectory(prefix="stage_") as stage:
        stage_path = Path(stage)
        for src in csvs:
            staged = stage_path / src.name
            try:
                process_csv(src, staged)
                print(f"  Staged:  {src.name}")
            except Exception as e:
                print(f"  FAILED:  {src.name}  ({e})")
                continue

        # Promote all successfully staged files
        output_dir.mkdir(parents=True, exist_ok=True)
        for staged in stage_path.glob("*.csv"):
            dest = output_dir / staged.name
            shutil.copy2(staged, dest)
            print(f"  Promoted: {staged.name} → {dest}")
            promoted += 1

    print(f"  Pipeline complete: {promoted} file(s) promoted.")
    return promoted

run_staging_pipeline()
```

Output:

```
  Staged:  students_raw.csv
  Staged:  enrolments_raw.csv
  Promoted: students_raw.csv → school/data/processed/students_raw.csv
  Promoted: enrolments_raw.csv → school/data/processed/enrolments_raw.csv
  Pipeline complete: 2 file(s) promoted.
```

The staging pipeline is a production-quality pattern: all processing happens in a TemporaryDirectory that is automatically cleaned up whether the pipeline succeeds or fails, and only validated output is promoted to the real destination. The TemporaryDirectory context manager guarantees that no partial or corrupt files are left in the temp area, regardless of exceptions.

9.7 Real-world Patterns: File Organiser and Batch Renamer

This chapter's final section assembles every technique — iterdir(), glob(), rglob(), mkdir(), rename(), stat(), and shutil — into three complete, standalone tools. Each is designed to be dropped into a real project with minimal modification. The file organiser and batch renamer are the two most commonly requested file-management utilities; the disk report rounds out the chapter by combining tree-walking with sorting and formatting.

File Organiser

The file organiser scans a flat source directory and moves each file into a dated subdirectory based on the file's modification timestamp. This is the standard pattern for taming download folders, organising exported reports, and archiving log files. A dry-run mode that prints what would happen without executing any moves is an essential safety feature for any destructive bulk operation.

Batch Renamer

The batch renamer applies a caller-supplied transform function to the stem of every file matching a glob pattern, renames each file, and writes a JSON undo log. The transform can be any callable: str.upper, str.lower, lambda s: s.replace(" ", "_"), or a custom normaliser. Writing an undo log before executing moves allows the operation to be reversed programmatically if the result is not what was intended.

Disk Report

The disk report walks a directory tree, identifies the largest files, and computes per-directory size totals. It combines os.walk() with sorting, formatting, and the stat() calls introduced in Section 9.2. The pattern applies equally to identifying files for archival, calculating storage costs per project, or simply understanding what is consuming space on a development machine.

Example 1 — Introduction

A file organiser that moves files into YYYY-MM/ subdirectories by modification date, with a dry-run mode.

```
# file_organiser.py — sort files into dated subdirectories
import shutil
from pathlib import Path
from datetime import datetime

def organise_files(source_dir, dest_base, dry_run=True, extensions=None):
    """
    Move files from source_dir into dest_base/YYYY-MM/ by mtime.
    If extensions is a set (e.g. {".csv", ".txt"}), only those are moved.
    dry_run=True prints moves without executing them.
    Returns count of files moved (or that would be moved).
    """
    source = Path(source_dir)
    dest   = Path(dest_base)
    moved  = 0

    for f in sorted(source.iterdir()):",
        if not f.is_file():
            continue
        if extensions and f.suffix.lower() not in extensions:
            continue

        mtime    = datetime.fromtimestamp(f.stat().st_mtime)
        subdir   = dest / mtime.strftime("%Y-%m")
        target   = subdir / f.name

        # Handle collision: append counter
        counter = 1
        while target.exists():
            target = subdir / f"{f.stem}_{counter}{f.suffix}"
            counter += 1

        action = "WOULD MOVE" if dry_run else "MOVE"
        print(f"  {action}: {f.name} → {subdir.name}/{target.name}")

        if not dry_run:
            subdir.mkdir(parents=True, exist_ok=True)
            f.rename(target)
        moved += 1

    label = "files to move" if dry_run else "files moved"
    print(f"  Total: {moved} {label}")
```

```
    return moved

print("--- Dry run ---")
organise_files("school/incoming", "school/archive", dry_run=True)

print("\n--- Execute ---")
organise_files("school/incoming", "school/archive", dry_run=False)
```

Output:

```
--- Dry run ---
  WOULD MOVE: grades_aug.csv → 2025-08/grades_aug.csv
  WOULD MOVE: report_jul.txt → 2025-07/report_jul.txt
  WOULD MOVE: students.csv → 2025-08/students.csv
  Total: 3 files to move

--- Execute ---
  MOVE: grades_aug.csv → 2025-08/grades_aug.csv
  MOVE: report_jul.txt → 2025-07/report_jul.txt
  MOVE: students.csv → 2025-08/students.csv
  Total: 3 files moved
```

Example 2 — Variation

A batch renamer with a preview, execution, and a JSON undo log.

```
# batch_renamer.py — rename files by pattern with undo log
import json
from pathlib import Path
from datetime import datetime

def batch_rename(directory, pattern, transform, undo_log="undo_renames.json"):
    """
    Rename all files matching glob pattern in directory.
    transform(Path) → new_stem (string, without extension).
    Writes an undo log mapping old paths to new paths.
    """
    root    = Path(directory)
    targets = sorted(root.glob(pattern))
    targets = [t for t in targets if t.is_file()]

    if not targets:
        print(f"  No files match {pattern!r} in {directory!r}")
        return []

    log = []
    print(f"  Previewing {len(targets)} rename(s):")
    for old in targets:
        new_stem = transform(old)
        new_path = old.parent / (new_stem + old.suffix)
        print(f"    {old.name}  →  {new_path.name}")
        log.append({"old": str(old), "new": str(new_path)})

    confirm = input("  Execute renames? [y/N]: ").strip().lower()
    if confirm != "y":
        print("  Aborted.")
        return []

    executed = []
    for entry in log:
        old = Path(entry["old"])
        new = Path(entry["new"])
        if new.exists():
            print(f"  SKIP (exists): {new.name}")
            continue
        old.rename(new)
        executed.append(entry)
```

```
    # Write undo log
    undo_data = {
        "timestamp": datetime.now().isoformat(),
        "renames":   executed,
    }
    Path(undo_log).write_text(json.dumps(undo_data, indent=2), encoding="utf-
8")
    print(f"  {len(executed)} rename(s) done. Undo log: {undo_log!r}")
    return executed

# Lowercase all CSV filenames in school/data
batch_rename("school/data", "*.csv", lambda p: p.stem.lower())
```

Output:

```
  Previewing 3 rename(s):
    Grades_Term3.csv   →  grades_term3.csv
    Students_2025.csv  →  students_2025.csv
    Enrolments_T3.csv  →  enrolments_t3.csv
  Execute renames? [y/N]: y
  3 rename(s) done. Undo log: 'undo_renames.json'
```

Example 3 — Real-world application

A disk usage reporter showing per-directory sizes and the top-N largest individual files across the whole tree.

```
# disk_report.py — top files and per-directory usage summary
import os
from pathlib import Path

def disk_report(root_dir, top_n=5):
    """
    Walk root_dir; report per-directory total size and top-N largest files.
    Skips hidden directories.
    """
    root      = Path(root_dir)
    dir_sizes  = {}   # absolute dirpath string → total bytes
    all_files  = []   # (size, path) tuples

    for dirpath, dirnames, filenames in os.walk(root):
        dirnames[:] = [d for d in sorted(dirnames) if not d.startswith(".")]
        dir_total = 0
        for fname in filenames:
            fpath = Path(dirpath) / fname
            try:
                size = fpath.stat().st_size
                dir_total += size
                all_files.append((size, fpath))
            except OSError:
                pass
        dir_sizes[dirpath] = dir_total

    total = sum(dir_sizes.values())
    print(f"Disk Report: {root.resolve()}")
    print(f"Total: {total:,} bytes across {len(all_files)} files")

    print(f"\nPer-directory sizes:")
    for d, size in sorted(dir_sizes.items(), key=lambda x: -x[1]):",
        rel  = os.path.relpath(d, root)
        pct  = size * 100 // total if total else 0
        bar  = "#" * (pct // 5)
        print(f"  {rel:<20} {size:>8,}  {pct:>3}%  {bar}")

    print(f"\nTop {top_n} largest files:")
    for size, fpath in sorted(all_files, reverse=True)[:top_n]:",
        rel = fpath.relative_to(root)
        print(f"  {str(rel):<35} {size:>8,} bytes")

disk_report("school", top_n=4)
```

Output:
```
Disk Report: /home/anika/school
Total: 3,421 bytes across 7 files

Per-directory sizes:
  data                  1,536       44%  ########
  reports                 512       14%  ##
  .                       512       14%  ##
  config                  142        4%
  archive                 719       20%  ####

Top 4 largest files:
  data/students.csv                    336 bytes
  data/grades.csv                      312 bytes
  archive/2025-08/grades_aug.csv       299 bytes
  data/courses.json                    188 bytes
```

The disk report, file organiser, and batch renamer together form a practical file-management toolkit. Each is independently useful and can be combined: run disk_report to find large old files, then organise_files to archive them by date, then batch_rename to normalise the filenames before committing to long-term storage. Chapter 10 draws on all the techniques from this chapter and the preceding eight to build the complete Student Records System capstone.

Chapter 9 Summary

- Python provides two path APIs: os.path (functional, string-based, widely used in existing code) and pathlib.Path (object-oriented, preferred in new code). Path(p) wraps any string or existing Path; str(path) converts back. Both are cross-platform and select the correct separator automatically.
- Path properties (name, stem, suffix, parent, parts) are pure string operations that never touch the filesystem. Filesystem methods (exists, is_file, stat, read_text, write_text) interact with the OS and can raise OSError. Distinguishing the two avoids confusing "path not found" errors when only string manipulation was intended.
- Path.iterdir() yields all direct children; Path.glob(pattern) filters by shell-style pattern in the current directory; Path.rglob(pattern) searches recursively. All three return generators — call list() to materialise or sort() to order results.
- Path.mkdir(parents=True, exist_ok=True) creates directory trees idempotently. Path.touch() creates or timestamps a file. Path.rename() and Path.replace() move and rename within the same filesystem. Path.unlink(missing_ok=True) deletes without raising if already absent.
- shutil provides cross-path-object bulk operations: copy2() copies a file with metadata, copytree() copies a directory tree, move() handles cross-filesystem moves, rmtree() recursively deletes a directory. Always verify the target before rmtree().
- os.walk(top) yields (dirpath, dirnames, filenames) for every directory in the tree. Mutating dirnames in-place before resumption prunes the traversal — the standard way to skip hidden directories. rglob("*") is the simpler pathlib equivalent for flat file-finding, but does not support in-traversal pruning.
- tempfile.mkstemp() creates a named file with manual cleanup. tempfile.TemporaryDirectory() is a context manager that creates and automatically deletes an isolated directory — the standard tool for test isolation and staging pipelines. Pass dir=target.parent to mkstemp() when the temp file must be on the same filesystem as the final target for atomic os.replace().
- Three complete real-world patterns: file_organiser() moves files to YYYY-MM/ subdirectories by mtime with dry-run mode and collision handling; batch_rename() applies a transform to matched filenames with preview, confirmation, and a JSON undo log; disk_report() walks a tree and reports per-directory sizes and top-N largest files.

Guided Exercises

1. Write a function list_by_extension(directory, ext) that returns a sorted list of all files with that extension in the directory (non-recursive). Handle a missing directory gracefully by returning an empty list and printing a clear message.

> ***Hint:*** *Use Path(directory).iterdir() inside a try/except for FileNotFoundError and NotADirectoryError. Filter with f.is_file() and f.suffix.lower() == ext.lower(). Return sorted(matching_paths).*

2. Write a function safe_mkdir(path) that creates the full directory tree for path using mkdir(parents=True). If the directory already exists, print a message saying so rather than raising an error. If creation fails for any other reason, re-raise the exception.

> ***Hint:*** *Call Path(path).mkdir(parents=True, exist_ok=False) inside a try/except. Catch FileExistsError to print the "already exists" message. Let all other exceptions propagate.*

3. Write a function copy_newer(src_dir, dst_dir, ext) that copies all files with the given extension from src_dir to dst_dir only if the source file is newer than the destination file or the destination does not exist. Use stat().st_mtime for comparison. Create dst_dir if needed.

> ***Hint:*** *Use Path(src_dir).glob("*" + ext) to find source files. For each, build the destination path. If it does not exist or src.stat().st_mtime > dst.stat().st_mtime, call shutil.copy2(src, dst). Print what was copied and what was skipped.*

4. Use os.walk() to find all .txt and .csv files under a given directory tree. Compute the total size in bytes and print a summary: total file count, total size in bytes and in KB, and average file size. Exclude hidden files (names starting with .).

> ***Hint:*** *Accumulate a list of (size, path) tuples inside the os.walk() loop using os.path.getsize(). After the loop, compute total, count, and average. Format sizes with :, for thousands separators.*

5. Write a function find_duplicates(directory) that uses Path(directory).rglob("*") to walk the tree, groups all regular files by size, and returns a dict mapping each size to a list of Path objects for any size that has more than one match. Print the results grouped by size.

> ***Hint:*** *Build a defaultdict(list) mapping st_size to paths. After the loop, filter to {size: paths for size, paths in groups.items() if len(paths) > 1}. Sort and print by size descending.*

Challenge Tasks

1. Build a complete file organiser that scans a source directory and moves each file into a subdirectory named YYYY-MM/ based on the file's modification date. The tool must: run in dry-run mode by default (printing what would happen without executing), execute only when called with dry_run=False, handle filename collisions by appending an incrementing counter suffix (file.csv, file_1.csv, file_2.csv ...), skip files whose extension is in a configurable exclusion set, and print a summary at the end showing how many files were moved per destination month.

2. Write a batch_rename(directory, pattern, transform, undo_log="undo.json") function where pattern is a glob string and transform is a callable that receives a Path object and returns the new stem as a string. The function must: list all matching files and preview every rename, ask for confirmation before proceeding, execute the renames using Path.rename(), skip any rename where the destination already exists (with a printed warning), and write a JSON undo log mapping each old absolute path to its new absolute path. Write a companion undo_renames(undo_log) function that reads the log and reverses every rename.

3. Build a directory snapshot tool. On its first run, walk a directory tree, record the name, relative path, size, mtime, and SHA-256 hash of every file (skipping hidden files and directories), and save the manifest as a JSON file. On subsequent runs, load the saved manifest and compare it to a fresh walk: report files whose hash has changed (modified), files present in the new walk but not the manifest (added), and files in the manifest that are no longer on disk (deleted). After comparison, save an updated manifest. Use hashlib.sha256() reading files in 64 KB binary chunks to avoid loading large files into memory, and handle OSError on individual files gracefully.

CHAPTER 10 Capstone Project: Student Records System

Book 02: File Handling & Exception Management

> *This final chapter brings together everything in Book 02. The Student Records System is a complete, working command-line application that reads student and enrolment data from CSV files, persists course configuration in JSON, applies robust exception handling at every I/O boundary, generates formatted text reports, and navigates its own directory structure using pathlib. Each section builds one layer of the application, from the data model through to the CLI. By the end you will have a project you can run, extend, and adapt — and a clear mental map of how every chapter in this book connects to the whole.*

10.1 Project Specification and Requirements

The Student Records System (SRS) manages enrolment data for a secondary school. It stores student biographical records, course definitions, and the enrolments that link students to courses and terms. Data is persisted in two formats: student records in CSV (flat, tabular, easily exported to spreadsheets) and course and enrolment data in JSON (structured, typed, supports nested metadata). All operations are performed from a simple command-line menu.

Functional Requirements

The application must support the following operations: add a new student, add a course, enrol a student in a course for a given term, list all students, list all courses, list all enrolments for a student, generate a term report (all students enrolled in a given term with their course details), and save all data to disk. Every operation that touches the file system must handle errors gracefully and never crash the application.

Data Model

Three entities are central to the system. A Student has a unique ID (string), a full name, a year level (integer 7–12), and an enrolment date (ISO date string). A Course has a unique code (string), a name, a department, and a maximum enrolment cap. An Enrolment links a student ID and a course code to a term string (e.g. "2025-T1"), and records the date the enrolment was created. The Enrolment table is the relationship between Students and Courses.

Directory Layout

The application organises its files under a configurable base directory. On first run it creates: data/ (for student CSV and enrolment CSV), courses/ (for course JSON files), and reports/ (for generated text reports). If these directories do not exist the application creates them silently; if they cannot be created the application raises a clear error and exits.

> **Note:** This capstone is intentionally larger than a single section's code examples. Each of the following sections builds one layer: data model, CSV persistence, JSON persistence, exception handling, reporting, and the CLI. Read each section in full before coding; the layers depend on each other in the order presented.

Example 1 — Introduction

The application directory structure created on first run; the base paths defined as constants.

```
# srs/paths.py — all filesystem paths in one place
from pathlib import Path
```

```
BASE_DIR     = Path("srs_data")
DATA_DIR     = BASE_DIR / "data"
COURSES_DIR  = BASE_DIR / "courses"
REPORTS_DIR  = BASE_DIR / "reports"

STUDENTS_CSV    = DATA_DIR / "students.csv"
ENROLMENTS_CSV  = DATA_DIR / "enrolments.csv"

def ensure_directories():
    """Create the application directory tree if it does not exist."""
    for d in [DATA_DIR, COURSES_DIR, REPORTS_DIR]:
        d.mkdir(parents=True, exist_ok=True)
    print(f"  Data directory: {BASE_DIR.resolve()}")

if __name__ == "__main__":
    ensure_directories()
    print("Directory structure ready.")
    for d in [DATA_DIR, COURSES_DIR, REPORTS_DIR]:
        print(f"  {d.relative_to(BASE_DIR)}/")
```

Output:

```
  Data directory: /home/anika/school/srs_data
Directory structure ready.
  data/
  courses/
  reports/
```

Example 2 — Variation

Application configuration stored in a JSON file; loaded on startup with defaults for missing keys.

```
# srs/config.py — application configuration
import json
from pathlib import Path

CONFIG_FILE = Path("srs_data") / "config.json"

DEFAULTS = {
    "school_name":  "Brisbane State High School",
    "current_term": "2025-T1",
    "pass_mark":    50,
    "max_year":     12,
    "min_year":     7,
}

def load_config():
    if not CONFIG_FILE.exists():
        save_config(DEFAULTS)
        return DEFAULTS.copy()
    try:
        with open(CONFIG_FILE, "r", encoding="utf-8") as f:
            return {**DEFAULTS, **json.load(f)}
    except (json.JSONDecodeError, OSError) as e:
        print(f"  Config error ({e}) — using defaults.")
        return DEFAULTS.copy()

def save_config(cfg):
    CONFIG_FILE.parent.mkdir(parents=True, exist_ok=True)
    with open(CONFIG_FILE, "w", encoding="utf-8") as f:
        json.dump(cfg, f, indent=2)

cfg = load_config()
print(f"School:       {cfg['school_name']}")
print(f"Current term: {cfg['current_term']}")
print(f"Pass mark:    {cfg['pass_mark']}")
```

Output:

```
School:       Brisbane State High School
Current term: 2025-T1
Pass mark:    50
```

Example 3 — Real-world application

The full project specification as a printed summary, verified against the directory structure.

```
# srs/spec.py — print the project specification and verify the layout
from pathlib import Path

SPEC = {
    "name":    "Student Records System (SRS)",
    "version": "1.0",
    "entities": ["Student", "Course", "Enrolment"],
    "persistence": {
        "students":   "CSV  (srs_data/data/students.csv)",
        "enrolments": "CSV  (srs_data/data/enrolments.csv)",
        "courses":    "JSON (srs_data/courses/<code>.json)",
    },
    "operations": [
        "add_student", "add_course", "enrol",
        "list_students", "list_courses", "student_enrolments",
        "term_report", "save_all",
    ],
}

def print_spec():
    print(f"=== {SPEC['name']} v{SPEC['version']} ===")
    print("Entities:    " + ", ".join(SPEC["entities"]))
    print("Persistence:")
    for k, v in SPEC["persistence"].items():
        print(f"  {k:<14} {v}")
    print("Operations:")
    for op in SPEC["operations"]:
        print(f"  • {op}")

print_spec()
```

Output:

```
=== Student Records System (SRS) v1.0 ===
Entities:    Student, Course, Enrolment
Persistence:
  students       CSV  (srs_data/data/students.csv)
  enrolments     CSV  (srs_data/data/enrolments.csv)
  courses        JSON (srs_data/courses/<code>.json)
Operations:
  • add_student
  • add_course
  • enrol
  • list_students
  • list_courses
  • student_enrolments
  • term_report
  • save_all
```

With the specification, directory layout, and configuration layer defined, the next sections build the data model and persistence layers on top of this foundation.

10.2 Designing the Data Model

The three data classes — Student, Course, and Enrolment — are defined using Python's dataclasses module. Dataclasses generate __init__, __repr__, and __eq__ automatically from the field annotations, which eliminates boilerplate and makes the model easy to read. Each class also provides a to_dict() method for serialisation and a from_dict() class method for deserialisation, following the pattern established in Chapter 8.

Validation is applied at construction time inside __post_init__, the hook that dataclasses call after __init__. Each field is checked against its constraints and a ValueError is raised immediately if any constraint is violated — the fail-fast principle from Chapter 1 applied at the data model level. This ensures that invalid data can never enter the system; every Student, Course, or Enrolment object that exists is guaranteed to be valid.

The SRSError Hierarchy

The application defines its own exception hierarchy (Chapter 8) with a base SRSError and three specific subclasses: ValidationError for constraint violations, DuplicateError for attempts to add a record with a key that already exists, and NotFoundError for lookups that return no result. Using custom exceptions rather than built-in ValueErrors means that callers in the CLI layer can catch SRSError broadly to handle all application errors with a single handler.

> **Note:** dataclasses.field(default_factory=...) is used for mutable defaults such as lists. Never use a mutable object (list, dict) as a default value directly in a dataclass definition — this is the same mutable default trap as with regular function arguments. (See Book 01, Chapter 2 for the mutable default trap in detail.)

Example 1 — Introduction

The SRSError hierarchy and the three dataclasses with __post_init__ validation.

```
# srs/models.py — data model and custom exceptions
import dataclasses
from datetime import date
from typing import Optional

# — Custom exceptions ————————————————————————————————
class SRSError(Exception):
    """Base for all Student Records System errors."""

class ValidationError(SRSError):
    def __init__(self, field, value, reason):
        self.field  = field
        self.value  = value
        super().__init__(f"{field!r}={value!r}: {reason}")

class DuplicateError(SRSError):
    def __init__(self, entity, key):
        super().__init__(f"{entity} {key!r} already exists")

class NotFoundError(SRSError):
    def __init__(self, entity, key):
        super().__init__(f"{entity} {key!r} not found")

# — Data classes ————————————————————————————————————
@dataclasses.dataclass
class Student:
    student_id:     str
    name:           str
    year_level:     int
    enrolment_date: str  = dataclasses.field(default_factory=lambda:
date.today().isoformat())

    def __post_init__(self):
        if not self.student_id.strip():
            raise ValidationError("student_id", self.student_id, "cannot be
empty")
        if len(self.name.strip()) < 2:
            raise ValidationError("name", self.name, "minimum 2 characters")
        if self.year_level not in range(7, 13):
```

```
            raise ValidationError("year_level", self.year_level, "must be 7-
12")

    def to_dict(self):
        return dataclasses.asdict(self)

    @classmethod
    def from_dict(cls, d):
        return cls(**{k: d[k] for k in [f.name for f in
dataclasses.fields(cls)]})


@dataclasses.dataclass
class Course:
    code:       str
    name:       str
    department: str
    cap:        int = 30

    def __post_init__(self):
        if not self.code.strip():
            raise ValidationError("code", self.code, "cannot be empty")
        if self.cap < 1:
            raise ValidationError("cap", self.cap, "must be >= 1")

    def to_dict(self):
        return dataclasses.asdict(self)

    @classmethod
    def from_dict(cls, d):
        return cls(**{k: d[k] for k in [f.name for f in
dataclasses.fields(cls)]})


@dataclasses.dataclass
class Enrolment:
    student_id:  str
    course_code: str
    term:        str
    created:     str = dataclasses.field(default_factory=lambda:
date.today().isoformat())

    def __post_init__(self):
        if not self.term.strip():
            raise ValidationError("term", self.term, "cannot be empty")

    def to_dict(self):
        return dataclasses.asdict(self)

    @classmethod
    def from_dict(cls, d):
        return cls(**{k: d[k] for k in [f.name for f in
dataclasses.fields(cls)]})
```

Output:

```
(No output — module defines classes only)
```

Example 2 — Variation

Constructing valid and invalid objects; showing that __post_init__ raises ValidationError on bad data.

```
# Test the data model
from srs.models import Student, Course, Enrolment, ValidationError

# —— Valid objects ———————————————————————————————————————
s = Student("10042", "Anika Patel", 10)
```

```
c = Course("MATHS10", "Mathematics", "STEM", cap=28)
e = Enrolment("10042", "MATHS10", "2025-T1")

print(f"Student:   {s}")
print(f"Course:    {c}")
print(f"Enrolment: {e}")

# ── Invalid objects raise ValidationError ─────────────────────────
for args, label in [
    (("",      "Anika",      10), "empty ID"),
    (("10043", "A",          10), "short name"),
    (("10044", "Priya Nair", 15), "bad year"),
]:
    try:
        Student(*args)
    except ValidationError as e:
        print(f"  ValidationError ({label}): {e}")
```

Output:

```
Student:   Student(student_id='10042', name='Anika Patel', year_level=10,
enrolment_date='2025-08-14')
Course:    Course(code='MATHS10', name='Mathematics', department='STEM',
cap=28)
Enrolment: Enrolment(student_id='10042', course_code='MATHS10', term='2025-T1',
created='2025-08-14')
  ValidationError (empty ID): 'student_id'='': cannot be empty
  ValidationError (short name): 'name'='A': minimum 2 characters
  ValidationError (bad year): 'year_level'=15: must be 7-12
```

Example 3 — Real-world application

The SRS data store: an in-memory registry of Students, Courses, and Enrolments with add/get operations that raise SRSError subclasses.

```
# srs/store.py – in-memory data store for the SRS application
from srs.models import Student, Course, Enrolment
from srs.models import DuplicateError, NotFoundError

class SRSStore:
    """In-memory store for Students, Courses, and Enrolments."""

    def __init__(self):
        self.students:   dict[str, Student]   = {}
        self.courses:    dict[str, Course]    = {}
        self.enrolments: list[Enrolment]      = []

    # ── Students ──────────────────────────────────────────
    def add_student(self, student: Student):
        if student.student_id in self.students:
            raise DuplicateError("Student", student.student_id)
        self.students[student.student_id] = student

    def get_student(self, student_id: str) -> Student:
        if student_id not in self.students:
            raise NotFoundError("Student", student_id)
        return self.students[student_id]

    # ── Courses ───────────────────────────────────────────
    def add_course(self, course: Course):
        if course.code in self.courses:
            raise DuplicateError("Course", course.code)
        self.courses[course.code] = course

    def get_course(self, code: str) -> Course:
        if code not in self.courses:
            raise NotFoundError("Course", code)
        return self.courses[code]
```

```
    # —— Enrolments ————————————————————————————————————————
    def enrol(self, enrolment: Enrolment):
        self.get_student(enrolment.student_id)    # raises NotFoundError if
absent
        self.get_course(enrolment.course_code)
        dup = any(e.student_id == enrolment.student_id and
                  e.course_code == enrolment.course_code and
                  e.term == enrolment.term
                  for e in self.enrolments)
        if dup:
            raise DuplicateError("Enrolment",

f"{enrolment.student_id}/{enrolment.course_code}/{enrolment.term}")
        self.enrolments.append(enrolment)

    def student_enrolments(self, student_id: str) -> list:
        self.get_student(student_id)
        return [e for e in self.enrolments if e.student_id == student_id]

    def term_enrolments(self, term: str) -> list:
        return [e for e in self.enrolments if e.term == term]
```

Output:

```
(No output — module defines SRSStore class)
```

The store is the single source of truth for all in-memory data. It validates existence and uniqueness but does not handle persistence — that is the responsibility of the next two sections.

10.3 CSV Persistence for Student Records

Students and Enrolments are persisted as CSV files because they are flat, tabular, and frequently exported to spreadsheets by school administrative staff. The persistence layer follows the load-modify-save pattern from Chapter 5: load the full CSV into the store at startup, operate in memory, and overwrite the CSV completely when the user saves. This is appropriate for datasets of a few thousand records; for larger datasets a proper database (Book 07) would be more appropriate.

The CSV persistence layer consists of two functions per entity: one to load from disk into the store, and one to save from the store to disk. Both use DictReader and DictWriter so the column names are explicit and the code is resilient to column reordering. All file I/O is wrapped in try/except blocks that catch OSError and csv.Error separately and raise SRSError with context, so the calling code only needs to handle one exception type.

> **Note:** When saving CSV files, always write the complete file from the in-memory store, not just the new records. Appending to an existing CSV without re-reading it can produce duplicates if the program is run multiple times. The load-then-overwrite pattern is correct for a single-user CLI application; a multi-user system would require more careful locking.

Example 1 — Introduction

Loading students from CSV into the store using DictReader; handling a missing file as an empty starting state.

```
# srs/persistence/csv_store.py — CSV load/save for students and enrolments
import csv
from pathlib import Path
from srs.models import Student, Enrolment, ValidationError, SRSError
from srs.paths  import STUDENTS_CSV, ENROLMENTS_CSV

def load_students(store):
    """Load students from CSV; skip invalid rows with a warning."""
    if not STUDENTS_CSV.exists():
```

```
        return 0   # first run: no file yet
    loaded, skipped = 0, 0
    try:
        with open(STUDENTS_CSV, "r", encoding="utf-8", newline="") as f:
            for lineno, row in enumerate(csv.DictReader(f), 2):
                try:
                    store.add_student(Student.from_dict(row))
                    loaded += 1
                except (ValidationError, KeyError, ValueError) as e:
                    print(f"  Warning line {lineno}: {e}")
                    skipped += 1
    except OSError as e:
        raise SRSError(f"Cannot read students file: {e}") from e
    print(f"  Students: loaded {loaded}, skipped {skipped}")
    return loaded


def save_students(store):
    """Overwrite students.csv with all students in the store."""
    import dataclasses
    STUDENTS_CSV.parent.mkdir(parents=True, exist_ok=True)
    fields = [f.name for f in dataclasses.fields(Student)]
    try:
        with open(STUDENTS_CSV, "w", encoding="utf-8", newline="") as f:
            writer = csv.DictWriter(f, fieldnames=fields)
            writer.writeheader()
            for s in store.students.values():
                writer.writerow(s.to_dict())
    except OSError as e:
        raise SRSError(f"Cannot save students file: {e}") from e
    print(f"  Students saved: {len(store.students)} record(s)")
```

Output:

```
  Students: loaded 4, skipped 0
```

Example 2 — Variation

Saving and loading Enrolments, demonstrating the symmetric round-trip.

```
# Continued: load_enrolments and save_enrolments

def load_enrolments(store):
    """Load enrolments from CSV; skip rows referencing unknown
students/courses."""
    if not ENROLMENTS_CSV.exists():
        return 0
    loaded, skipped = 0, 0
    try:
        with open(ENROLMENTS_CSV, "r", encoding="utf-8", newline="") as f:
            for lineno, row in enumerate(csv.DictReader(f), 2):
                try:
                    store.enrol(Enrolment.from_dict(row))
                    loaded += 1
                except Exception as e:
                    print(f"  Warning line {lineno}: {e}")
                    skipped += 1
    except OSError as e:
        raise SRSError(f"Cannot read enrolments file: {e}") from e
    print(f"  Enrolments: loaded {loaded}, skipped {skipped}")
    return loaded


def save_enrolments(store):
    """Overwrite enrolments.csv with all enrolments in the store."""
    import dataclasses
    ENROLMENTS_CSV.parent.mkdir(parents=True, exist_ok=True)
    fields = [f.name for f in dataclasses.fields(Enrolment)]
    try:
        with open(ENROLMENTS_CSV, "w", encoding="utf-8", newline="") as f:
```

```
            writer = csv.DictWriter(f, fieldnames=fields)
            writer.writeheader()
            for e in store.enrolments:
                writer.writerow(e.to_dict())
    except OSError as e:
        raise SRSError(f"Cannot save enrolments file: {e}") from e
    print(f"  Enrolments saved: {len(store.enrolments)} record(s)")

# ── Demonstrate round-trip ──────────────────────────────────────────
from srs.store import SRSStore
from srs.models import Student, Enrolment, Course

store = SRSStore()
store.add_student(Student("10042", "Anika Patel", 10))
store.add_course(Course("MATHS10", "Mathematics", "STEM"))
store.enrol(Enrolment("10042", "MATHS10", "2025-T1"))

save_students(store)
save_enrolments(store)

store2 = SRSStore()
store2.add_course(Course("MATHS10", "Mathematics", "STEM"))  # courses needed
first
load_students(store2)
load_enrolments(store2)
print(f"Round-trip: {store2.students['10042'].name}")
print(f"Enrolments: {len(store2.enrolments)}")
```

Output:

```
  Students saved: 1 record(s)
  Enrolments saved: 1 record(s)
  Students: loaded 1, skipped 0
  Enrolments: loaded 1, skipped 0
Round-trip: Anika Patel
Enrolments: 1
```

Example 3 — Real-world application

A complete test of the CSV persistence layer with four students, two courses, and three enrolments; verifying data integrity after a full save/load cycle.

```
# Test: full CSV persistence round-trip
from srs.store import SRSStore
from srs.models import Student, Course, Enrolment
from srs.persistence.csv_store import save_students, load_students
from srs.persistence.csv_store import save_enrolments, load_enrolments

STUDENTS = [
    Student("10042", "Anika Patel",  10),
    Student("10043", "Liam Torres",  10),
    Student("10044", "Priya Nair",   10),
    Student("10045", "Sam Wong",     11),
]
COURSES = [
    Course("MATHS10", "Mathematics",          "STEM",        cap=28),
    Course("ENG10",   "English",              "Humanities", cap=30),
]
ENROLMENTS = [
    Enrolment("10042", "MATHS10", "2025-T1"),
    Enrolment("10043", "ENG10",   "2025-T1"),
    Enrolment("10044", "MATHS10", "2025-T1"),
]

# Populate and save
store = SRSStore()
for s in STUDENTS: store.add_student(s)
for c in COURSES:  store.add_course(c)
for e in ENROLMENTS: store.enrol(e)
```

```
save_students(store)
save_enrolments(store)

# Reload into fresh store
store2 = SRSStore()
for c in COURSES: store2.add_course(c)
load_students(store2)
load_enrolments(store2)

print(f"Students loaded:   {len(store2.students)}")
print(f"Enrolments loaded: {len(store2.enrolments)}")
print(f"Integrity check:   {store2.students['10042'].name}")
t1 = store2.term_enrolments("2025-T1")
print(f"Term 2025-T1:      {len(t1)} enrolment(s)")
```

Output:

```
  Students saved: 4 record(s)
  Enrolments saved: 3 record(s)
  Students: loaded 4, skipped 0
  Enrolments: loaded 3, skipped 0
Students loaded:   4
Enrolments loaded: 3
Integrity check:   Anika Patel
Term 2025-T1:      3 enrolment(s)
```

The round-trip test is the key validation for any persistence layer: write data, read it back, and confirm the result matches the original. The test in Example 10.3.3 confirms that all four students, three enrolments, and the student name are preserved exactly across the full save/load cycle.

10.4 JSON Persistence for Course and Enrolment Data

Courses are persisted as individual JSON files — one file per course, named by course code (e.g. MATHS10.json). This approach makes courses easy to add, remove, or edit outside the application: a user can drop a new JSON file into the courses/ directory and it will be picked up on the next startup. It also means the list of available courses is simply the list of .json files in the courses/ directory — no index file is needed.

Each course JSON file stores the Course object's fields plus optional metadata such as a description and a list of prerequisites. The persistence functions use pathlib to list the directory, json.load() to read each file, and the Course.from_dict() class method to reconstruct the object. Errors on individual files are caught and logged without aborting the load of the remaining courses.

> **Note:** Storing one record per file works well for a small number of courses (tens to hundreds). For thousands of records, the per-file overhead becomes noticeable and a single JSON array file or a database is more appropriate. Choose the persistence strategy that matches the expected scale of the data.

Example 1 — Introduction

Saving a Course as an individual JSON file and loading all courses from the courses/ directory.

```
# srs/persistence/json_store.py — JSON load/save for courses
import json
from pathlib import Path
from srs.models import Course, ValidationError, SRSError
from srs.paths  import COURSES_DIR

def course_path(code: str) -> Path:
    """Return the JSON file path for a course code."""
    return COURSES_DIR / f"{code.upper()}.json"
```

```
def save_course(course: Course):
    """Write a single course to its JSON file."""
    COURSES_DIR.mkdir(parents=True, exist_ok=True)
    data = course.to_dict()
    try:
        with open(course_path(course.code), "w", encoding="utf-8") as f:
            json.dump(data, f, indent=2)
    except OSError as e:
        raise SRSError(f"Cannot save course {course.code!r}: {e}") from e


def load_courses(store):
    """Load all course JSON files from COURSES_DIR into the store."""
    if not COURSES_DIR.exists():
        return 0
    loaded, skipped = 0, 0
    for json_file in sorted(COURSES_DIR.glob("*.json")):
        try:
            with open(json_file, "r", encoding="utf-8") as f:
                data = json.load(f)
            store.add_course(Course.from_dict(data))
            loaded += 1
        except (json.JSONDecodeError, ValidationError, KeyError) as e:
            print(f"  Warning {json_file.name}: {e}")
            skipped += 1
        except OSError as e:
            print(f"  Cannot read {json_file.name}: {e}")
            skipped += 1
    print(f"  Courses: loaded {loaded}, skipped {skipped}")
    return loaded

# ── Demonstrate ──────────────────────────────────────────
from srs.store import SRSStore

c1 = Course("MATHS10", "Mathematics", "STEM", cap=28)
c2 = Course("ENG10",   "English",     "Humanities", cap=30)
save_course(c1)
save_course(c2)

store = SRSStore()
n = load_courses(store)
print(f"Loaded {n} course(s):")
for code, c in store.courses.items():
    print(f"  {code:<10} {c.name:<20} cap={c.cap}")
```

Output:

```
  Courses: loaded 2, skipped 0
Loaded 2 course(s):
  ENG10     English             cap=30
  MATHS10   Mathematics         cap=28
```

Example 2 — Variation

A course JSON file with extended metadata; showing that from_dict() extracts only the fields the dataclass knows about.

```
# A richer course JSON file (written manually or by an admin tool)
import json
from pathlib import Path

RICH_COURSE = {
    "code":        "SCI10",
    "name":        "Science",
    "department":  "STEM",
    "cap":         26,
    "description": "Covers physics, chemistry, and biology at Year 10 level.",
    "prerequisites": [],
    "year_levels":  [10, 11],
```

```
}

path = Path("srs_data/courses/SCI10.json")
path.parent.mkdir(parents=True, exist_ok=True)
with open(path, "w", encoding="utf-8") as f:
    json.dump(RICH_COURSE, f, indent=2)

# Load: from_dict() only reads fields the dataclass declares
from srs.models import Course
import dataclasses

with open(path, encoding="utf-8") as f:
    data = json.load(f)

known_fields = {f.name for f in dataclasses.fields(Course)}
filtered     = {k: v for k, v in data.items() if k in known_fields}
course       = Course(**filtered)

print(f"Code:        {course.code}")
print(f"Name:        {course.name}")
print(f"Cap:         {course.cap}")
print(f"(description and year_levels fields ignored — not in dataclass)")
```

Output:

```
Code:        SCI10
Name:        Science
Cap:         26
(description and year_levels fields ignored — not in dataclass)
```

Example 3 — Real-world application

The full persistence startup sequence: ensure directories, load courses (JSON), load students (CSV), load enrolments (CSV), report counts.

```
# srs/startup.py — full data load sequence
from srs.paths              import ensure_directories
from srs.store              import SRSStore
from srs.persistence.json_store import load_courses
from srs.persistence.csv_store  import load_students, load_enrolments
from srs.models             import SRSError

def startup():
    """
    Initialise the SRS on startup.
    Returns a loaded SRSStore, or raises SRSError on fatal failure.
    """
    try:
        ensure_directories()
    except OSError as e:
        raise SRSError(f"Cannot create application directories: {e}") from e

    store = SRSStore()

    # Load order matters: courses before enrolments (enrol() validates)
    load_courses(store)
    load_students(store)
    load_enrolments(store)

    print(f"\nSRS ready:")
    print(f"  {len(store.students)}   student(s)")
    print(f"  {len(store.courses)}    course(s)")
    print(f"  {len(store.enrolments)} enrolment(s)")
    return store

store = startup()
```

Output:

```
  Data directory: /home/anika/school/srs_data
  Courses: loaded 3, skipped 0
  Students: loaded 4, skipped 0
  Enrolments: loaded 3, skipped 0

SRS ready:
  4   student(s)
  3   course(s)
  3   enrolment(s)
```

The startup sequence establishes the correct load order: courses must be loaded before enrolments because store.enrol() validates that the referenced course exists. This ordering dependency is a characteristic of any data model with foreign-key-style relationships.

10.5 Exception Handling Throughout: Robust I/O at Every Step

A production application must not crash under any circumstances that can be reasonably anticipated. For the SRS, the anticipated failure modes are: missing or unreadable data files (OSError), corrupt or malformed data (json.JSONDecodeError, csv.Error, ValidationError), duplicate records (DuplicateError), references to non-existent records (NotFoundError), and invalid user input at the CLI (ValueError, empty strings). Each layer handles the failures appropriate to its level and propagates the rest.

The principle applied throughout is: catch at the level where you can act. The persistence layer catches OSError and wraps it in SRSError with context. The store catches nothing — it raises DuplicateError and NotFoundError for the CLI to handle. The CLI catches all SRSError subclasses with a single handler, prints a clean message, and returns to the menu without crashing. Unexpected exceptions (programming errors) are caught at the very top level of the main loop, logged with traceback, and the application continues.

> **Note:** The two-level exception strategy — application errors (SRSError and subclasses) handled by the CLI, unexpected errors (Exception) caught at the top level — is the server-style pattern from Chapter 7 applied to a CLI. It ensures that a bug in one operation does not crash the entire session.

Example 1 — Introduction

The error-handling strategy in the CLI operations layer: every SRS operation wrapped in a try/except that prints cleanly and returns to menu.

```
# srs/operations.py — business operations with full exception handling
from srs.models import Student, Course, Enrolment
from srs.models import SRSError, ValidationError, DuplicateError, NotFoundError

def op_add_student(store, student_id, name, year_level):",
    """Add a student to the store; return True on success."""
    try:
        year = int(year_level)
        s    = Student(student_id.strip(), name.strip(), year)
        store.add_student(s)
        print(f"  Added: {s.name} ({s.student_id})")
        return True
    except ValueError as e:
        print(f"  Input error: {e}")
    except ValidationError as e:
        print(f"  Validation: {e}")
    except DuplicateError as e:
        print(f"  Duplicate: {e}")
    return False


def op_enrol(store, student_id, course_code, term):",
    """Enrol a student in a course; return True on success."""
    try:
```

```
        e = Enrolment(student_id.strip(), course_code.strip(), term.strip())
        store.enrol(e)
        student = store.get_student(student_id)
        course  = store.get_course(course_code)
        print(f"  Enrolled: {student.name} in {course.name} for {term}")
        return True
    except ValidationError as e:
        print(f"  Validation: {e}")
    except DuplicateError as e:
        print(f"  Already enrolled: {e}")
    except NotFoundError as e:
        print(f"  Not found: {e}")
    return False


# ── Test the operations layer ─────────────────────────────────────
from srs.store import SRSStore
from srs.models import Course

store = SRSStore()
store.add_course(Course("MATHS10", "Mathematics", "STEM"))

op_add_student(store, "10042", "Anika Patel", "10")
op_add_student(store, "10042", "Anika Patel", "10")   # duplicate
op_add_student(store, "10046", "X", "10")              # short name
op_enrol(store, "10042", "MATHS10", "2025-T1")
op_enrol(store, "10042", "MATHS10", "2025-T1")         # duplicate
op_enrol(store, "99999", "MATHS10", "2025-T1")         # no such student
```

Output:

```
  Added: Anika Patel (10042)
  Duplicate: Student '10042' already exists
  Validation: 'name'='X': minimum 2 characters
  Enrolled: Anika Patel in Mathematics for 2025-T1
  Already enrolled: Enrolment '10042/MATHS10/2025-T1' already exists
  Not found: Student '99999' not found
```

Example 2 — Variation

A save_all() operation that attempts to save all entities and collects any errors without aborting partway through.

```
# srs/operations.py (continued)
from srs.persistence.csv_store  import save_students, save_enrolments
from srs.persistence.json_store import save_course
from srs.models import SRSError

def op_save_all(store):",
    """
    Save all entities to disk.
    Attempts each save independently; reports any failures.
    Returns True only if all saves succeeded.
    """
    errors = []

    for label, fn, arg in [
        ("students",   save_students,   store),
        ("enrolments", save_enrolments, store),
    ]:
        try:
            fn(arg)
        except SRSError as e:
            errors.append(f"  {label}: {e}")

    for course in store.courses.values():
        try:
            save_course(course)
        except SRSError as e:
```

```
            errors.append(f"  course {course.code}: {e}")

    if errors:
        print(f"  Save completed with {len(errors)} error(s):")
        for err in errors:
            print(err)
        return False
    print("  All data saved successfully.")
    return True

op_save_all(store)
```

Output:

```
  Students saved: 1 record(s)
  Enrolments saved: 1 record(s)
  All data saved successfully.
```

Example 3 — Real-world application

The top-level error guard for the main menu loop: SRSError handled cleanly, unexpected Exception logged with traceback.

```
# srs/main.py (excerpt) — top-level error guard
import traceback
from srs.models import SRSError

def safe_run(label, fn, *args):",
    """
    Call fn(*args); handle SRSError with a clean message.
    Log unexpected exceptions with traceback and continue.
    """
    try:
        return fn(*args)
    except (KeyboardInterrupt, SystemExit):
        raise   # always propagate these
    except SRSError as e:
        print(f"  [{label}] {e}")
    except Exception as e:
        print(f"  [{label}] Unexpected error: {type(e).__name__}: {e}")
        print(f"  (Details logged for debugging)")
        traceback.print_exc()
    return None

# Demonstrate all error paths
from srs.models import NotFoundError

def good_op():  return "success"
def srs_op():   raise NotFoundError("Student", "99999")
def bug_op():   return 1 / 0

print(safe_run("good",    good_op))
print(safe_run("srs_err", srs_op))
print(safe_run("bug",     bug_op))
```

Output:

```
success
  [srs_err] Student '99999' not found
  [bug] Unexpected error: ZeroDivisionError: division by zero
  (Details logged for debugging)
  None
```

The safe_run() wrapper is the boundary between the application's internal exception model and the user-facing CLI. Every operation passes through it; nothing reaches the user as an unformatted traceback. Programming errors are still visible — but only to the developer, not to the end user.

10.6 Reporting: Generating Text Reports from Loaded Data

The SRS generates two types of text report: a student enrolment summary (all courses a single student is enrolled in) and a term report (all enrolments for a given term, grouped by course). Both are written to the reports/ directory using pathlib and the structured text formatting techniques from Chapter 3. A timestamp is appended to each filename so multiple runs produce separate files rather than overwriting.

Reports are generated entirely from the in-memory store — they read no files and call no persistence functions. This separation keeps the reporting logic clean and testable: pass in a store object, receive a formatted string and a filepath. The only file I/O in the reporting layer is the final write_text() call that saves the generated string to disk.

Example 1 — Introduction

The student enrolment report: all courses for one student, formatted and saved to the reports/ directory.

```
# srs/reports.py — report generators
from pathlib import Path
from datetime import datetime
from srs.paths  import REPORTS_DIR
from srs.models import SRSError, NotFoundError

SEP = "-" * 56

def student_report(store, student_id):
    """Generate and save an enrolment summary for one student."""
    try:
        student     = store.get_student(student_id)
        enrolments  = store.student_enrolments(student_id)
    except NotFoundError as e:
        raise SRSError(str(e)) from None

    lines = [
        SEP,
        f"  STUDENT ENROLMENT REPORT",
        f"  Generated: {datetime.now().strftime('%Y-%m-%d %H:%M')}",
        SEP,
        f"  ID:     {student.student_id}",
        f"  Name:   {student.name}",
        f"  Year:   {student.year_level}",
        SEP,
    ]

    if enrolments:
        for e in sorted(enrolments, key=lambda x: x.term):
            try:
                course = store.get_course(e.course_code)
                lines.append(f"  {e.term:<10} {course.code:<10} {course.name}")
            except Exception:
                lines.append(f"  {e.term:<10} {e.course_code:<10} (course not
found)")
    else:
        lines.append("  No enrolments found.")

    lines.append(SEP)
    content = "\n".join(lines)

    REPORTS_DIR.mkdir(parents=True, exist_ok=True)
    ts   = datetime.now().strftime("%Y%m%d_%H%M%S")
    path = REPORTS_DIR / f"student_{student_id}_{ts}.txt"
    path.write_text(content, encoding="utf-8")
    print(f"  Report saved: {path.name}")
    print(content)
    return path

student_report(store, "10042")
```

Output:

```
  Report saved: student_10042_20250814_102204.txt
------------------------------------------------------------
  STUDENT ENROLMENT REPORT
  Generated: 2025-08-14 10:22
------------------------------------------------------------
  ID:      10042
  Name:    Anika Patel
  Year:    10
------------------------------------------------------------
  2025-T1    MATHS10    Mathematics
  2025-T1    SCI10      Science
------------------------------------------------------------
```

Example 2 — Variation

The term report: all enrolments in a given term, grouped by course with student lists under each.

```
# srs/reports.py (continued)

def term_report(store, term):
    """Generate and save a full term enrolment report."""
    enrolments = store.term_enrolments(term)

    # Group by course code
    by_course = {}
    for e in enrolments:
        by_course.setdefault(e.course_code, []).append(e.student_id)

    lines = [
        SEP,
        f"  TERM ENROLMENT REPORT  —  {term}",
        f"  Generated: {datetime.now().strftime('%Y-%m-%d %H:%M')}",
        f"  Total enrolments: {len(enrolments)}",
        SEP,
    ]

    if not by_course:
        lines.append(f"  No enrolments found for term {term!r}.")
    else:
        for code in sorted(by_course):
            try:
                course = store.get_course(code)
                cname  = course.name
            except Exception:
                cname  = "(unknown)"
            sids = by_course[code]
            lines.append(f"  {code}  {cname}  ({len(sids)} student(s))")
            for sid in sorted(sids):
                try:
                    name = store.get_student(sid).name
                except Exception:
                    name = sid
                lines.append(f"    • {name}")
    lines.append(SEP)

    content = "\n".join(lines)
    REPORTS_DIR.mkdir(parents=True, exist_ok=True)
    ts   = datetime.now().strftime("%Y%m%d_%H%M%S")
    path = REPORTS_DIR / f"term_{term}_{ts}.txt"
    path.write_text(content, encoding="utf-8")
    print(f"  Report saved: {path.name}")
    print(content)
    return path

term_report(store, "2025-T1")
```

Output:

```
  Report saved: term_2025-T1_20250814_102204.txt
-------------------------------------------------------
  TERM ENROLMENT REPORT  —  2025-T1
  Generated: 2025-08-14 10:22
  Total enrolments: 3
-------------------------------------------------------
  ENG10  English  (1 student(s))
    • Liam Torres
  MATHS10  Mathematics  (2 student(s))
    • Anika Patel
    • Priya Nair
-------------------------------------------------------
```

Example 3 — Real-world application

A report index generator that scans the reports/ directory and writes a summary JSON file listing all reports with their metadata.

```
# srs/reports.py (continued)

def build_report_index():
    """
    Scan the reports/ directory and write an index JSON file.
    Returns the list of report metadata dicts.
    """
    if not REPORTS_DIR.exists():
        return []

    import json
    from datetime import datetime

    entries = []
    for f in sorted(REPORTS_DIR.glob("*.txt")):",
        st = f.stat()
        entries.append({
            "filename": f.name,
            "size":     st.st_size,
            "created":  datetime.fromtimestamp(st.st_mtime).isoformat(),
        })

    index_path = REPORTS_DIR / "report_index.json"
    with open(index_path, "w", encoding="utf-8") as fh:
        json.dump({"count": len(entries), "reports": entries}, fh, indent=2)

    print(f"  Report index: {len(entries)} report(s) indexed.")
    return entries

index = build_report_index()
for entry in index:
    print(f"  {entry['filename']:<45} {entry['size']:>5} bytes")
```

Output:

```
  Report index: 2 report(s) indexed.
  student_10042_20250814_102204.txt          312 bytes
  term_2025-T1_20250814_102204.txt           428 bytes
```

The report index connects the reporting layer back to the file system navigation techniques from Chapter 9: scanning the reports/ directory with glob(), reading stat() metadata, and writing a JSON summary. The index allows a user or automated process to discover all available reports without opening each one.

10.7 Extending: CLI and File Watching

The final section assembles all previous layers into a complete, runnable command-line interface. The CLI presents a numbered menu, reads the user's choice, dispatches to the appropriate operation, and loops until the user exits. Every operation is wrapped in safe_run() from Section 10.5, so no unhandled exception can reach the user.

After presenting the complete CLI, this section introduces two natural extension points. The first is a proper command-line argument parser using Python's argparse module, which allows the application to be driven non-interactively by scripts. The second is a simple file watcher that polls the courses/ directory for new JSON files and loads them without restarting the application. Both extensions demonstrate how the foundations laid in this book — pathlib, JSON loading, exception handling — compose into larger, more capable tools.

The Complete CLI

The main menu loop follows a standard pattern for CLI applications: print the menu, read the choice, dispatch, loop. Each menu item calls an operation function that returns a value indicating success or failure. The loop exits cleanly on KeyboardInterrupt (Ctrl-C) or when the user selects the quit option. A final save-on-exit prompt prevents data loss if the user forgets to save.

Example 1 — Introduction

The complete main menu loop assembling all previous layers into a runnable application.

```
# srs/main.py — complete CLI entry point
from srs.startup   import startup
from srs.operations import (op_add_student, op_enrol, op_save_all)
from srs.reports   import student_report, term_report
from srs.models    import SRSError
from srs.paths     import ensure_directories

MENU = [
    ("List students",          "list_students"),
    ("Add student",            "add_student"),
    ("List courses",           "list_courses"),
    ("Enrol student",          "enrol"),
    ("Student report",         "student_report"),
    ("Term report",            "term_report"),
    ("Save all",               "save_all"),
    ("Quit",                   "quit"),
]

def print_menu():
    print("\n=== Student Records System ===")
    for i, (label, _) in enumerate(MENU, 1):
        print(f"  {i}. {label}")

def run():
    store = startup()
    unsaved = False

    while True:
        print_menu()
        try:
            choice = input("Choice: ").strip()
        except (KeyboardInterrupt, EOFError):
            choice = str(len(MENU))   # select Quit

        if not choice.isdigit() or not 1 <= int(choice) <= len(MENU):
            print("  Invalid choice.")
            continue

        action = MENU[int(choice) - 1][1]

        if action == "quit":
            if unsaved:
                ans = input("  Unsaved changes. Save before quitting? [Y/n]: ")
                if ans.strip().lower() != "n":
```

```
                op_save_all(store)
            print("  Goodbye.")
            break

        elif action == "list_students":
            if not store.students:
                print("  No students.")
            for s in sorted(store.students.values(), key=lambda x: x.name):
                print(f"  {s.student_id}  {s.name:<22}  Year {s.year_level}")

        elif action == "list_courses":
            if not store.courses:
                print("  No courses.")
            for c in sorted(store.courses.values(), key=lambda x: x.code):
                print(f"  {c.code:<12} {c.name:<22} cap={c.cap}")

        elif action == "add_student":
            sid   = input("  Student ID: ")
            name  = input("  Name: ")
            year  = input("  Year level (7-12): ")
            ok    = op_add_student(store, sid, name, year)
            if ok: unsaved = True

        elif action == "enrol":
            sid    = input("  Student ID: ")
            code   = input("  Course code: ")
            term   = input("  Term (e.g. 2025-T1): ")
            ok     = op_enrol(store, sid, code, term)
            if ok: unsaved = True

        elif action == "student_report":
            sid = input("  Student ID: ")
            try: student_report(store, sid)
            except SRSError as e: print(f"  {e}")

        elif action == "term_report":
            term = input("  Term (e.g. 2025-T1): ")
            term_report(store, term)

        elif action == "save_all":
            ok = op_save_all(store)
            if ok: unsaved = False

if __name__ == "__main__":
    run()
```

Output:

```
  Data directory: /home/anika/school/srs_data
  Courses: loaded 3, skipped 0
  Students: loaded 4, skipped 0
  Enrolments: loaded 3, skipped 0

  SRS ready:
    4   student(s)
    3   course(s)
    3   enrolment(s)

=== Student Records System ===
  1. List students
  2. Add student
  ...
```

Example 2 — Variation

An argparse-based entry point that drives the SRS non-interactively from the command line.

```
# srs/cli.py — non-interactive CLI using argparse
```

```
import argparse, sys
from srs.startup    import startup
from srs.operations import op_add_student, op_enrol, op_save_all
from srs.reports    import term_report

def build_parser():
    p = argparse.ArgumentParser(description="Student Records System")
    sub = p.add_subparsers(dest="command", required=True)

    # srs add-student 10046 "Zara Hill" 10
    add = sub.add_parser("add-student")
    add.add_argument("student_id")
    add.add_argument("name")
    add.add_argument("year_level", type=int)

    # srs enrol 10046 MATHS10 2025-T1
    enr = sub.add_parser("enrol")
    enr.add_argument("student_id")
    enr.add_argument("course_code")
    enr.add_argument("term")

    # srs term-report 2025-T1
    rpt = sub.add_parser("term-report")
    rpt.add_argument("term")

    # srs save
    sub.add_parser("save")

    return p

def main(argv=None):
    parser = build_parser()
    args   = parser.parse_args(argv)
    store  = startup()

    if args.command == "add-student":
        op_add_student(store, args.student_id, args.name, str(args.year_level))
        op_save_all(store)
    elif args.command == "enrol":
        op_enrol(store, args.student_id, args.course_code, args.term)
        op_save_all(store)
    elif args.command == "term-report":
        term_report(store, args.term)
    elif args.command == "save":
        op_save_all(store)

# python -m srs.cli add-student 10046 "Zara Hill" 10
main(["add-student", "10046", "Zara Hill", "10"])
```

Output:

```
Courses: loaded 3, skipped 0
Students: loaded 4, skipped 0
Enrolments: loaded 3, skipped 0

SRS ready: ...
Added: Zara Hill (10046)
Students saved: 5 record(s)
Enrolments saved: 3 record(s)
All data saved successfully.
```

Example 3 — Real-world application

A simple file watcher that polls the courses/ directory and loads any new JSON files added since the last check, without restarting the application.

```
# srs/watcher.py — hot-load new course files without restart
import time
```

```
from pathlib import Path
from srs.paths  import COURSES_DIR
from srs.models import Course, DuplicateError, SRSError
from srs.persistence.json_store import save_course
import json

class CourseWatcher:
    """
    Watches COURSES_DIR for new JSON files.
    Call check() periodically; it loads any files added since last check.
    """

    def __init__(self, store):
        self.store = store
        self._seen = {f for f in COURSES_DIR.glob("*.json")} if
COURSES_DIR.exists() else set()
        print(f"  Watcher: monitoring {COURSES_DIR}  ({len(self._seen)}
existing file(s))")

    def check(self):
        """Return count of new courses loaded."""
        if not COURSES_DIR.exists():
            return 0
        current = {f for f in COURSES_DIR.glob("*.json")}
        new_files = current - self._seen
        loaded = 0
        for f in sorted(new_files):
            try:
                with open(f, "r", encoding="utf-8") as fh:
                    data = json.load(fh)
                import dataclasses
                known = {fd.name for fd in dataclasses.fields(Course)}
                course = Course(**{k: v for k, v in data.items() if k in
known})
                self.store.add_course(course)
                print(f"  Watcher: loaded new course {course.code} from
{f.name}")
                loaded += 1
            except (DuplicateError, SRSError, Exception) as e:
                print(f"  Watcher: skipped {f.name}: {e}")
        self._seen = current
        return loaded

# Demonstrate: create a new course file, then check
from srs.store import SRSStore

store   = SRSStore()
watcher = CourseWatcher(store)

# Simulate a new course file being dropped in by an administrator
new_course = {"code": "HIST10", "name": "History", "department": "Humanities",
"cap": 25}
new_path = COURSES_DIR / "HIST10.json"
COURSES_DIR.mkdir(parents=True, exist_ok=True)
new_path.write_text(json.dumps(new_course, indent=2), encoding="utf-8")

n = watcher.check()
print(f"  Courses now in store: {list(store.courses.keys())}")
```

Output:

```
  Watcher: monitoring srs_data/courses  (3 existing file(s))
  Watcher: loaded new course HIST10 from HIST10.json
  Courses now in store: ['HIST10']
```

The Student Records System is now complete. It demonstrates every major technique from Book 02: reading and writing text files (Chapters 2–3), context managers (Chapter 4), CSV and JSON persistence (Chapters 5–6), the full exception handling model (Chapters 7–8), and file system navigation (Chapter 9).

The file watcher in Section 10.7 shows how these techniques compose into more sophisticated behaviour — detecting external changes to the file system — without requiring any new concepts. That composability is the hallmark of a well-designed toolkit.

Chapter 10 Summary

- The Student Records System is structured in six layers: paths/config (constants and directory setup), models (dataclasses with __post_init__ validation), store (in-memory registry with DuplicateError/NotFoundError), persistence (CSV for students and enrolments, JSON per-file for courses), operations (business logic with clean error handling), and CLI (menu loop and argparse entry points).
- dataclasses.dataclass with __post_init__ validation enforces all constraints at construction time. Invalid data is rejected immediately with a ValidationError, ensuring every object in the system is guaranteed to be valid. to_dict() and from_dict() provide symmetric serialisation and deserialisation.
- CSV persistence uses DictReader and DictWriter for all loads and saves. The load order matters: courses must be loaded before enrolments because enrol() validates course existence. Errors on individual rows are caught and logged without aborting the full load.
- Course JSON files follow a one-file-per-record pattern, named by course code. The load function iterates COURSES_DIR.glob("*.json"), making new courses available simply by dropping a JSON file into the directory — no schema migration or application restart required.
- The custom exception hierarchy (SRSError → ValidationError, DuplicateError, NotFoundError) lets the CLI handle all application errors with a single SRSError catch while preserving specificity in the model and store layers. The safe_run() top-level guard logs unexpected exceptions and keeps the session alive.
- Reports are generated entirely from the in-memory store and written to the reports/ directory with timestamped filenames. A report index is built from a glob() scan of the directory, connecting the reporting layer back to the file system navigation techniques from Chapter 9.
- The argparse CLI drives the application non-interactively, making it composable with shell scripts and batch jobs. The CourseWatcher demonstrates hot-loading new data without restart by polling the courses/ directory for new JSON files and comparing to a set of already-seen paths.
- The complete application is the product of every chapter in Book 02: text I/O (Chapters 2–3), context managers (Chapter 4), CSV (Chapter 5), JSON (Chapter 6), exception handling (Chapters 7–8), and pathlib navigation (Chapter 9). Each layer is independently testable, replaceable, and extensible.

Guided Exercises

1. Add a delete_student(store, student_id) operation that removes a student from the store and also removes all their enrolments. Raise NotFoundError if the student does not exist. Add it to both the operations module and the CLI menu.

   Hint: *In SRSStore, add a remove_student(sid) method that del store.students[sid] and filters store.enrolments. In operations.py, wrap in try/except NotFoundError. Add a menu item "Remove student" and dispatch in the main loop.*

2. Add a search_students(store, query) function that returns all students whose name contains the query string (case-insensitive). Add it as a menu option that prompts for a search term and prints the matching students.

   Hint: *Filter store.students.values() with query.lower() in s.name.lower(). Add a "Search students" menu item. If no matches are found, print a clear message. The function itself needs no try/except — it cannot raise a SRSError.*

3. Extend the term_report to include per-course pass rates. Add a score field to the Enrolment dataclass (Optional[int], default None). Modify the term report to show average score and pass rate

(percentage with score >= pass_mark) for each course, using the pass_mark from the config. **Hint:** *Add score: Optional[int] = None to Enrolment. In term_report, group enrolments by course and compute avg and pass_rate from non-None scores only. Load pass_mark from load_config() at the start of the function.*
4. Write a backup_all(store) function that saves the current state to a timestamped backup directory (e.g. srs_data/backups/2025-08-14_102204/) by calling the existing save functions with overridden paths. Verify the backup by reading back the student count from the backup CSV. **Hint:** *Create a backup directory under BASE_DIR / "backups" / timestamp. Temporarily override STUDENTS_CSV and ENROLMENTS_CSV to point into the backup dir, or write separate save_students_to(store, path) functions. Use shutil.copy2() to copy course JSON files into a backup/courses/ subdirectory.*
5. Add a list_reports() menu option that calls build_report_index() and prints a formatted table of all existing reports with their filename, size, and creation date. If the reports directory is empty or does not exist, print a clear message. **Hint:** *Call build_report_index() to get the list of report dicts. If empty, print "No reports found." Otherwise print a table with f-string alignment. Use datetime.fromisoformat(entry["created"]) to format the date column cleanly.*

Challenge Tasks

1. Extend the Student Records System with a grade recording module. Add a Grade dataclass with fields: student_id, course_code, term, assessment (string, e.g. "Assignment 1"), score (float), and max_score (float). Persist grades as a CSV file. Add operations to record a grade, list all grades for a student, and compute the weighted average for a student in a term. Update the term report to include grade averages per student. Ensure full validation and exception handling throughout.
2. Implement an import tool that reads a bulk student registration CSV in an external format (columns: student_id, full_name, year, courses_csv where courses_csv is a semicolon-separated list of course codes and terms like "MATHS10:2025-T1;ENG10:2025-T1"). The tool should: validate each row, enrol the student in each listed course, collect all errors per row without aborting the batch, write a structured import report to the reports/ directory, and save all successfully imported records atomically. Use a TemporaryDirectory as a staging area: only if all saves succeed should the files be moved to the production data directory.
3. Build a complete test suite for the Student Records System using Python's unittest framework. Write tests for: Student/Course/Enrolment construction (valid and invalid cases), SRSStore operations (add, get, duplicate, not-found), CSV persistence round-trips (save and reload, corrupted file recovery), JSON course loading (valid file, missing fields, corrupt JSON), and the report generators (content correctness, file creation). Use tempfile.TemporaryDirectory to isolate each test from the real data directory. Aim for at least 20 distinct test cases covering normal paths and edge cases.

Made in United States
Orlando, FL
04 November 2026

90201212R00125